THE
WORLD
IS
SOUND:
NADA
BRAHMA

THE WORLD IS SOUND:

Joachim-Ernst Berendt

With a Foreword by Fritjof Capra

Translated by Helmut Bredigkeit

NADA BRAHMA

MUSIC
AND THE LANDSCAPE
OF CONSCIOUSNESS

DESTINY

BOOKS

ROCHESTER, VERMONT

Destiny Books
One Park Street
Rochester, Vermont
www.InnerTraditions.com

LIBRARY OF CONGRESS CATALOGING-IN-PUBLICATION DATA

Berendt, Joachim Ernst.
    [Nada Brahma. English]
    The world is sound, Nada Brahma : music and the
landscape of consciousness / Joachim-Ernst Berendt :
foreword by Fritjof Capra.
      p. cm.
    Translation of: Nada Brahma.
    Includes bibliographical references and index.
    ISBN 0-89281-318-0 (pbk.)
    1. Music—Philosophy and aesthetics. 2. Music and
society. I. Title.
ML3845.B3713 1991
780'.1—dc20   91-12309
                                                CIP
                                              MN

Printed and bound in the United States.

10   9   8   7   6   5

Design by Dede Cummings, *Irving Perkins Associates*

Contents

All music, based upon melody and rhythm, is the earthly
representative of heavenly music.

> PLOTINUS

Open spaces—nothing holy!

> BODHIDHARMA

How unbelievably modest are human beings who bind themselves
to only one religion! I have very many religions, and the one
overriding them is only forming throughout my life.

> ELIAS CANETTI

The universe and I exist together, and all things and I are one. As
all things are one, there is no need for further speech. But since I
just said that all things are one, how can speech be not important?
. . . .
Behind the divisible there is always something indivisible. Behind
the disputable there is always something indisputable. You ask:
What? The wise man carries it in his heart.

> CHUANG-TZU

Hear, and your soul shall live.

> ISAIAH 55:3

IN MEMORY
OF
John Coltrane
Jean Gebser
Hermann Hesse
Sufi Hazrat Inayat Khan
Hans Kayser

FOREWORD

THE DISCOVERIES OF modern science and the ideas developed in various social movements are now radically changing our view of the world. A new vision of reality is slowly emerging that will form the basis of our future sciences, philosophy, technology, economics, and politics. This new vision of reality, or new paradigm, is a holistic view of the world. The universe is no longer seen as a mechanical system composed of elementary building blocks but rather as a complex web of interdependent relationships. The network of relationships, moreover, is intrinsically dynamic. All forms are associated with processes, all interrelations with interactions, and opposites are unified through oscillations. In quantum physics, the science that pioneered the new vision of reality, subatomic particles are recognized as being merely patterns in an inseparable cosmic process. Matter, at the subatomic level, consists of energy patterns continually changing into one another —a continuous dance of energy.

To unify recent insights in physics and in the life sciences into a coherent description of reality, a conceptual shift from structure to rhythm seems to be extremely useful. Rhythmic patterns appear throughout the universe, from the very small to the very large. Atoms are patterns of probability waves, molecules are vibrating structures, and living organisms manifest multiple, interdependent patterns of fluctuations. Plants, animals, and human beings undergo cycles of activity and rest, and all their physiological functions oscillate in rhythms of various periodicities. The components of ecosystems are interlinked through cyclical exchanges of matter and energy; civilizations rise and fall in evolutionary cycles, and the planet as a whole has its rhythms and recurrences as it spins around its axis and moves around the sun.

It has been said since ancient times that the nature of reality is much closer to music than to a machine, and this is confirmed by many discoveries in modern science. The essence of a melody does not lie in its notes; it lies in the relationships between the notes, in the intervals, frequencies, and rhythms. When a string is set vibrating we hear not only a single tone but also its overtones—an entire scale is sounded. Thus each note involves all the others, just as each subatomic particle involves all the others, according to current ideas in particle physics.

The present book explores the ancient proposition that "the world is sound"—*Nada Brahma* in the classical Sanskrit of India—with countless examples from modern science, art, philosophy, and from many spiritual traditions. Having dedicated his entire professional life to music, with a long and distinguished career as a jazz critic and producer of records, concerts, and radio shows, Joachim-Ernst Berendt is uniquely qualified to guide such an exploration. In a majestic sweep he takes the reader through the macro- and microcosm, from the "harmony of the spheres" to the songs of dolphins and whales and other "sounds of the sea," the "entrainment" of rhythmic patterns in human communication, and the vibrations of molecules and atoms. Berendt extends the notion of rhythm also to the "static rhythms" of crystals, the regular structural patterns of living organisms, and the "sacred geometry" encoded in Europe's great cathedrals. Thus, "planetary orbits, the shapes of leaves and bodies, churches and cloisters, obey the laws of harmonics."

For Joachim Berendt, the universal dynamic pattern is not just vibration. The world is *sound,* which means to him that it vibrates in harmonic proportions. He notes that from billions of possible vibrations the universe chooses with overwhelming preference those few thousand that make harmonic sense, which leads us to the question: why is the world so harmonious? A recently developed theory of living systems may provide a surprising answer to this intriguing question. According to the theory, we do not perceive an independently existing world, but rather create a world in the processes of perception and cognition. These processes differ in different living organisms—plants, animals, or human beings—who are endowed with different organs of perception and thus create different worlds. From this point of view, it is not surprising that we observe only harmonic vibrations in the universe. If our sense organs are harmonic, then the world they create, naturally, will "make harmonic sense."

For the author of this book the realization that the world is sound has profound implications not only for science and philosophy but also for our everyday lives and our society. He argues that for the past several hundred years our Western culture has overemphasized seeing and neglected listening. Therefore our current change of paradigms includes for Berendt an essential shift of emphasis from the eye to the ear. He shows with impressive examples that such a shift from eye to ear would be consistent with the shift from masculine to feminine values that has often been associated with our cultural transformation—from analysis to synthesis, from rational knowledge to intuitive wisdom, from domination and aggression to nonviolence and peace.

FRITJOF CAPRA

Introduction

IT IS WITH DEEP emotion that I revise this book for its publication in the English-speaking world, because it is this world we look to when we talk about the "paradigm shift" and the "growth of a new consciousness" in the last phase of the twentieth century. To be sure, the idea of a "new man" was not born in the United States. The first modern thinker to concern himself with it was Friedrich Nietzsche. Later, and from different points of origin, it was developed by writers as far apart as Teilhard de Chardin, Hermann Hesse, and Jean Gebser (who demanded the creation of an "integral consciousness"). Even so, the idea is closer to the American way of life than to the European. Walt Whitman, that American phenomenon *par excellence*, who knew so much about "integral consciousness," was accepted in America from the beginning, while Nietzsche, Chardin, Hesse, Gebser, and so many others have remained "aliens," outsiders in Europe. It is no coincidence that Hesse's works have been so much more popular in the United States (and in Japan) than in Germany, the country in whose language he wrote.

Above all, it was in the United States that the New Consciousness grew into a movement, into the much-cited "New Age"—which, when you think about it, is not such a bad name after all. Objectionable are only the fact that it has become something like a trademark, and the agility and speed with which Americans have turned this "brand name" into what they understand so well: a business.

· No doubt, many of the important thinkers of the "New Age" (an expression I shall discontinue using) are either Americans or Europeans or Indians residing in North America. Nowhere in the world are more books published about the "New Paradigm" and the "New Consciousness" than in the United States. It is for this reason that I feel deeply moved to see *The World is Sound: Nada Brahma* selected for presentation to the reading public of the English-speaking world. The book will thus find its place in a world that has left its mark in recent years on all of us who belong to the "family" of the New Consciousness, whether we live in the United States, Europe, or Japan—or anywhere else.

II.

It is necessary to clarify the position of the author. *Nada Brahma* is a mantra. A mantra has no author. Reflections on a mantra can claim to have an author only insofar as the author is a "catalyst." In many chapters of this book, its author holds the function of "com-poser," someone who "puts together." It is not a single author who speaks here: there are many.

The sound with which this book deals is also a "sounding together," a chord formed by many voices: from Lao-tzu to Niels Bohr, from Pythagoras to John Coltrane, from the biblical psalmists to Hermann Hesse, from the Zen master Hakuin to Werner Heisenberg.

Everything—or almost everything—put forth in this book has always been part of humankind's knowledge, even when we have repressed it and preferred not to know it. All we have to do is rediscover it, make it conscious again. That is the main task of this book.

III.

This work deals with a new consciousness whose growing presence is felt today even by those who scoff at it.

Futurologists, ecologists, peace researchers, cybernetically-minded scientists who have not yet been atrophied by specialization, doctors who are able to look beyond the barbed-wire fences of their textbook medicine—all these experts have been telling us repeatedly: It is five minutes to twelve.

In an age in which humankind spends 2.3 million dollars per minute for its own potential destruction, our end, the end of us all, has become "feasible." And experience has shown that whatever is "feasible" for human beings, they will end up doing. Preparations for an atomic war are well under way. Systematically, but without informing the public, Western military leaders are transforming our technology—which is supposedly defensive in nature, and a clear case of madness at that —into "first-strike capability," which means: into a tool of atomic aggression. But even if we are spared the fate of atomic destruction, ecological and biological disasters (AIDS) seem clearly programmed.

Every year, a piece of land as large as France turns into desert. By the year 2000, a minimum of between 437,000 and 1.4 million biological species (about sixty percent of all existing species) will have become irreversibly extinct. (Between the early sixteenth century and the beginning of World War II only 100 species of mammals and 150 bird species were destroyed by human beings.) It can only be seen as an expression of our inexhaustible optimism that most people still believe that the general process of dying will exclude their own species—and this at a time when the concept of the "megacorpse" (one million dead), created by the perverted brain of the military, is slowly but surely taking over the thinking of our politicians. "Looking at the true state of the world is psychologically unbearable" (as East German author Christa Wolf wrote).

IV.

We have all heard it and read about it again and again in recent years: A new consciousness is our only salvation. But we have also heard this question: What good will it do to develop this consciousness in my own soul (by changing my way of acting and thinking and by meditating and all the other possibilities we know of); what value is there in retiring into my own shell, forever working on myself, if things outside and around me are deteriorating at an unbelievable pace? Under these circumstances, is it not much more realistic to help others before working on myself? Is it not narcissistic and egotistical to be only engrossed in myself? This question has been given the following answer by the many wise people quoted in this book, from the Asian thinkers and the Japanese Zen masters to Hermann Hesse, from Socrates to Erich Fromm: *We* are the world. Which means: We cannot change the world if we do not change ourselves first. Any other way would be absurd, would not improve things but rather would worsen them, because we would carry our own problems into any political, economic, or social "solution" we might try to implement. That is the reason why yesterday's revolutionaries are tomorrow's dictators. And why each and every nineteenth-century social proposal has been proven unsound by twentieth-century history, and why each and every proposal of twenty or twenty-five years ago is being proven unsound by what is happening now.

But how can we change the world by changing ourselves? For centuries there was no answer to this question. We only knew that this was the way it was. All great upheavals in the course of documented history were initially upheavals in consciousness. This can be easily recognized in the Renaissance and the Reformation periods or the French and Russian Revolutions, but it can also be seen even before that, during the upheavals when a new and different world emerged from the world of Greek and Roman antiquity. Revolutions, new lifestyles, new social systems, new paradigms—they all start in the head.

Whatever has undergone complete change, began as a change in the consciousness of individual human beings. Only thereafter was it possible for the world to change.

Perhaps today we know why this is so—and that, too, is a topic of this book. "All is one," said the sages of Asia and ancient Egypt. One might believe that was so—or not. Today, however, modern nuclear physics (the phenomenon of holography, and other concepts that I will discuss) bear out that, indeed, "all is one," in a way that may not be open to our intellect but at the same time is subject to scientific, mathematical, experimental proof. If, however, "all is one", then *my* consciousness can bring on change—then the consciousness of one person can change the consciousness of a thousand people, the consciousness of a million people can change the consciousness of one hundred million people, and the consciousness of one hundred million people can change the consciousness of a billion people.

Physicists speak of the "law of small numbers." This law holds true not only in physics but in society, too. Again and again in the course of history, humankind has experienced the power of this law. We are experiencing it now. Yet the "small number" is no longer as small as it was five years ago. We are in the midst of the "paradigm shift."

V.

Many outstanding scholars, scientists, psychologists, philosophers and writers have described and circumscribed the New Consciousness. An entire body of literature deals with it. But one aspect has not been pointed out: that it will be the consciousness of hearing people. That is: No longer will our eyes have precedence over our ears, as is the general case today; on the contrary, our ears will have priority over our eyes. The audible, the sound, will be more important than the visible. (The point is simply the relationship between them, the disproportionate way we favor our eyes and disregard our ears; of course both the eyes and the ears are precious, indispensible sense organs.)

The seeing person analyzes, takes things apart—as becomes immediately clear when seeing is taken to its extreme, looking through an electron microscope. There, even those things that seem "indivisible" are taken apart. The eyes are wonderful organs, but the better they are, the "sharper" they are; "sharpness" is a quality of knives and of cutting, which for the New Consciousness means a negative, destructive, possibly even murderous quality. For prehistoric people, the symbol of the eye was the arrow; the arrow, however, is capable not only of hitting its target but also of killing.

Human beings with their disproportionate emphasis on seeing have brought on the excess of rationality, of analysis and abstraction, whose breakdown we are now witnessing. In the age of television, seeing people have allowed themselves to be led *ad absurdum*. No longer do we see the world, we see its images—and unbelievably enough, we are content with that, content with looking at moving pictures. Living almost exclusively through the eyes has led us to almost not living at all.

To put it provocatively (all this will be dealt with in more detail later on): The highest, most admirable ideal of the "eye person" is to possess an "eagle eye." The eagle spots its prey, dives, and seizes it. This is a fitting ideal for Western man, who has become accustomed to looking at the entire world as his potential prey. It is a beautiful ideal, but an aggressive one—and in today's world that means a dangerous one.

The ears, on the other hand, are symbolized by a mussel or a conch, which in turn symbolize the female sex organ, itself a symbol for receiving and engulfing—for becoming one.

To the ancient Chinese, the eyes constituted a *yang* type of sense organ: male, aggressive, dominating, rational, surface-oriented, analyzing things. The ears, on the other hand, are a *yin* sense: female, receptive, careful, intuitive and spiritual, depth-oriented, perceiving the whole as one.

It is the *yin* kind of perception that is required—and offered—in this work, which was written by an "ear person." The whole is

more important to him than its parts. Synthesis is more important than analysis, context more important than specialization.
"Behind the divisible there is always something indivisible. Behind
the disputable there is always something indisputable." (Chuang-
tzu).

VI.

A starting point for me was my interest in hearing, my experience that
modern human beings have lost themselves in such a hypertrophy of the
visual that they no longer are able to listen adequately. I had wanted to
write a book about listening, but—to my initial surprise—it turned out
to be a spiritual book. It will become obvious why this is so, why it had
to be that way inevitably.

The deterioration of our sense of hearing has run remarkably parallel
with the process of secularization, which has been referred to as the
Western world's "uncoupling from God." The fact that modern human
beings "no longer listen to God," is so commonplace a realization that I
would not have written it down were it not equally true that the words
"to God" can be dropped from that sentence so easily. Modern human
beings no longer listen to God. Modern human beings no longer listen.
The first sentence is a theological statement. The second one is
proven by, for example, the fact that in spite of all our advanced technology we obviously do not consider it necessary to supply our
television sets with a sound system that reflects the technical possibilities. And yet these two statements are related. That, too, will
become clear.

Wherever God revealed Himself to human beings, He was heard.
He may have appeared as a light, but in order to be understood, His
voice had to be heard. "And God spoke" is a standard sentence in
all holy scriptures. The ears are the gateway. On the other hand:
"Thou shalt not make unto thee any graven image." No image for
the eyes. Many religions make such a demand, Judaism and Islam in particular.

VII.

My eyes are looking at this sheet of paper I am writing on. They are
incapable of penetrating the paper even for a tenth of an inch. The field
of the visible is the surface. Our eyes scan surfaces. Our ears, however,

immerse themselves deeply into the spheres they investigate by hearing. The "ear person" thus has better chances of penetrating his object's depth than the "eye person."

Whatever has been said in recent years about the New Consciousness is correct and relevant, but one point has always been overlooked: The New Man will be Listening Man—or will never be at all. He will be able to perceive sounds in a way we cannot even imagine today. These are the sounds discussed in *Nada Brahma*. These sounds *are Nada Brahma*.

To be sure, listeners and readers have rightfully pointed out to me that we will also have to learn to see correctly again. But we already suffer from an overemphasis on the sense of seeing, and in the Western world there is an admirable tradition and culture of the eye, of seeing, and of light, dating back to the Renaissance and, further back, to ancient Greece. There is nothing comparable in our world in reference to the ear and to hearing.

A *deeper* change in consciousness (and I think it is uncontested that we do need a different kind of awareness, a new perception of the world) will be reached when we have learned to use our sense of hearing fully; just as we have been using our eyes and our sense of seeing for centuries. Once we have learned to hear again, we will be able to correct our ocular hypertrophy. Then we will comprehend the statement made by Goethe (an eye person) that "the eye of the spirit must see in unison with the eyes of the body, for otherwise there is the danger that one will see something and yet look past it."

VIII.

When I was working on *Nada Brahma*, I had no idea what an enormous response the book would receive in Europe. On the contrary, I thought that after the many successful books I had written on jazz and music, I could allow myself the luxury of a book addressed to a smaller circle of readers—a book that is a fruit of the spiritual path I have been following since the early sixties, since my meeting and work with the jazz musician John Coltrane, and since my travels in Asia (and the period when I lived on Bali for some time). I was (and still am) surprised that very soon more people were reading *Nada Brahma* than I would have ever dreamed.

Especially intense was the response to the chapter on listening, "Temple in the Ear." No other chapter was reviewed, discussed, and quoted more often than this one. Clearly, readers understood the appeal from Isaiah: "Hear, and your soul shall live." Listen, and you shall survive! In this vein I continued to work. The chapter "Temple in the Ear" was the germinating cell for a further book, *The Third Ear*, in which I attempt to answer some of the questions that *Nada Brahma* raised for me and many readers as well:

Why has our sense of hearing been so carefully differentiated by evolution, much more so than our sense of seeing?

Why did evolution select that particular sense to harbor our capacity for measuring, for the mathematical? And why is our capacity for transcendence also located in our sense of hearing? And why is our sense of balance, of equilibrium placed there also?

Why are the data we receive from our ears so much more precise than that from our eyes? Why is the range of what we can hear so much wider—by exactly tenfold—than the range of what we can see? What is that meant to signal to us?

Why have we been unable to understand these signals for the last three centuries, since the time of Galileo, Descartes, and Bacon? What do we stand to gain from learning to comprehend these signals again? How may we profit if in fields like biology, evolutionary theory, anthropology, linguistics, or sociology we learn to work as precisely and conscientiously with our ears as scientists have been working with their eyes ever since Aristotle?

Why don't men listen to women? Why do men interrupt women so much more frequently (according to a careful study conducted at an American university: twenty-five times more often!) than women interrupt men?

Why is it that the sentence "You're not even listening to me!" has become a standard reproach in modern relationships? How might society (and that also means: politics) change if this sentence were to become less often necessary?

Why do women have higher voices than men? Why has conventional science ignored a fact that is so obvious: Everywhere in nature and in music the higher voices have a leading function. Instruments with a higher pitch (violins, flutes, trumpets) carry the melody, while those with a lower pitch (in the "male" range: cellos, basses, trombones, tubas) usually have accompanying functions. They are perceived as melody instruments only when the higher ones are silent or kept transparent and reserved. The same is true in street traffic: If it's a matter of survival, we choose signals with a high, "female" pitch: police cars, ambulances, and other warning signals. In fact, even an army sergeant (the traditional symbol for patriarchal supremacy) lifts his voice to higher ranges when he wants to be obeyed: "Present arms!" In most cases, the word "arms" is shouted in a voice higher than the normal voice of the officer. What are nature and evolution trying to tell us with this phenomenon? Why has the male-dominated field of science overlooked—or "overheard"—such questions? Why does science in general tend to ignore questions related to hearing, even though it has diligently investigated optical problems for centuries?

IX.

A collection of Zen koans compiled in 1783 in Kyoto by the Japanese monk Genro contains the following sentence: "A doctrine that ignores everyday life is not the true doctrine." Whatever may seem too theoretical in the main body of this book will come alive in the chapters of part 2. If you have not realized it by then, the chapter "Zen and Modern Japan" will certainly make it clear that *Nada Brahma* is not something esoteric. Living is permitted—in fact, living is required. For me, too, the path to *Nada Brahma* was a path of living. Only later was life experience followed by reading and theoretical understanding.

Of course, the sound that this book deals with is also a musical sound. That's why we have to speak about music. In no profession do you find more adherents of the New Consciousness than among musicians. Collin Walcott, the late percussionist of the group Oregon, once said that many players of the new "World Music" today anticipate that type of human being that we all will have to become someday if we want to survive on this shrinking, ever more crowded planet. I myself came to *Nada Brahma* from the world of jazz, and in much of my work I have combined my jazz and my *Nada Brahma* experiences (as on many of my record productions, or at the World Music Festivals I have directed in Berlin, Baden-Baden, Donaueschingen, and Tokyo, or at the 1982 Lincoln Center concert "Jazz and World Music" in New York—a concert whose success gave me tremendous joy). The chapter "India and Jazz" will show how the musical and spiritual dimensions are closely bound in a "marriage" that will become even more intimate in future generations.

In this, the closing phase of the twentieth century, the sciences have become part of our life—in fact, they have become too much a part of it. The "Postscript on Science" will show how the claim staked by science must be relativized. In general, *Nada Brahma* is a very peaceful book, but here you may sense an aggressive note. Since the early 1970s we have come to understand that science without wisdom can be dangerous. No longer should science be the determinant force in our lives.

And yet a new kind of science has emerged, a unified and participatory one, at peace with the "perennial philosophy." This is my point of reference. It first appeared in the findings and theorems of the physicists of our century, but it has also become obvious in most other sciences, especially in biology. That is why physics is important to me (also for another reason: Physics was the first major subject I studied as a young man before turning to music).

X.

Finally, let me make a few remarks about the page of epigraphs with which this book begins.

The first epigraph comes from Plotinus, the great descendant of Plato in the era of Hellenism. It is characteristic of Pythagorean thinking.

The words "Open spaces—nothing holy!" come from Bodhidharma, who in the late fifth or early sixth century made a pilgrimage from his Indian homeland to China to become the founder of Chinese Zen. Impoverished, tattered, and emaciated after years of begging and wandering, the sage was received by Emperor Wu in his throne room. (Question: Why don't the leaders of today's Western world-power nations ever receive such people?) The Emperor asked: "What is the deepest meaning of the holy truth?" Bodhidharma's answer consisted of just these four words: "Open spaces—nothing holy!" The Emperor asked for clarification. The sage declined. Wu did not understand him, and Bodhidharma is said to have gone "across the river northward." Emperor Wu, however, pondered the pilgrim's answer all his life and found enlightenment at a very old age. Open and wide. Nothing holy.

The epigraph taken from Elias Canetti should be supplemented by another statement by this Nobel Prize–winning writer: "There is always something shady about subscribing to a faith that very many people have shared beforehand. There is more resignation in that act than could be framed in human words. Faith is a human faculty that can be *expanded*, and anyone who can do so ought to contribute to this expansion." Religion has to do with man's creative powers. Dogmas and everything dogmatic—in other words, established religions that hardly change anymore—are noncreative. They do not move; above all, they no longer move the creative and spiritual powers and imagination of the individual.

The next epigraph comes from Chuang-tzu, the Chinese sage and philosopher of the second half of the fourth century who, with his powerful language, wrote the most beautiful account we have of Taoism. He stated the problem of *Nada Brahma* most succinctly: "As all things are one, there is no need for further speech. But since I have just said that all things are one, how can speech be not important?"

XI.

In closing this introduction, I would like to add a remark that I have inserted in many of my books over the last twenty years: I cannot hope to have avoided every possibility of error, nor do I expect that my personal interpretations will be accepted by all readers. I feel that this book—more than any other book I have written—is a very personal one. I am grateful to those who join me on this way, but I respect those who decline to do so.

Baden-Baden, West Germany
Spring 1987

PART ONE

PART ONE

I ✍

What Does "Nada Brahma" Mean?

Nada Brahma is a primal word in Indian spirituality, a primal word that also refers to India's great classical music. That is where the answer must begin. But before going any further, let me make the following remarks to prevent misunderstanding: This book is not about India —or only inasmuch as Indian spirituality is part of the spirituality of humankind. This is a book about us. It refers to modern Western man. Whatever will be said here about foreign cultures and ancient times, understood correctly, will correspond with the findings of modern science: cosmology, morphology, biology, mythology, harmonic studies, astrophysics and nuclear physics.

To be sure, the sages of Asia knew many of the things we shall be talking about (and that modern science claims to have discovered) as much as two or three thousand years before our times.

To *Nada Brahma*, then: *Nada* is a Sanskrit word meaning "sound." Dictionaries also list renderings such as "sounding, droning, roaring, howling, screaming." But the related word *nada* also means "bull." A roaring bull. In other words, "roaring" was a kind of bridge over which the meaning expanded from "sound" to include "bull." Before that took place, there had been yet another change in meaning: to the related word *nadi*, meaning "river" or "stream" but also "rushing" or "sounding." From the rushing river to the rushing sound. As the eminent paleolinguist Richard Fester has shown, the syllable *nad-*

(or some variant: *nar-*, *nid-*, etc.) is hidden in the names of rivers all over the world, from the German Nidda and the Polish Nida to the Norwegian Nid and the British Nidd, from the Italian Niete to the Nidwan in Afghanistan, from the Italian Nera to the Russian Ner, Nara, Narova, and Narym, and from the German Nahe to the African Nahil and the Spanish Narcea.

The term *nadi* is also used to mean "stream of consciousness," a meaning that goes back four thousand years to the oldest of India's four sacred Vedic scriptures, the *Rig-Veda*. Thus the relationship between sound and consciousness has long been documented in language. The "stream of sound" has been a prime concept in man's imagination ever since he started to use language. Martin Buber expressed it in a single sentence: "We may listen to our inner self—and still not know which ocean we hear roaring."

In one single paragraph, we have thrown together these elements: tone, sound, drone, roaring bulls, rushing rivers, and oceans. The Greek term meaning "to throw together" is *symbállein*. It also means: to provoke an argument, lend money, draw a bill, interpret, explain, meet, fall together, exchange blows, fight—and finally, to *understand*. The word *symbol* derives from *symbállein*. We have created symbols. Symbols for what? The answer to this question is provided by the second part of this book's title, the word *Brahma*.

Along with Shiva and Vishnu, Brahma is one of the three main deities of Hinduism. All other deities next to them or below them, are basically merely reincarnations of these three gods. In India, this trinity of the three main deities is referred to as the *Trimurti*, and theologians have discovered in it parallels to the Christian trinity of Father, Son, and Holy Spirit, and to spiritual trinities the world over.

In Hinduism, as in Christianity, as in all other religions involving a trinity, speaking of this trinity makes sense only when, in the final analysis, the triad means oneness. Whoever speaks of Christ means God; whoever speaks of God also means the Holy Spirit; whoever speaks of the Holy Spirit means Christ *and* God. Whoever speaks of Brahma—or Shiva or Vishnu—ultimately means the Highest Divine Principle of the Hindu world. In this sense, as the eminent Indologist Heinrich Zimmer has shown, Hinduism is a monotheistic religion. On the island of Bali, in the particular "primal" form of Hinduism of the Balinese people, you can still sense that the large number of main, accessory, and subordinate gods (which are of animistic as well as Hindu origin) were amalgamated in the One God.

In one dictionary I find the following: *"Brahma* (Sanskrit): originally a magic formula in India, later understood as the primal creative word, source of the world and sacred knowledge, Brahma became the central concept of Indian interpretation of the world. It is one with man's inner consciousness." Thus for one thing, *Nada Brahma* means: *Sound is God.* Or, vice versa: God is Sound.

But Brahma, the All-Creator, is more than God. He is identical with that which He has created and in which He is constantly present. For that reason, He is so often depicted as having four heads, which look toward the four cardinal points of the world. In this way, Brahma also means: the universe. Brahma: the cosmos.

The principle of Brahma, the so-called *Brahman*, is the prime power of the cosmos, the inner consciousness of man and of all living things. The Upanishads (together with the Vedas—of which they are a part—the oldest and most important written documentation of Indian philosophy) have only one great central theme, which is varied again and again with an inexhaustible wealth of ideas: Brahman is everything.

> Brahman is the absolute.
> Everything that exists is Brahman or the Sacred Word,
>   which cannot be explained.
> It is without condition and without properties.
> It is the world-soul containing all single souls,
>   as the ocean contains all drops of water
>   of which it consists.
> Brahman is life.
> Brahman is joy.
> Brahman is void. . . .
> Joy is truly the same as void.
> Void is truly the same as joy.

Following our Western rationalism, my dictionary puts it into these words: *"Brahman . . . .:* Basic element and active force of all natural and historic things and events."

Brahma about himself (in the Upanishads):

> I am the creator, the womb of the world,
>   acquired from my own being,
>   the only Lord,
>   highest word without beginning.
> He who worships me as such will be saved.
>   I cause all gods to become and I end their reign,
>   and no one is to be found anywhere in the worlds
>   who would tower above me.

The words *Brahma* and *Brahman* come from the Sanskrit root *bri,* meaning "to grow" but also "to praise." Everything that is growing, everything that is alive (and in the cosmologies of the ancient Brahman sages as well as those of modern astrophysicists, everything is growing, even the universe), is *Brahma* and *Brahman:* the indivisible oneness of all beings.

So *Nada Brahma* means not only: God, the Creator, is sound; but also (and above all): Creation, the cosmos, the world, is sound. And: Sound is the world.

But it also means: Sound is joy; sound praises. And even: Emptiness is sound. And finally: Spirit and soul are sound.

It is obvious that the word *nada* (sound) is just as important as the word *Brahma* or as the cosmic principle *Brahman* (which means: as important as the word *God*).

So much is already clear. Sound is the central concept: the World-*nada*, the *nada*-World, the *Brahma*-Sound, the Sound-Word. The word "is" between "world" and "sound" as well as between "Brahma" and "sound" and "word" can just as easily be left off. *Nada Brahma* is one singularity: the primal sound of being. Being itself.

Here is where the "trip" of this book begins. We have taken note of the meaning of *Nada Brahma* (but hardly more than that: taking note). Now we shall start on our trip—through macrocosm and microcosm and through the world in which we live. We shall put our questions to nuclear physicists and astronomers, cosmologists and mathematicians, biologists and specialists in evolution, chemists and botanists, logicians and cyberneticists, mystics and rationalists, specialists in Buddhism and Zen, in Hinduism, Islam, and Christianity; we shall be asking musicologists and musicians in East and West, ethnologists and linguists, scholars of the legends, myths, and tales of the world's peoples; we shall be asking scientists and those who reject science, even those who deem science dangerous; we shall be asking contemporary people and the sages and seers of the past in both East and West; we shall ask our questions as we travel through Japan and China, to Bali and the Polynesian Islands, to India and Tibet, to Persia and Egypt, North and South America and Africa: Is the world really sound? And if so, in what way is it sound? Is the world a single, unimaginably huge cosmic musical instrument? And the structure of the microcosm, with its electrons and photons—is it primarily sound, too? Are the shapes of leaves and crystals, are human and animal bodies also sound? Words and language—are they, above everything else, sound? Are we ourselves sound? Is that which we call spirit and soul sound? And the relationship we call love—is it controlled by sound progressions? Are *we* the players of the instrument? Or is it all a matter of chance? Or—what else?

2 ❧ Nada Brahma— as Koan and as Mantra

Including an Excursion into Logic

THE WORLD IS sound. Immediately the question arises: What kind of sound? It is a key question; because if the world is sound, then to ask this question means the same as to ask about the prime substance of the world—in the physicist's terms, about atoms, neutrons, and positrons, about photons, quarks, and leptons, and all the other elementary particles of which the atomic nucleus consists and the universe consists and we consist. As we shall see, there is in fact a close relationship between these two questions.

Japanese Zen masters ask their disciples this question:

If you blot out sense and sound—
   what do you hear?

One of the great eleventh-century Zen masters thought up this question. It has a great tradition; it has been asked for centuries in Japanese Zen monasteries. The Japanese call it a *koan*. Originally, *koan* (Chinese, *kung-an*) meant "public document" or "public announcement." To be sure, the koan, as used in Zen, is no longer a public "bulletin," but it is helpful to keep this meaning in mind. Koans are matters of fact; they are given to the meditator, who then has to live by them, to deal with them.

Koans are formulas, questions, or problems that seem to be rational and yet have no rational solution. You can solve them only by meditating. And you can solve them only for yourself. No one can use anyone else's solution. Were I to know the answer and write it down here, it would be absolutely meaningless for others, even if that solution had changed my life—and that's what the answer to a koan does: it changes one's life.

You have to pose such a question, your koan, many times over. Posing the question is more important than answering it. Asking is the answer. Zen masters say: Asking is the way. The word *way* (*tao* in Chinese, *do* in Japanese) itself has a spiritual meaning—even before anything is said about which way is meant and where the way leads.

The Zen disciple goes along "the" way. He asks his question many times. He sits in meditation, in the appropriate posture, and meditates on the koan given to him. If he sits for only half an hour (the minimum daily requirement), he may have considered his koan one hundred, perhaps one hundred and fifty, times. If he sits for four hours a day (most disciples sit for longer periods), he will have posed the question twelve hundred times. There are meditators who need a year—or even many years—to "crack" their koan. In our computation, that would mean asking oneself the question about one million times:

> If you blot out sense and sound—
> what do you hear?

Asking this question can take a lifetime. When you finally find the answer, it takes only a few seconds. This is often described as a "bolt of lightning." For centuries, one main point was argued among the various Zen sects: whether one became aware of the solution gradually in a slow process of increasing approximation, or in a sudden, single flash. Eventually, the lightning-bolt faction prevailed.

Hakuin, the great Japanese Zen master, born in 1685, who carried the koan technique to its modern perfection, wrote:

> When you take a koan and examine it persistently, your spirit will die and your ego will be destroyed. It is as if a bottomless, empty pit were to open up before you and your hands and feet can find no hold. You feel as if you were looking at the face of death and as if your heart were going up in flames. Then suddenly you are one with the koan, and you are freed of body and spirit. . . . That is the vision into your own nature. You must carry on relentlessly, and with this perfect composure you will invariably reach the prime ground of your nature . . .

Richard de Martino compares the koan with a fiery ball that the meditating person swallows, only to try to spit it out again immediately. But the ball grows and grows until it is so large that the ego itself becomes a single glowing ball. "Ego has at last become koan." At this point, the ego dies the "great death" (the Zen term is *taishi*), and enters into the "great birth" *(daigo)*. "The ego bursts like a bubble of water."

Since koans have to do with experience, let me relate my own experiences with a koan—although they are in no way comparable to the findings of the great practitioners of Zen meditation. My first Zen master in Kyoto gave it to me:

> Nothing evil. Nothing good.
> My original face now!

Or, more comprehensively: "Don't think of anything evil or of anything good. Do only one thing: find out what your face looked like before you entered into this world. Find out *now*."

What happens—what can happen—when you devote yourself to this problem?

The first thing seems obvious: No one should think of anything evil. One is tempted to assume that by doing so one is supposed to make room for the good, to have all the more good thoughts. But your koan says: No. And that is the beginning of Zen absurdity, albeit only its beginning: you are not supposed to think of anything good either.

After dealing with the koan for an appropriate length of time, you will reach the following conclusion in a "logical" and yet also totally "extralogical" way: The equation of the two phrases "Nothing evil/ Nothing good" can only mean the equation of evil and good. Both, says the koan, are equally unimportant when measured against the real point.

Evil and good form *the* (or at least one very important) primal polarity. Here is the next step then: Polarities are unimportant. They only seem to exist. You will dwell on unimportant matters if you give too much meaning to all the tension fields we fall into: evil and good, light and dark, God and Devil, heaven and hell, top and bottom, warm and cold. . . . Forget all that.

Forget it, because the second part of the problem—at least, so you hope—will help you along: Your original face! What did you look like earlier? The question inevitably takes you further: What did you look like before that—and before that?

At first, you actually look for a face, perhaps for months. You go back further and further. You see many faces, you sense them; and seeing them often brings you to tears. But prior to any of the faces you see or sense, there must have been an even earlier one. Until there are no more faces. After all, you know—you learned it in school—human faces have existed only for so and so many hundred thousand years. But what existed before that? Genes? Cells? And before those: Molecules? Atoms? And before the atoms: Particles? Elementary entities? Photons? The primal light that plays a role in the cosmology of modern physics as well as in the Bible ("In the beginning was light")? Photon soup. Light slush.

You can take this direction, or any other one, of course. If you take this one, however, at a certain point—whether gradually or all at once—the search for light becomes primary. Is light becoming your original face? You go deeper and deeper and you search and search and search for—*light!* Perhaps you will keep searching for light; but it is also possible that you may experience it. Perhaps you are not sure, perhaps the result lies somewhere between search and experience. The masters know for sure, but you are not a master. You say to yourself: If the masters are certain, why can't I be? I want to be sure, too. And you do not give up; you carry on.

I, too, carry on with my description. But what am I describing? Basically, except for the pains I felt from sitting still, I can describe only one thing: what I was thinking. But that is exactly the unimportant part, the part you are supposed to overcome!

You lie in your koan as if it were a river. The koan carries you along. You are lying on your back, surrounded by the water of your koan. Only your mouth and your nose stick out so you can breathe: breathe thoughts. All the other parts of your body—of your being, your essence—are surrounded by the koan-water so densely and so closely that thoughts cannot reach you. Precisely that is the relationship between the thoughts and all the other things you cannot describe: the relationship between the tip of your nose and the rest of your body. Or the relationship between the ten minutes it takes to read what I am trying to describe here and the two years of my dealing with this koan: three *seshins* (meditation workshops), one in Kyoto and two in Germany, consisting of eight hours daily spent in seated meditation; for the rest of the time, thirty minutes twice a day spent meditating on this koan, not only at home in Baden-Baden but also on all business trips and private travels to lectures and concerts, festivals and conferences, in Europe and the United States and once for two weeks in Brazil: Nothingevilnothinggoodmyoriginalfacenow.

Somewhere along the line you realize that you are doing something quite ordinary. The Zen master is far away in Kyoto. You can forget him. There was a sentence you once heard in school from your Greek teacher—but even if you had never learned Greek you would know

Socrates' call: *Gnothi seautón.* Know thyself. You've heard it, read it—too often, you think. Forget Socrates, too. You remember: It is also an entirely modern prescript. Freud, Jung, Adler, Reich, Fromm, Fritz Pearls—the whole of psychology, psychoanalysis, and psychotherapy comes down to the same statement, whether they put you on the couch, or on the chair of Gestalt therapy, or in the darkened room of Primal Scream therapy: Know thyself. From this angle, too (even though it is quite a different angle), you end up with the same question that has faced you all these months: Who are you? What do you really look like? What did you originally look like? Again you see faces, and again there are tears. But you don't have any answer yet. Or you could give this answer: Nothing. You do think certain things; you are a thinking human being, you cannot exist without thinking—and yet thinking in a meditative state is different from everyday, intellectual thinking: you have "sat on it," and for that reason alone it has also to do with experience. So you think: Nothing. You think: The atoms that you consist of—compress them and they will be smaller than a dust mote. Aside from this piece of dust there is: nothing. But the dust mote itself dissolves into atoms, and the atoms into elementary particles and frequencies and energy and into still less. Into nothing.

Once you have had a bit of experience with Zen, you remember: "Nothing"—Japanese, *mu*—is also an exercise; just as "light" is an exercise, the great exercise in the Tibetan Book of the Dead: "My consciousness, luminous and pure, inseparable part of the Great Radiating Body, knows neither birth nor death. It is the unrelenting light."

Nothing. Nothing. Nothing. Light. Light. Light. Original Face. Original Face. Original Face. And you realize that all these problems amount to the same thing.

When I had dealt with the Tibetan word for a while, my Christian heritage came through. More and more I had to think of these words from the Book of Isaiah:

> Arise, shine;
> For thy light is come,
> And the glory of the Lord is risen upon thee.
>
> (Isaiah 60:1)

I sensed that these two statements, the Tibetan one and the one from the Old Testament, in the final analysis mean the same. The light that "is come" to you when you become light yourself, when you realize that your *own* consciousness is "luminous and pure," is "part of the Great Radiating Body." But it comes only if you follow the command of the first two words: "Arise, shine." You cannot wait for things to come to you. Get up on your own, and only then will you experience the "unchangeable light" that to the prophet Isaiah is "the glory of the Lord." This light, this "glory," knows neither birth nor death—and all of a sudden you are back where you were before: This is part of the problem you are supposed to solve, to break down the barrier between death and birth. What was before that? Your original face as a face of light?

There still remains the third part of your problem, the word "Now!"

You are supposed to see your original face *now*. But doesn't that mean you may as well quit? You know you don't see it now. You can't go on living a lie day after day, telling yourself, "Now—Now—Now," while nothing happens "now." No Zen master can be stupid enough to believe that you will fall for that. What, then, is meant by "Now"? Why "Now"? Why not tomorrow, because if anything at all is going to happen, it will be tomorrow at the earliest—or in a couple of months or years—after repeating for the ten thousandth time

NOTHINGEVILNOTHINGGOODMY
ORIGINALFACENOWNOTHINGEVIL
NOTHINGGOODMYORIGINALFACE
NOWNOTHINGEVILNOTHINGGOOD
MYORIGINALFACENOW
NOTHINGEVIL . . . NOWNOWNOW . . .

Somewhere along the line you have begun to realize (is that the reason why you are still hanging on?) that this word *Now* is the most important part of your problem. Nothingevilnothinggood *NOW!* Forget everything else. Do just this one thing. But do it fully. Whatever it may be. You've read it in ancient Zen scriptures: Shit and piss and love and eat and sleep. And feel the pain from sitting in the Buddha posture for hours: pains in your legs, in your back, sometimes all over—all of you is pain—feel this and nothing else. But when you have done it long enough, you feel exactly that: nothing at all. The pain dissolves. Just do one thing at a time—but do that one thing fully: Now! Gradually you understand that Now and Yesterday and Tomorrow are the same, that time doesn't exist, that it dissolves, just like your pain. The only thing left is "Now."

Now you feel your leg. Your pain. Now you are meditating. Now you are thinking—no, you are *being:* Nownownownownow . . . "Now" is what you have sometimes said at the climax of lovemaking, and in this "Now," too, everything else falls away. The only thing left is Now. And you realize, of every type of experience you have ever had, the sexual is the only experience halfway comparable to this one. Here, too, Now is Everything. And One. And here, too, the Now— sometimes at least—becomes Everything.

But you leave that behind, too, because the similarity is only approximate. And you realize: Now is just like Evilandgood, like the Original Face and like Nothing and like Light—they all amount to the same thing. You have already realized that where there is only Now, there is no more time—which means that your original face does not lie so far back in the past. Neither do Nothing and Light. So this is Now. And everything else is in this Now: the Original Face and Nothing and the Light and all the rest to which your path has led you.

Perhaps your path has led you also to a sound. Your koan has become a sound after you have repeated it a few thousand times. The seven words of your exercise are like the seven notes of a scale—or of a chord. You hear them and speak them as One. You don't need the words anymore. The sound is enough. It sounds always and now. It *is* now. It is the fiery ball that your ego swallows, and then it expands and expands—and the ego bursts.

It might happen that way. But at the same time: No. That is not the way it takes place, because it does not take place through words and concepts, through thoughts and abstractions. That was the reason you were given the problem, to transcend the concepts. How do you describe transcendence?

You describe around it, inadequately and approximately—as I have tried to. Lao-tzu said: "The *tao* that can be expressed in words is not the eternal *tao*. The name that can be pronounced is not the name of the eternal *tao*."

The *Genro*, the book of koans mentioned earlier, says: "A koan is a strange thing. When you engage yourself in it, you will be led into a world of experience. The more you experience, the deeper will be your look into the Buddha-nature."

Think about this last sentence. The Christian parallel to it would be something like this: "The stronger your belief, the deeper your understanding of the essence of Christ." Experience and belief confront each other. Zen is not about things you can—or cannot—believe in. Zen is about things one experiences. And the things you have experienced you know. Period. That is why the word *belief* plays no role in Zen texts. It is unnecessary. It is necessary in Western religion—beginning with early Christianity, the apostle Paul in particular, and becoming increasingly important as man became increasingly rationalistic, "brain-oriented," and began to block his own path toward religious experience. For Martin Luther, belief stands in the center of religion—no wonder, because the Reformation and the beginning of the modern age fall together: If religion is to have any chance at all, then the hypertrophy of *ratio*, of Western rationalism, requires the hypertrophy of belief.

What is astounding is the fact that a Zen master can tell whether his disciple has really "cracked" his koan, has really experienced its solution. Outsiders will wonder how he can be sure. It happens quite often that a student of meditation will blissfully run to his *roshi* (his Zen master) to report that he has solved his koan, but the master will send him away again, explaining that the disciple has fallen for what was only an apparent solution and will have to continue meditating. Zen masters are strict, and they can become quite irritated when they are offered such apparent-solutions too frequently.

"Appearances" are frequent in meditation—for instance, the "appearance of beauty." The meditating disciple will hang on to it as a drowning person will cling to a piece of straw. In the end it will become clear that it was indeed only a piece of straw; it was *maya*.

> If you blot out sense and sound—
> what do you hear?

Again, the goal is not to be able to write down an answer. But one thing is obvious: The sound asked for in this koan is a sound "beyond sense and sound," a sound also beyond all music. And yet it is the sound that is the base and the goal of all music. Remember the explanation of the term *Nada Brahma*, given in the preceding chapter: The sound that is left—*now*—when sense and sound are taken away, is *nada*, the primeval rushing, the primeval roaring of the primal *nadi*, the primordial river that is the world. This sound itself *is* the world. Again and again we will have to come back to this point.

We have already noted that almost all koans amount to the same thing. Lies Groening, a German respiratory therapist, for four years the only woman meditating among Zen monks in the Shokoko-ji monastery in Kyoto, was given the task by her master to make the sounding of a bell stop while it was ringing. Here, too, the problem was to take away sense and sound. What did she hear then? Lies Groening had to ask herself whether she had really ever heard at all. Only then did she learn to hear. She became one with the sound of the bell. Only now did she really hear it. She had to "hear so totally" that she herself became the ringing of the bell. Only at that point was she able to make it stop. And only at that point did silence become "the great instrument into which all choirs of life flow."

Many people meditate not on a koan but on a mantra (or—what is best of all, of course, if you can do it—on nothing). A mantra is a sacred sound that may be an entire phrase, a single word, or even a syllable. As we shall see, it is because mantras are sound that they are so effective. What does the word *mantra* mean? The syllable *man* means "intelligence," also "thinking" or "feeling"—everything that distinguishes a human being. The English word *man* is related to it. *Tram* is the helping and protecting power, the "wings" of the psalmist: "He shall cover thee with his wings. And His truth shall be they shield and buckler" (Psalm 91:4). That is *tram*. A *man-tram* spreads its wings over intelligence, thinking, and feeling, over man. The German-born Tibetan Buddhist Lama Anagarika Govinda calls mantras "mental tools . . . tools of the mind."

Mantras emerge from the mantric sound, in Sanskrit *bija,* or "seed." Mantras are germinating seeds that sprout oneness. They are "tools of becoming one." Probably the word *bija* is related to the Sanskrit root *brih* ("to grow"), mentioned in chapter 1, the source of the names for the god Brahma and the cosmic principle, *Brahman.* They are all part of the same linguistic context. The seed from which the mantras sprout is the same as the one from which Lord Brahma grew.

Lama Govinda speaks of the "mantra as primordial sound and as archetypal word symbol." Mantric formulas are "pre-linguistic." They are "primordial sounds which express feelings but not concepts, emotions rather than ideas." From the *bijas,* the germ cells of the mantras, language grew. From the mantras language grows.

The greatest of all mantras is "OM." It is spoken and sung in an especially impressive manner by Tibetan monks, wherever they are living today in their worldwide diaspora, in the Kashmir and Swiss mountains, in the valleys of Colorado and those of northern India. Their singing is marked by the ability to produce with a single human voice entire chords—and what chords they are! Chords that seem to come from the deepest depths and that truly express the meaning of that word, the fact that it contains the Latin word *cor,* "heart."

Western listeners marvel at these Tibetan voices, but they are marvelous to us mainly because we have abstracted the sound (as with many other things), tearing it out of its natural context. When a string is set vibrating (the archetype of all sound production, including that of our human vocal chords) what vibrates is not only the entire string but also inevitably half of the string (the next higher octave, that is); as well as two-thirds of the string (the fifth), three-quarters (the fourth), three-fifths (the major sixth), four-fifths (the major third), five-sixths (the minor third), and so on. In other words: the entire scale is sounded, but as an overtone scale, which of course is the only "natural" scale, the only "true" one. Each note contains all others. Just as in Indic mythology Indra's pearl, although no larger than all other pearls, contains all pearls of the world—and just as, according to recent ideas in particle physics, the events in a single electron "contain" all the nuclear events in the world.

Certain musical cultures exist that are clearly based on the internal connections between all notes. And there are instruments that are especially rich in overtones and whose players do not try to suppress those overtones or at least neglect the vibrations of the overtones (as most Western musicians do), but who develop, cultivate, and accent them: the players of the Indian string instruments, for instance, the sitar, the sarod, the vina, or the surbahar; or those of wind instruments with a similar wealth of overtones, such as the shenai or the nagaswaram. In this way they constantly underline the context of each and every tone with the totality, the "cosmos of all tones," reminding you and themselves of it again and again. ("Cosmos of all tones": the last three words can just as easily be left off.) Above all, however, there are singers—the Tibetan monks, for example—who cultivate the overtones and often also the much less audible, much more difficult to produce undertones. In this way they produce the impression of many-voiced chords, even of polyphony, because different independent melody lines are created. To do this, you need complete relaxation of palate, pharynx, tongue, lips, windpipe, and chest cavity. Nowhere is meditation practiced so much as in Tibet, and meditation particularly promotes this type of relaxation.

This type of overtone singing is also part of the religious tradition of the Mongolian Tuvan, a people living in Siberia. The tradition is guarded by the shamans, the magically and mediumistically gifted priests. Traces of polyphonic-overtone singing, however, can be found in many cultures: among South American Indians, on the island of Sardinia, and in Bulgaria; recently even musicians of contemporary Western Europe and America have become wonderful overtone singers. These particular musicians were able to do so because they meditate.

The ancient scriptures of Tantric Buddhism say the following about OM: "This mantra is the most powerful one. Its power alone can bring enlightenment." And in the Upanishads: "Whoever speaks this mantra thirty-five million times, the mantra of the sacred word, shall be released from his karma and from all his sins. He shall be freed of all his bonds and shall reach absolute liberty."

Nada Brahma, the world is sound: The sages of India and Tibet as well as the monks of Sri Lanka feel that if there is a sound audible to us mortals that comes close to the primal sound that is the world, then it is the sound of the sacred word OM.

Once more a quote from the Upanishads:

> The essence of all beings is earth,
>   the essence of earth is water,

the essence of water are plants,
the essence of plants is man,
the essence of man is speech,
the essence of speech is sacred knowledge,
the essence of sacred knowledge is word and sound,
the essence of word and sound is OM.

And in a different context: "God Brahma spoke: 'You are the holy sacrificial call *Svaha,* you are the power of life, you are the holy call *Vashat*—sound is your essence. You are the draught of immortality, o Everlasting One; your essence lies determined in the three times of the holy syllable OM, you are determined in the halftime which follows the fading syllable OM as silence, o Eternal One who cannot be expressed through differences."

Swami Sivananda Sarasvati cites a well-known Vedic metaphor: "OM is the bow, the mind is the arrow, God or Brahman is the target. . . . Strike the target!"

Elsewhere he adds:

OM is the inner music of the soul. . . .
Become yourself through OM.
Always think of OM.
Sing OM.
Recite OM.
Practice OM.
Meditate OM.
Enter the ship OM.
Sail safely on it . . .
And safely land in the wonderful city
    of the Eternal Brahma.

Speaking and meditating on OM is irresolvably connected with the correct method of breathing. OM "happens" while exhaling. The *M* has to vibrate for a long time—extending as much as possible into the space between exhaling and inhaling, which is the actual moment of emptiness and becoming one. OM signifies that point where "breath" becomes "word" and where "word" becomes "breath," along with everything that belongs to these two words: *atma* ("the self") to breath, and the Greek *logos* to the word.

OM is one of the four great mantric "seed syllables." Lama Govinda names three others: AH, HUM, HRIH. They contain the four basic Sanskrit vowels *o, a, u,* and *i,* which correspond to the "four movements: the circular (all-inclusive), the horizontal, the downward, and the upward movement." Thus it can be said of the four prime mantras, too, that they encompass the universe—like Lord Brahma, who looks into the four cardinal directions, and like the principle of Brahman.

Govinda writes: "OM is the ascent towards universality, HUM the descent of universality into the depth of the human heart."

HUM is the mantric measure for what is human; and so it joined with the *man* (which, as we know, means "intelligence, thinking, feeling") to form *human*.

Govinda: "OM and HUM are like counterpoints in a musical score."

The mantra AH, in contrast, is "the expression of wonder and direct awareness," of marvel, praise, and adoration, which befit us, but also of the cry of pain. And the sound of love.

The seed-syllable HRIH, Govinda says, has "the nature of the flame: it has its warmth, its intensity, its upward movements, its radiance and its color. . . . In [meditating on] OM [the meditator] makes himself as wide as the universe. . . . The movement [of the *O*] is like opening one's arms . . . , so as to make room for the Infinite . . . Light. . . . In [meditating on] HRIH he kindles the upward-leaping flame of inspiration and devotion."

The vowels have a cosmic reference. They correspond to the planets: A to Jupiter, I to Mars, O to Venus, U to Saturn, and E to Mercury. In other words, there is a correlation between the vibrations of the vowels and those of the planets, as was pointed out by the great astronomer Johannes Kepler (see chapter 4). We shall be hearing more about this connection of all things with everything; in chapter 6 I will discuss it in detail. That is also something the great mantric seed-syllables OM, AH, HRIH, and HUM do: they enquire into this connection.

There is also a type of mantra, however, that the meditator has all to himself. It is given to him by his master, or by the person who introduced him to meditation; and it would break the mantric power were he to ever speak about his mantra—except, of course, with his master. When you meditate on such a personal mantra for years, an almost perfect synchronization can develop between the vibrations of the mantra given to you and your own personal vibrations. That is another point we will get back to: man *is* vibration, just as everything else is—not only in a spiritual sense but also physically.

You meditate on your mantra, aloud or only in your subconscious, for years until your master gives you a different task, or until you find a different task yourself.

One of the great mantras of Indian mysticism is "Om mani padme hum" (the Tibetans pronounce it "Om mahni Pay Mae Hoong"). The question as to its meaning brings you only indirectly further. It means: "Hail to the jewel in the lotus!" or: "Hail to him who is the jewel in the lotus!" The lotus blossom, beauty born out of swamp and decay, is one of the great symbols of Asian spirituality. It is not being suggested here that we adopt such a symbol, for we have our own—the rose, for example (whose symbolism, to be sure, also originated in Asia).

The analysis of a mantra, its intellectual interpretation, can only have a crutchlike function. Once more Lama Govinda:

> Just as written music cannot convey the emotional and spiritual impact of heard or performed music, so the sound-symbol of a mantra and its intellectual analysis cannot convey the experience of an initiate and of the profound effects it creates in the course of prolonged practice.

Of the powerful six-syllable mantra "Om mani padme hum," which is "embraced" by the seed-syllables OM and HUM, Govinda says that it has "filled a millennium of Tibetan history with a superhuman aspiration, relected by millions of inscriptions carved on stones and rocks and displayed in gigantic letters on mountainsides."

A mantra frequently used in Zen meditation is the Japanese word MU, in English: "no thing." MU signifies the state the disciple wants to reach in meditation: emptiness, so that he may be filled with being. In MU vibrates the "sound of no thing," that sound which you hear when you "blot out sense and sound."

When used as a mantra, MU illustrates that koan and mantra can blend into each other. As a matter of fact, MU originally was a koan, one of the most famous:

> A monk asked Master Joshu: Can a dog have the Buddha-nature? The *roshi* answered: "Mu."

The reasoning behind this answer is as follows: If everything has Buddha-nature and if Buddha is in everything then, of course, also a dog (or a worm, or a rat) should share in the nature of Buddha. Why, then, did Joshu answer "Mu," meaning "No," "No thing," or "Not being"? —why didn't he say "U," which means "Yes," especially since Master Joshu again and again had pointed out the Buddha-nature of all living things, in different contexts?

The answer is that Joshu did not answer the monk's question but rather disallowed it. His "Mu" wants to express: Do not worry about metaphysics; or: Don't worry about things that are none of your business. So again, as we encountered it earlier, we have the attitude "Shit and piss and eat and sleep," which is in fact an instruction given by a Zen master to his disciple. The following dialogue, between another master and his disciple, has been passed on to us: "Where are you going to go after death?" Answer: "Excuse me for a moment, I have to go to the toilet." Or the instruction: "Name in one breath the Five Moral Principles and the Five Cardinal Virtues" (in Christian Zen, this instruction would be: "In one breath, speak the Ten Command-ments."). The answer: "It's a nice day today."

The court lady Kasuga delivered a spirit from the world of suffering by filling a teacup with water. How did she do that? Quite simply by filling the cup with such inimitable perfection that nothing, not even Buddha, could have been more perfect, and by concentrating her entire being, all her charm and her beauty, even her sexuality (which must have been dazzling, otherwise nobody would remember Lady Kasuga today) and her energy on this act of filling up the teacup just as light rays are focused through a prism—with the result that time and the world (and quite certainly also the polarity of Lady Kasuga and her teapot made of precious ceramic) fell together in a single, all-encompassing "Now!" That is what is meant when Zen demands that a thing be done, but *only* this one thing, in a complete and perfect way. That is what Master Joshu meant to say: It is worthier to piss, but to do that attentively, than to meditate while at the same time thinking about the potential Buddha-nature of a dog. And that is why, taking his koan a step further, he demanded of his disciple, "Hand me MU." The disciple took any object in his reach and gave it to the master—because everything is MU. Everything is nothing. Form is emptiness. "Tell me the size of MU," Joshu asked. And the disciple named his own height, because the disciple is entirely MU—or at least: he is supposed to become MU. MU is the measure of all things, including the size of a human being.

A koan that develops in a dialogue between master and disciple is called a *mondo*. The master asks: "How old is Amida Buddha?" And the disciple answers: "As old as I am." That is a mondo. If he misses the answer, he must continue to meditate on that special mondo until he finds the answer—even if it takes years.

I will never forget how I heard MU for the first time. It was in Kyoto, the old Japanese temple city. I was living in the Miyako Hotel, because I had read about it in a novel by Kawabata, the Japanese Nobel Prize winner in literature. From the hotel I crossed the street to the Nanzen-ji, one of the main temples of the Rinzai sect of Zen. In the *sammon*, the temple gate, I was looking at a painting depicting angels and birds that has become quite famous in Japanese art history, and I was thinking about what this painting wants to say: that the birds' song is no different from that of the angels, that their function is to make audible the angelic message—when suddenly a message was sounded in a side building which was everything else but angelic: MU. I was shocked by the deep droning sound coming from a multitude of male voices and filling the entire temple area. At the time I did not know what it meant. Years later, after I became involved in Zen, this MU with its dark vibrating power exploded within me again. That's the kind of sound it is: You hear it once, and failing to understand it, you actually should forget it again, like so many other things you hear and don't understand—and yet it remains within you, forever unforgettable. A primal sound.

What the mantra is to the Indians and Tibetans, what the koan is to the Chinese and Japanese, that is the *wazifah* to the Sufis. The first mystical Sufi order was founded in the tenth century B.C.E. in Persia. The great Persian poets Jelaluddin Rumi, Hafiz, and Farid al-Din Attar were Sufis. Sufism can be called the esoteric side of Islam, but its veneration of nature goes back to the influence of Zoroaster; Hindu philosophy and Brahmanism flowed into it along with the thinking of Jewish mysticism and of Christianity (especially of the Gospel of John). The Sufis are well aware of all these influences; and this awareness is the source of the Sufi sense of tolerance that distinguishes them from the majority of Muslims. Sufis pray in mosques as well as in Christian churches, in synagogues as well as in Hindu or Buddhist temples.

What makes the Sufis important for our journey is their highly developed sense of sound and music. They call both *Ghiza-i-ruh:* food for the soul. The transition from the sound to the mantra and to the word and from there to music and to poetry is flowing in the minds of the Sufis. In fact, for the famous Sufi Hazrat Inayat Khan (who was a renowned master of the music of northern India before going to the Western world to spread Sufism in the United States and in Europe), this line begins even earlier, with breathing:

> When we study the science of breath the first thing we notice is that breath is audible; it is a word in itself, for what we call a word is only a more pronounced utterance of breath fashioned by the mouth and tongue. In the capacity of the mouth breath becomes voice, and therefore the original condition of a word is breath. If we said, "First was the breath," it would be the same as saying, "In the beginning was the word." . . .
> . . . the first sign of life that manifested was the audible expression, or sound; that is the word. When we compare this interpretation with the Vedanta philosophy, we find that the two are identical. All down

the ages the Yogis and seers of India have worshipped the Word-God, or Sound-God. . . . All occult science, all mystical practices are based upon the science of the word or sound. . . . There are words that echo in the heart, and there are others that do so in the head. And again others have power over the body.

Vilayat Inayat Khan, Hazrat's son, who has carried on his father's work, adds the following words:

Work with the sound until you are absolutely amazed that you could produce such a sound and it seems to you that you are just the instrument through which the divine pied piper blows the whisper of the incantations of his magic spell. . . .
   Use the scale of overtones as a Jacob's ladder to climb. Jacob's ladder is like listening to the echo of an echo. . . .
   Become yourself pure vibration beyond space. If the sound generated by the vocal chords into the vibratory network of the universe has the faculty of tuning one, it is because it links one with the cosmic symphony. The repetition of a physical sound sets off a sound current, a vibration tidal wave in the ether, by building up energy. . . .
   We live on several planes at the same time. It is said in the *Heikhaloth*, the Jewish book of the heavenly spheres, that each time a new soul descends in the ocean of the manifested realm, it generates a vibration which is communicated to the entire cosmic ocean. . . .
Each creature is a crystallization of a part of this symphony of vibrations. Thus we are like a sound petrified in solid matter which continues indefinitely to resound in this matter
      and the word became flesh
        and the word became flesh
          and the word became flesh
            and . . .
   So you must become pure vibration and pass on through the other side.

Mantras are also important in Tantric sexual practices, those techniques that are being practiced more and more also in the Western world, which make it possible "to experience more desire, to give more desire than any desire that mortals know about," and to transcend sexuality into mental and spiritual spheres. The Tantras (literally meaning "fabric") are dialogues, originally written in Sanskrit, between Lord Shiva as the highest potency of male power and his partner Shakti as the personification of the highest female power. The mantras used there are the linguistic archetypes of this dialogue.

   There are three types of mantras in the Tantric tradition: mantras of perception, of control, and of channeling. The first kind *(Ommm Aahdi Ommm)* enhance the sensitivity and the ability to experience desire. They can become so powerful that they begin to show an effect when they are merely uttered or merely thought of, before any body contact takes place, because, as Shiva explains in the Tantric texts, "the center of desire is the mind."

The mantras of control *(Pahhh Dahhh O-Mahmmm)* are used to increase self-discipline, to delay orgasm, and to abide by the "one hour rule" of the Tantrics: orgasm should not be attained any earlier than one hour after beginning union. Practiced frequently enough, these mantras are effective even beyond the "point of no return," when they "ignite the bodies to such heights of ecstasy that they sink into a dreamlike state wherein they are held for hours at the border of an orgasm that does not take place."

The most difficult Tantric technique is that which comes closer and closer to orgasm but remains at that point with the aid of the control mantra and avoiding actual orgasm. In Tantric language: "diving into the ocean's depth without getting wet." Or: "Riding the tiger" but not getting thrown off even by the wildest jumps, because for the rider that would mean getting torn apart by the tiger. Together rider and tiger roar the mantra which has grown out of the tiger's primal scream.

For Taoists, the tiger is *yin*, a symbol for the woman. The *yang* symbol for the man is the kite: Having mastered the control ritual, it is able to fly and fly and fly without coming down. If it has not mastered it, however, it will crash, be smashed to pieces and devoured by the tiger. Tantrics have only to evoke these images, "riding the tiger" and "flying the kite," and insiders know what is meant.

The third of these mantras, the channeling mantra *(Ahhh Nahhh Yahhh Taunnn)*, transcends the sexual power into the mental and spiritual sphere "so that the power is directed not downward but up," creating a union between the couple making love and the universe. The techniques of channeling (often practiced after using the control ritual for hours) make it possible to lift the sexual consciousness into spheres where it transcends into cosmic consciousness, otherwise reached only by meditation.

In recent times, Tantra workshops and courses have been held also in the Western world, so that Tantric techniques are employed much more frequently than before. In this way, Western men and women are now able to experience the effectiveness of mantras with a verifiable force that they no longer question.

Koans . . . mondos . . . mantras . . . wazifahs . . . prayer . . . wherever we look, there is knowledge of the power of sound, syllable, and word. For Japan's Pure Land Buddhists it is the *Namu Amida Butsu:* the word *namu* (the English word "name" comes from the same root) signifies "self-power" and *amida* the "other-power," the divine one.

"*Namu Amida Butsu* symbolizes the unification of . . . self-power and other-power" (D. T. Suzuki).

The mantra of Nichiren Shoshu Buddhism, which many contemporary musicians in jazz, rock and concert music profess, is "Nam Myoho Renge Kyo," the "roaring of the lion," as it is called. In this expression of "adoration to the *Lotus Sutra*" (the literal translation of "Nam Myoho Renge Kyo," referring to the Buddhist scripture held as foremost by Nichiren followers), the syllable *nam* signifies the bodily and mental "self-power" of the meditating person; *myoho* is the "law of the hereafter"; *renge* is the name of an especially precious lotus flower (but the word also stands for the karmic law of cause and effect); and *kyo* is word and sound, language and voice, sutra, vibration. These four words together, according to the thirteenth-century Japanese priest Nichiren Daishonin, literally "embrace" the entire *Lotus Sutra*—eight volumes, a total of twenty-eight chapters. They stand for the entire giant work. It is noteworthy in our context that *sutra* (that is, the form of the most sacred scriptural tradition of *Shakyamuni,* of Gautama Buddha), in Japanese *kyo,* means "word, language, voice, sound, vibration." The sound of *Nam Myoho Renge* "embraces" the world. It is *Nada Brahma.*

Once again: There is no need to know exactly what a mantra means. It is effective beyond the conscious intellect, and only for that reason is it able to "compel the transcendentation of the mental, rational concept." "You must become pure vibration" (Vilayat Inayat Khan).

The following mondo has been handed down from ninth-century China: The Zen disciple asks his *roshi:* "How should I hear correctly?" The master answers: "Not with your ears." The disciple asks for further explanation, but the master says only: "Do you hear now?" Now! At this moment the disciple finds enlightenment.

Tozan, a Zen monk of the ninth century, wrote:

> Let your eye catch the sound.
> Then you will finally understand . . .

—which certainly does not imply a preference for the eye over the ear. Tozan could just as well have said: "Let your ear catch the colors. Then you will finally understand." The point is to transcend what everybody does, to attack the obvious and the superficial in the conventional ways of behavior. The point is to experience the inaudible of the sounds, the invisible of the colors, the visible of the sounds, the audible of the colors. The Mu.

For centuries, the sages of India and Tibet have referred to the power that comes from mantras. The Tibetans say that the entire universe came into being out of the primal sound OM, the primal mantra, the primal syllable that again and again renews the command "Let there be . . ." Nor is this a concept foreign to those of us born in the Judeo-Christian tradition, because for us, too, the world came into being through a mantra, through God's "Let there be . . ." (Genesis 1:3).

"Let there be . . ." That is a mantra—and a mantra is: word! That is why the Gospel according to John says: "In the beginning was the word. And the word was with God. And the word was God" (John 1:1). This knowledge of the mantric power of God's word exists not only in the Book of Genesis at the beginning of the Old Testament and again in the Gospel according to John. This knowledge is the very foundation of the Holy Scripture. That is why it is the "word of God."

Goethe, that giant of eighteenth-century German letters, knew nothing of mantras. Yet the hero of his most important drama, Faust, appears on the stage poring over a translation he is making of the Gospel of John, and stops at the first verse to proclaim:

> I cannot hold the word in such high esteem,
> I have to translate it a different way. . . .
> . . . "In the beginning was the deed"!

In having Faust replace the word with the deed, Goethe formulated the problems that our scientific-technological age experiences with word and mantra, a troubled attitude that has become common in Western culture. In particular many Protestants exhibit this kind of attitude toward the mantra and to prayer by repetition. They look on the Tibetan prayer-wheel and on the Catholic rosary alike with misapprehension and arrogance, seeing both as a mindless rattling off, a parroting. Yet they never bother to attempt to penetrate what is really taking place here, namely the unconditional observation of Christ's word: "Men ought always to pray" (Luke 18:1). For those who pray continually, prayer becomes a mantra.

Mantras and wazifahs are symbols of the primal sound. If the world is sound, and if this sound which is the world is rationally unattainable for mortal humans, then we need reflections, symbols, parables. We need them also in order to make ourselves understood, for ourselves and for others.

Mantras and their seed syllables, the *bijas*, stand at the beginning not only of language but also of music. In fact, any music that is conscious of its spiritual source is nothing other than a variation of the primal mantra, the primal sound that it seeks—in everything that sounds within it. The literature of spirituality is filled with such interpretations of music. In the Tibetan Book of the Dead, the deceased, on his migration through the intermediate state between death and rebirth, hears "innumerable kinds of musical instruments that fill entire world-systems with music and cause them to vibrate, to quake and tremble, with sounds so mighty as to stun one's brain. . . ."

Over and over again I have found that the concepts "primal sound" and "primal tone" are for many people so within the realm of the plausible that, even when they are heard for the first time, they need no explanation. They are archetypal concepts.

In the Upanishads the "primal sound" is called *Sabda Brahman*, the sound of Lord Brahma, the cosmic sound whose power resides in all words that express the essential. In the Vedas, it is the *anahad*, the "unlimited tone." And for the musicians and sages of India since the times of the Moguls, *Nada Brahma* is the primal sound, understood as "Brahma-sound," "world-sound," or "god-sound." In order to understand it, one needs *Nada Yoga:* drill and exercise and training through sound. Sufis call the primal sound *Saute Surmad*, the tone that fills the cosmos. Muhammad perceived it when he was enlightened in the cave of Gare-Hira. So Islam also knows the sound that says, "Let there be. . . ." Sufi Hazrat Inayat Khan writes:

> This sound is the source of all manifestation. . . . The knower of the mystery of sound knows the mystery of the whole universe.

The Hebraic-Jewish world has a sense of these matters too. The trumpets that brought down the walls of Jericho are symbols of the power of the primal sound and of primal music. The "trumpeting cherub" is a Hebrew and Christian prime concept, and what he blows is primal music.

Of course, mantras also exist in the realm of Christianity. *Amen,* the *Hail Mary* of the rosary, *Hallelujah, Hosanna, Kyrie Eleison*—these are all mantras. The last named—"Lord have mercy"—is the "Jesus prayer" of the Orthodox tradition, used by wandering monks, many of whom meditate on it for years. If one is skeptical of mantra stories from Asia, one can find an impressive report on the methods and effects of using mantras in a work that is closer to our Western European tradition: in *The Way of a Pilgrim,* the classic account by a devout nineteenth-century Russian peasant who learns from a monastic elder the practice of the "ceaseless Jesus prayer":

> The elder opened the *Philokalia* to the account of St. Simeon the New Theologian and began reading: "Sit alone and in silence; bow your head and close your eyes; relax your breathing and with your imagination look into your heart; direct your thoughts from your head into your heart. And while inhaling say, 'Lord Jesus Christ, have mercy on me,' either softly with your lips or in your mind. Endeavor to fight distractions but be patient and peaceful and repeat this process frequently."

Whether consciously or not, the many translators of the Old and New Testaments must have felt that *Amen, Hallelujah,* and *Hosanna* are mantras, because these words—and these words alone—are commonly left untranslated, as are many sacred words in the Catholic Mass *(Kyrie Eleison, Sanctus, Agnus Dei,* etc.).

Many of the translated words and sentences of the Holy Scriptures, however, also have to be understood as mantras: the "word" of the Gospel of John, "peace on earth" in the Christmas story, and, of course, "Let there be . . ." of the Book of Genesis. Above all though, the divine and sacred names are mantras: God, Jesus, Christ, Mary, Lord, Creator . . . We shall see that the name has magic power —which is why *nam* is a primal syllable: It exists all over the world, as far away as in Japan in the *namu* of the Amida Buddha.

An echo of the primal sound and the primal tone has resounded in more recent times also. For instance, in nineteenth-century German Romanticism: E. T. A. Hoffmann, A. W. Schlegel, Clemens Brentano, Ludwig Tieck, and Novalis are some of the pertinent names. Jean Paul, one of the great exponents of this genre, spoke of music as the "echo from a distant harmonical world," as "the angel's sigh within ourselves."

More recently than that, the theologian Dietrich Bonhoeffer, a member of the resistance movement in Nazi Germany, just a few weeks before he was hanged by the Gestapo wrote in his cell in a Berlin SS prison about "the rich sound of the world that invisibly spreads itself around us"—a sound which becomes audible only in stillness, even the stillness of a prison cell.

"Magic words" play an important role in the tales and sagas of almost all peoples of the world. The "magic word" is the mantra. It is the primal tension, the "tone" that created the world. Greek *tónos* and

Latin *tonus* mean not only "tone" or "sound" but also "tension." *Teino* in Greek means "I tense." Hence *tónos* also means: "rope, silk, effort, power, stress, earnestness." It is the tension of the string whose one tone makes all other tones vibrate in sympathy. Thus even etymologically the primal tone is primal tension. Indeed, it will become a key practice on this journey to listen for the sound and the sense of language in its primal syllables and primal words.

Quite impressively, Heinrich Zimmer has pointed out the fluency of transition from sound to mantra, and from mantra to the magic word and to the power of great poetry: "As in its first sounding immediacy came over the seer-poet in the form of images and words with mystic compulsion (a compulsion through which the poet came to terms with immediacy as image and word), so it will be a mystic compulsion, a magic tool, for any future generation conversant in the use of mantra words to create immediate reality: manifestation of deities or the play of forces. Indeed, this is the characteristic of the true poet: that his word creates indisputable reality, that it directly summons and unveils real things. His word does not speak, it creates reality."

For a long time, Western rationalists smiled at the notion that the sound of a single word, a single syllable should have a formative, shaping, creative power. The smile seems to have faded from their faces, however: more people meditate today in the West than in the East. Here too, millions of people have experienced the power of mantra in themselves and in others. And above all, modern science has made physical, physiological, and psychological findings that verify the strength immanent in mantras.

Mantras consist of vibrations. Our nerves, our ganglia, and our cells also vibrate. The law of resonance teaches us: Anything that vibrates reacts to vibrations, even (as recent discoveries have shown) to the most minute vibrations, and to those that only a few years ago could not be measured—brainwaves, for instance—and hence logically also to vibrations that have yet to become measurable. Considering the fact that scientists have been discovering new waves and rays for a century and a half, we must conclude that new waves and rays and vibrations will continue to be discovered; in fact, any discovery of a new kind of vibration is evidence that countless others await discovery as well. Only the rationalist sees things differently: Unconvinced, in each generation, he believes himself to be in possession of the last and final word; and he simply cannot see that his sons and successors will have a different "last" and even more "final" word, which in turn will be surpassed or disproved by their sons and successors. That is one of the most absurd aspects of the behavior of Western science: for centuries on end it has patted itself on the back every twenty or thirty years for having reached the pinnacle of scientific inquiry and in this arrogant pose has passed its findings on to its students and successors. Still, no doubt, the fact that certain vibrations and currents have been perceived for centuries is more significant than its measurability, which may be verified even tomorrow.

Vilayat Inayat Khan: "In the Mantram practices one actually kneads the very flesh of our body with sound. The delicate cells of these elaborate bundles of nerve fibers that are the plexi or ganglia . . . are subjected to a consistent hammering. . . . There is a kind of seizure of the flesh by the vibrations of sound."

The Tibetans are a practical people. Were they merely the esoteric mystics that they are in the eyes of the Western world, they could never have survived in their harsh mountain world of snow and ice. They would not recite mantras for half a lifetime (as Tibetans have been doing for centuries), had they not tested and experienced again and again the power of such syllables and sounds in themselves.

In his book *Mantras: Sacred Words of Power* John Blofeld tells of an old monk who was asked where his cheerful serenity came from. His answer was that it was the sound of the mantras that enabled him to experience his inner harmony with the *tao,* the primal path and sense of existence. Blofeld continues:

> I was able to recognize the superiority of mantric utterance to prayer, for prayers convey a conceptual meaning and by evoking thought mar the stillness of the adept's mind. One's mind cannot attain a calm, untroubled state reflecting the serenity of the Source for as long as it dwells on such dualisms as "I, the worshipper; He, the worshipped." Prayer is at best an elementary form of mystical communion; as for prayers that contain petitions, what can be more unspiritual and self-seeking than to pray for victory, a particular state of weather or good fortune that can be attained only at the expense of others?

The superiority of mantric praying over Christian prayer is pointed out also by Lama Govinda. He compares the *mudras,* the prayer gestures of the Buddha and the Buddhist world (for example, that in which the palms of the hands are placed toward each other in front of the chest, with the fingertips pointed upward and thus receiving from above) with the folded hands of Christianity:

> In contrast to this natural gesture of praying [i.e., the Asian] is another gesture, in which the fingers are interlocked in such a way that it appears as if the praying person were shackled or straining in a feeling

of helplessness and despair, or struggling to obtain something by sheer force of will. It is significant that this gesture . . . has now, as it seems, been generally adopted in Western countries. Does it not reflect the tense, if not cramped, attitude of the Western individual?

Since in recent times the Western world has gradually begun to acquire an awareness of the power of mantras, it should now become possible to rediscover and put into practice the essence of the mantras also of the Christian world, for instance, the mantric power of a *Hallelujah* or a *Hosanna* by Johann Sebastian Bach. We shall have to realize that such a *Hosanna* (one of the most beautiful ones is that of Bach's *Mass in B minor*) can be heard in a completely new way if in all its notes we listen for the mantric content of the word *Hosanna* (in its pure form, Osanna), feeling its primal sound. In fact, we will *have* to learn to listen to such music in a state of mantric consciousness if we want to avoid either losing it altogether in the course of the coming generations or perceiving it as merely something exotic. That is the negative side of our new consciousness: Whatever does not go along consciously on the journey of change, whatever is merely dragged along the beaten track of tradition, we shall lose.

In the koan—and in the mondo—the spiritual power of Buddhism meets the rationality of Chinese Confucianism. China's Sung masters of the twelfth century were the first to use koans in our contemporary sense, but it was—characteristically enough—the Japanese who, beginning in the thirteenth century, perfected the koan technique. Koans are intensely, practically effective. They would be unthinkable without the Chinese sense of practicality and the Japanese sense of efficiency. D. T. Suzuki reminds us that the absurdity, the nonsense of many koans ("Walk by riding a donkey" or "Use the spade you are holding in your empty hands") first and foremost challenges man's rationalistic leanings by provoking, even insulting them.

This is, in fact, one of the fundamental problems in Zen meditation: The disciple says to himself, If the *roshi* has given me this task and says that it can be solved, then it must be so, I must be able to solve it. Of course it is only human to continue this train of thought by concluding that the solution has to be found with force, will, and the clarity of reason. But that's the trick of the koan: As for days, weeks, or years the disciple's reason probes the question given to him, he realizes on his own that reason is getting him nowhere. There is no more rational method of recognizing and, more importantly, directly experiencing the bounds of rationality than to work on a koan. Anyone who has managed to solve a koan no longer finds it a matter of discussion, because he has experienced it for himself: Reason is not enough, reason will inevitably lead you into a dead-end street. Suzuki, who uses the expression "dead-end street" in this context, writes:

> To expect any final answer from the intellect is asking too much of it, for this is not in the nature of intellection. The answer lies deeply buried under the bedrock of our being. . . . Whatever we may say about the intellect, it is after all superficial, it is something floating on the surface of consciousness. The surface must be broken through. . . . The intellect is needed to determine, however vaguely, where reality is. And the reality is grasped only when the intellect quits its claim on it. Zen knows this and proposes as a koan something which in disguise looks as if it demanded a logical treatment, or rather looks as if there were room for such treatment.

From a Western point of view, it may be surprising to read that in China and Japan the rational element nevertheless plays a role that goes beyond anything comparable in the Christian world. Indeed, Christianity reaches the limits of reason much sooner than East Asian spirituality. In Christianity you stand at the boundary from the beginning. Christ's crucifixion and resurrection for the salvation of the world—all this is beyond reason. Christianity and rationality contradict each other much more than do Zen and rationality. It is important for us to be reminded of this fact, because European rationalists are naturally convinced of the opposite. They feel that their own world of Western Christianity has a monopoly on rationality, whereas Zen and irrationality are inseparable. That is the position of people who are so fearful of the irrational that they fail to take a close look. It is characteristic of Western scientific thinking to give up its rationality, its discipline, its security, and its methods as soon as it approaches a field that eludes its grasp, or seems to do so. Zen is such a field.

It is a special outrage to the followers of rationalism that with the very aid of logical reasoning one can perceive its inadequacies all the more indisputably. In this disturbing situation they prefer from the outset to operate without logic and rationality, just like traditional Christian believers.

One way to experience the relativity and the limits of logic and *ratio* leads through the realization that what Western civilization calls "logic" is only one of several possible "logics." This is characteristic of our arrogant Western concept of logic: the plural form "logics" is not even grammatically permissible. According to our textbooks there is only one logic, "our" Aristotelian logic.

Just as a reminder: Aristotelian logic is based on the law of identity

(A equals A), the law of contradiction (A cannot be equal to non-A), and on the law of the excluded third (A cannot be equal to A as well as to non-A). Beside it stands (and has stood since ancient times) what is known as paradoxical logic, which postulates that A and non-A can both be predicates of X. Chuang-tzu, the ancient Chinese sage, wrote: "What is one, is one. What is not-one, also is one." And Erich Fromm notes: "Paradoxical logic was predominant in Chinese and Indian thinking, in Heraclitus' philosophy, and then again under the name of dialectics in the thought of Hegel and Marx."

Rational Western man thinks that the world "logically" functions solely according to Aristotelian logic. Western man is so subject to this "Aristotelitis" that he fails to realize that even in his closest surroundings paradoxical logic is constantly dominant. Sigmund Freud created the concept of ambivalence: You can feel love and hatred for the same person at the same time. We tend to think this is "illogical," and yet many of us experience such feelings daily. It is "illogical" only from the standpoint of Aristotelian logic; from the viewpoint of paradoxical logic, it is utterly "logical."

In reference to the work of the mathematicians and physicists John von Neumann and Garrett Birkhoff, Carl Friedrich von Weizsäcker has pointed out that quantum mechanics has long developed its own "quantum logic." In his essay "Quantenlogik und mehrfache Quantelung" (Quantum Logic and Multiple Quants), von Weizsäcker has compiled and further elaborated its equations and postulates. He writes: "The suspicion that classical logic might fail stems from the failure of the classical theory of probability in the field of quantum theory . . . The failure lies in the theorem of addition of probabilities." Weizsäcker points out that quantum logic "has to do with the changed attitude of quantum theory to the methodology of the separation of subject and object"—that same separation that Zen also recognizes as illusory. One of the main tenets of the Zen master Hakuin states: "The difference between subject and object exists only as long as there is ego consciousness." Any modern nuclear physicist could unconditionally subscribe to this tenet—with the one difference that Hakuin posited it around the year 1720, whereas quantum mechanics came to similar conclusions only in 1927, when Heisenberg formulated his famous "uncertainty principle." Heisenberg's "observer" is Hakuin's "ego consciousness."

Still another form of logic (or, *de facto,* several "logics") will be demanded by the phenomenon of multidimensions, which developed out of the theory of relativity and Hermann Minkowski's space-time equations. Lama Govinda remarks that "there are as many different kinds of logic as there are dimensions"—a statement that is completely in line with the British physicist David Bohm's theories about multidimensional worlds. Govinda calls for an effort to overcome "our one-dimensional logic which—while proceeding in a straight line towards any given object—cuts the world apart with the knife of its 'Either-Or,' in order to build from the lifeless pieces of a dissected world a merely conceptual and totally abstract universe." Heisenberg and Bohm come to the same conclusion.

Govinda reminds us that "logics" similar to those that modern theoretical physics has rendered irrefutable have been in existence in Indian Hinduism and Buddhism for several millennia. Indian logic is based not on the law of contradiction and that of the excluded third, but on a fourfold logic that admits the following propositions about an object:

1. It is
2. It is not
3. It is and is not
4. It neither is nor is not

Indian logic, in other words, postulates four possibilities:

1. Being (or "existence" of the object)
2. Not-being
3. Being as well as Not-being
4. Neither Being nor Not-being

Our Western concept of logic is strongly conditioned by Western language. It cannot be an accident that Aristotelian logic came into being in classical Greece, in whose language the separation of subject and object, common to all Western languages, found its first clear expression and was immediately realized, in a magnificent, graphic manner that was never duplicated by subsequent systems. Carl Friedrich von Weizsäcker speaks of the "language dependency of the thought systems of the great cultures." He points out that "the philosophies are closely related to the grammatical structures of their language. The subject-predicate scheme of Aristotelian logic corresponds to the grammatical structure of the Greek declarative sentence."

In his time, Nietzsche noted that the "astounding family likeness" seen in Western philosophies could be explained "simply enough," namely by their "unconscious domination by the same grammatical functions."

By way of contrast, the thinking behind the Chinese and Japanese languages, does not move in a straight line from the subject to the object with the aid of the verb. It circles around its object and envelops it until it is specified as precisely as the objects in our Western languages (which presupposes an *inner* predicate); in fact, specialists feel that these Asian languages are even more precise since they do not simply "objectivate" but rather let subject and object "become one" so that the active and the passive mode fall together.

This phenomenon shows itself impressively in the treatment of "I", the "subject of all subjects." There are ten different ways to express "I" in Japanese; which, however, does not mean that this wealth of expressions is extensively used. On the contrary, they are suppressed. The Japanese language not only avoids the "I," the subject, but also the "you," the object. No Japanese will say to his or her lover "I love you." He or she will say "Aishiteru," which means: "Loving." There is no need for "I" and "you"; they form a union in "loving." There isn't even a need for a verbal ending. To be sure, the Japanese lover who says "Aishiteru" is unusually modern and direct. Usually he or she will find much more cautious wordings (as I said, circuitous ones that express a union) to express the emotion "I love you."

The Japanese linguist Ryogí Okochi, from whose work the above remarks are derived, cites an example from an old collection of Japanese poetry, the *Manyoshu* (eighth century). Translated into English, the poem is something like this:

> When I eat melons I have to
>   think of my son. He is dead.
> When I eat chestnuts I think of him
>   even more.
> He loved chestnuts even more than melons.
> Why is my child's face so much on
>   my mind?
> His face is constantly in front of my eyes,
>   so that I cannot find sleep even at night."

The original Japanese version says much less:

Uri hameba kodomo omohoyu—	Eating melons, thinking son.
kuri hameba masthite shinobayu	Eating chestnuts, even more.
izuku yori kitarishi monozo	How come?
managaini motona kakarite	In front of eyes hanging always.
yasuishi nasanu	No restful sleep.

Note that there are almost no subjects and objects. But the strange thing is that they have not been excluded but rather have become fused. This becomes particularly clear in the very first sentence: In "thinking son," the "son" is not an object anymore; it forms a union with the "thinking." And since the word "I" seems to "slip into" this union, the point we are talking about finds a perfect image: the union of the mother with the thinking with the son.

We note that the "becoming one" demanded in Zen has a linguistic base. Of course, it must be much easier for a person speaking this language to reach the state of "being one" than for somebody who, from childhood, has been trained to disassemble even the simplest fact into subject, predicate, object.

Furthermore: not only are subject and object one; the difference between the active and the passive mode is also unnecessary. The Japanese say: "Yama ga mieru," and the English would translate: "The mountain is seen." Or: "I see the mountain." But "Yama ga mieru" simply means: "Mountain seeing." The English language has no choice but to translate this sentence into either active or passive tense. "In reality however," writes Ryogí Okochi,

> it speaks neither in the active nor in the passive mode; the act of speaking and that which is spoken take place beyond the separation of active doing and passive suffering, that is, in pure motion "through themselves." . . . Seeing and being seen, the looking at and the showing itself of the thing-seen belong inseparably together. . . . The mountain is not an object in the Western sense, but the topic that indicates what we now [!] have to do with. . . . The act of "seeing" includes both aspects, the seer and that which is seen. Doing and suffering, seeing and being seen are indistinguishably one in this act."

A favorite symbol of Zen is the circle. At the end of a *seshin* many *roshi*s give their disciples a circle drawn with ink on a precious piece of rice paper. The circle is a symbol meaning: All is one. The symbol of the Western way of speaking and of Western logic is the straight line, certainly not "written" freehand with ink but drawn with a ruler—a line for which the German writer and filmmaker Herbert Achternbusch discovered the perceptive metaphor "super-highway through the brain"; in fact straightline thinking is slapped on our brain nodes as violently and insensitively as super-highways are slapped over the countryside.

Argument and discourse in our Western way of speaking and thinking can be symbolized by two intersecting lines drawn with arrows at their ends, one pointing to the left and the other one pointing to the right. The two directions contradict each other, struggle with each other. Struggle is part of the plague of "Aristotelitis." The circle, however, leads contradictions toward each other, assimilating contrasts and embracing them—as, by the way, Hegel's dialectic does (or should do!). Struggle, however, is so much a part of our Western mode that those thinkers who come from Hegel (Marx and the Marxists as well as most sociologists), instead of realizing the unifying message of the theory of dialectics, made it the foundation of an even fiercer struggle than had existed before.

The German scholar Frederic Vester has shown that the processes and ways of thinking of contemporary cybernetics also contradict our conventional logic. They do not develop along the line of Aristotelian logic, connecting cause and effect, past and future on a straight line, but operate in circular motion, in "closed control loops," whereby an effect can become a cause and where the past can be controlled by the future (!). The cause can be anywhere, wherever we "enter" the "loop." The same is true about the past. Effect and future are just as arbitrary. They exist at that point where the "control loop" is left again. Someone else may enter the "loop" at exactly that point. "My" effect will then be "his" cause, "my" future will become "his" past.

We have all observed how, when children fight with each other, each will say of the other that "he started it." It is an observation that in cybernetics gains scientific status. The children are right: Cause and effect are not "objectively defined"; they depend on the "point of entry," where I "started it"—which no doubt is a different point than the "starting point" of the other person.

Thinking and planning in "control loops" in economics, ecology, medicine, biology, and urban development, for instance, is much more efficient, saves costs and energy and in the long run produces more organic effects than processes planned with the aid of conventional logic (where only singular symptoms are controlled and where, in the long run, the total complex system is destroyed).

The idea of unlimited growth, for example, is a "logical" idea. Cybernetic thinking, however, knows that complex systems can grow only up to a certain limit. Once they grow beyond that point, they destroy themselves—and usually their neighbor systems along with them. Essentially, it is "logical" thinking that has brought about many of the problems that seem unresolvable today: the chaos in our streets, the ungovernability of our cities, the cost explosion in conventional medical care, our inefficient protection of our natural resources, the coincidence of inflation and high rates of unemployment, the planning errors in the electric power industry, the inescapably erroneous prognoses of economists, the almost inevitable deterioration of the original state of affairs caused by large-scale construction projects designed to improve that very state (some of the prime examples: the large dams in Aswan, Egypt, and in Kariba gorge of the Zambezi River, South-central Africa; the development of the Okavango Valley in West-central Africa; or the billions of dollars worth of bad investments in European uranium enrichment plants). If in the fifties, for instance, politicians and scientists had learned to think and plan in circles and loops and to understand systems, they would have never built the Aswan High Dam, which not only failed to improve Egypt's economic and agrarian situation but indeed brought about an alarming deterioration.

In diverse publications, Vester has cited hundreds of examples in which conventional logical thinking has not only not solved the integral problems of today's world, but rather made them even worse (with especially disastrous results in the medical field, as for instance in the treatment of cancer). Vester relates a discovery he made at a cybernetics conference in Japan: To the Japanese—not only scientists but "average" people—thinking in "control loops" as it is done in cybernetics comes naturally and thus creates far fewer problems for them than for Westerners, who are still used to thinking along straight lines. Thinking and speaking in a circular motion has always been part of the Japanese language, tradition, and spirituality.

Thinking causally, however, can be replaced not only by operating with loops, but also through thinking teleologically and/or in analogies. We shall see that thinking by analogy is much more effective in harmonic contexts, which are a main point of this book, than conventional causal thinking. Its results are just as correct from a scientific viewpoint as the results reached by causal thinking; and the same holds true of teleological thinking. If I say of a table that its "cause" is the wood, or of a letter that its "cause" is the pen, then I am thinking along the lines of nineteenth-century science, with its strictly material orientation. This kind of thinking is still prevalent in almost all fields of science. If I determine table or letter "teleologically," however (in terms of their *raison d'être* or their desired effect), I can make far more relevant statements about them. It is necessary to consider how much Western man and his science limit themselves, how much they have narrowed their field of vision by using Aristotelian logic and causal thinking almost exclusively and by disdaining any other form of perceiving reality.

I feel that this excursion into "logics" is necessary in light of what we have said about koans and mantras and their effects. The Western rationalist position that what has been said here "can't be correct," because it is "absurd," no longer bears out. Not only koans are absurd.

The statements of the new physics are also absurd. And there are exact parallels between these absurdities. Today's rationalists must recognize that they are not well informed, that they live in the thinking of the last century, unaware that advanced Western science has finally found its way to systems of paradoxical logic corresponding to those in existence in Asia for thousands of years. At a later point I shall return to the following statement, made by Fritjof Capra: "Quantum mechanics are the Zen koan of our times."

MUSIC FOR LISTENING TO THE SECOND CHAPTER

The Music of Tibet: The Tantric Rituals ("OM"). Record 6 of *An Anthology of the World's Music.* Anthology AST 4005 (Anthology Record and Tape Corp., 135 West 41st St., New York, NY 10036).

Tibetan Ritual Music. Chanted and played by lamas and monks. Lyrichord LLST 7181.

The Songs of Milarepa. Tibetan sacred music performed at the Mahayana Buddhist Nunnery, Tilokpur. Lyrichord LLST 7285.

Padmasambava Chopa. A Tibetan Buddhist Rite from Nepal. Lyrichord LLST 7270.

Tibetan Songs of Gods and Demons. Lyrichord LLST 7291.

Tibetan Mystic Songs. Lyrichord LLST 7290.

Tibetan Bells II, by Henry Wolff and Nancy Hennings. Celestial Harmonies CEL 005.

Buddhist Tantras of Gyuto (Tibet). Nonesuch 72 064.

The Singing Bowls of Tibet. Saydisc 326.

Ritual Music (Tibet). Lyrichord LLST 7181.

Mystery of the Bulgarian Voice. Disques Cellier 008.

Shomyo-Buddhist Ritual from Japan. Zen songs recorded in various monasteries of the Shingon sect. Philips 6586021.

Zen: Inner Gates. Ceremonies, songs, and sounds, recorded in four temples of the Rinzai sect, including the Daitoku-ji, Kyoto. Philips PH 1513/14 (2 LPs with detailed text).

Zen: Head Sounds. Philips CD-4.

Buddhist Chant. A recorded survey of actual temple rituals: Zen, Shomyo, Goeika, Nembutsu, Yamabushi. Lyrichord LLST 7118 (2 LPs).

Japanese Temple Music. Zen, Nembutsu, and Yamabushi chants. Lyrichord LLST 7117.

Buddhist Drums, Bells and Chants. Recorded at actual services in the temples of Kyoto, Japan. Lyrichord LLST 7200.

Zen: Goeika and Shomyo Chants. Lyrichord LLST 7116.

3 🐚   In the Beginning
        Was the Sound

To facilitate comprehension of this chapter, try reading the next few pages out loud while listening to the sound of the words. Besides, it will be more enjoyable that way.

On Sound, Logos, and Rose

En àrchên en ho lógos—"In the beginning was the word"—is written in the Gospel of John. "In the beginning was OM" is what the Tibetans say. The two ideas are related. In the preceding chapter we saw that the transition between mantric sound and the spoken word is fluid. When human sound takes on a mentally comprehensible meaning, it becomes a word. Wassily Kandinsky found that "the word is an inner sound." Jean Gebser writes:

> As we come closer to the magic structure, the images fade away. . . . Only one means remains for approaching it more closely: sound. Or, if you will, we must attempt to render audible certain specific and highly differentiated primordial sounds. . . . The question is, How do we find these values? It would not be amiss if we were to seek them in the sound of the word-root.

51

The German linguist Arnold Wadler writes: "The opening of the Gospel of John, 'In the beginning was the word, and the word was with God,' meant an entirely real truth for ancient man; he was still aware of the nature and origin of the word."

In the Book of Genesis we read: "And God said. . . ." The word spoken by God was the word *light:* "And there was light." (I cannot think of this passage without hearing the radiant *fortissimo* major chord with which Haydn celebrates the word *light* in his oratorio *The Creation.* Whatever is expressed in this chord—as if it were *nadi,* a stream breaking through from a narrow passage into freedom and brightness—: that is the mantric power of the word *light.*)

This word *light,* as well as English *loud* and Greek *"logos"* (which, if you remember, means both "sound" and "word") all go back to the same primal root *leg.* Gebser has pointed out the central importance of this root. Some of the countless words stemming from it are: *Lux* (Latin, "light"), *light, logos, lychne* (Greek, "lamp"), *lex* (Latin, "law"), *language, legein* (Greek, "to gather, to collect, to talk, to read, to count"); the last-named, in turn, is the root of the Latin word *re-ligio* (which became our word *religion*). All this, and more, has developed out of the syllable *leg.* On the other hand, it also gave rise to the Germanic word *lug,* which is related to our English *lie!* One should bear that in mind: *Light* and *logos, loud,* and *lie* all go back to the same primal root, a root that left its traces in many kinds of languages on all continents. The same word is *liuhat* in Gothic, *l'ikhuta* among the Aymara Indians in Peru, *laki* in Melanesia, *lang* in Micronesia, *langit* among the Khmer of Cambodia, *langgit* in Malaysia, *lucidus* in Latin—; and (by way of the common substitution of *r* for *l*) *rucit* in Sanskrit, *langi* and *rangi* in Polynesia, *ra* in ancient Egypt, *la'atu* in Assyria, *larang-ai* in one of the Aboriginal languages of Australia, *lagat* in Cornish-Celtic, *llygat* in Cymric (which became our English *look!*)—and all these words stand for related concepts: for light and heaven and sun, for lightning and look and eye.

Linguists have shown that many primal roots have a so-called mirror root, which does not simply negate the meaning of the primal root but rather reflects it into new dimensions. The mirror root of *leg* is *regh.* (In many languages, *l* and *r* are interchangeable. Some cultures—those of the Japanese, the Chinese, and certain South American Indians—do not even differentiate between them.) From it developed the Latin words *rex* ("king") and *regula* ("rule"), but also our *right* (for both "law" and the opposite of "left") and the Greek word *orégein* ("to stretch or pull, to endeavor") which, in turn, is related to the word *árchè* ("beginning").

Bearing all this in mind, we find that *En àrchên en ho lógos,* "In the beginning was the word," is an etymological tautology: The word *is* the beginning. Both crucial elements of the sentence grew out of the syllable *leg* and its mirror syllable, *regh:* "beginning" = Greek àrchê (from *orégein*), and "word" = Greek *lógos,* related to *light* and to the Egyptian sun god Ra, but also to *loud* ("sound"), the mantric germ cell.

We need to take language literally ("by the word"). Language has known from the beginning that the word *is* light *is* loud (sound) *is* the beginning.

This process of considering linguistic-semantic-philosophical connections has been known to mankind for as long as human beings have dealt with the mysteries of language. As the American Sinologist Sukie Colgrave has pointed out, Confucius considered that

> while words contain genuine meanings which reflect certain absolute truths in the universe, most people have lost contact with these truths and so use language to suit their own convenience. This led, he felt, to lax thinking, erroneous judgements, confused actions and finally to the wrong people acquiring access to political power.

Although coming from a different word source, the following example also flows directly into the stream of this chapter: The Latin word *cantare* is generally translated as "to sing." Its original meaning, however, was "to work magic, to produce by magic." One can sense the transition that must have taken place somewhere in time: in the process of working magic through primal sounds, evoking metamorphoses through sounds, man musicalized these sounds—he sang. *Carmen,* the Latin word for "poem," originally meant "magic formula," and it still is that today in many cultures. Mexico's Huichol Indians use the Spanish word *cantor* to mean "magician, shaman." Thus they have taken it back to where it had come from in Latin. Clearly they listened to the language, to the primal meaning of its words.

The words for "poet," "singer," and "magician" go back to the same linguistic root not only in Latin but in many other languages. Quite often they all have the same meaning, which makes sense when one considers the magician's main tool, language—or more precisely: the word. More than magic potions or charms, more than gestures or magic herbs, it is the word that produces the magic: usually not a complete sentence, but a single word that becomes effective as sound and as mantra. In this aspect, too, the sound possesses the effective power: in the world religions as *logos* and mantra, for magicians and shamans as magic word or magic formula, with all imaginable intermediate stages and shadings from one extreme, the divine word that creates the world, to the other, the shaman's sounds that produce magic for love or for hunting.

All this, again, is true for all languages and word stems. It is the "name" which has the power. For example, let us look at the English word *name*. In this word, too, (just as in the wholly different word *cantare*) lies the changing, "magic" power of the word. In Hebrew, *nam* mean not only "to speak" but also the solemn proclamation of an oracle; *nabha* and *nawa* still mean the prophetic word, the creative vision. In Latin, *numen* not only referred to the heavenly sign but also to the "omen" written in the sky that wields power over human fate. And even in the *Edda,* the ancient Germanic myth, we find *nef-na,* which not only means "to name" but also "to solemnly proclaim." The word stem *nam, nef, num* also appears in Far Eastern languages, most impressively in the *nembutsu* of Japanese Buddhism, the "name of the Buddha." This term signifies precisely what we have been talking about: *naming* alone invokes the Buddha; merely pronouncing the divine name is sufficient. The word as such has the power, all the more so when it is the word *Buddha (Butsu).* In Nichiren Buddhism, *nam* is the first sound of the "roar of the lion": *Nam Myoho Renge Kyo,* the mantra that leads to enlightenment.

Even in our contemporary brains there smolders a remnant of awareness that name is not mere designation: that behind the act of giving someone a name there lies something meaningful and mysterious, something creative. It would be difficult to find a mother or father who really did not care whether her or his daughter was named Mary, Nancy, or whatever—although in purely rationalist terms the name really has no other function but to differentiate one child from another. In reality, however, the name does have a deeper meaning; few know today what it is, but parents sense its influence when with each new birth they discuss the question in all seriousness: What shall we name our child?

Carl Friedrich von Weizsäcker writes: "It is never enough to speak about language. One has to have a conversation with the language about what language is saying." Let's do just that, let's talk with and about the word *speak.* In Latin, *preces* means "prayer" (as well as its opposite, "curse"; the related Sanskrit word is *brihaspati,* which is related in turn to *Brahma,* to whom people *pray:* and *Brahman* is the sacred word! The *spoken* (the prefixed *s* is a later addition) language knows: God creates with His word. Man prays (or: should pray?) when he speaks. *Brahma* is phonetically related to the name *Bragi,* the son of Odin, who in Germanic mythology is the god of the word and of poetry. In Hebrew,

Brahma became *beracha,* a blessing! The spoken word prays. Both key words in this sentence, *speaking* and *praying,* go back to the same root. Thus, the mere word already signals that the spoken word is to be treated with veneration, not merely chattered forth.

Despite the claims of certain narrow-minded linguists, one should not believe that a word series of this sort—which Wadler traced to the Aztecs, to Australia, and to the South Sea Islands—came into being "by chance." Since the advent of the computer, we can now figure out with the aid of the laws of probability whether an event can possibly be accidental. If we do so here, we will find that "chance" would not have had enough time, because the phenomenon of human language is simply not old enough. For the god of chance to have created not only sporadic, random word similarities across our planet but a series of the complex order described above, the dinosaurs would have had to have a language—a human language—long before *Homo sapiens* came into existence, millions of years before the appearance of *Homo erectus.*

The old concept of relationships existing solely between languages of the so-called "Indo-European family" cannot be upheld any longer. As the new science of paleolinguistics has shown, there is only one language family, the family of human languages—period. Like so many other myths, the myth of the Tower of Babel is true: In the beginning, there was only one language!

However, let us continue to listen to the primal words—with Confucius's words in mind—to the word *word.* Where does it come from? Astonishingly, the answer to this question leads us to the same result that we reached earlier when following the series *logos—light —loud—beginning.*

Two of the three Norns, the ancient Norse goddesses of fate, had names derived from the same stem: *Urth* and *Verthandi.* Gothic *wairth,* Anglo-Saxon *weordh,* and Old Nordic *verdh* all go back to the Sanskrit root *vrt.* All these words mean: "to unroll, to become, to come into being." Aramaic *varda* and Arabic *vard* signify the rose, and the Hebrew word *wered* means both the bud (that which comes into being) and the rose (that which has become). In the (literal) sense of the word, *word* is rose, bud, and flower. The word is *urth* ("fate") and *verthandi* ("future"). And in everything I have just said lies the Indian root *vrt;* it is as if I had been repeating the same word over and over again. As improbable as it may seem, this Indian root can be found even in the word *rose.* In Greek it is still *rhódos*—by way of linguistic deterioration of the *v* (which often becomes *t, d, s,* etc.) and by advancing the *r.* In tracing this development, we can still sense the Arabic *vard* (rose) in it, along with its Aramaic, Hebrew, Gothic, and Old Nordic relatives. The "feedback" (as linguists call such etymological lines) goes like this: *vrt—vard—wered—wairth—wort—word—rod(hos)—rose*.

Arnold Wadler concludes his pioneering work on primal words with the following statement: "As the deepest, mightiest expression of this primeval stem, as widest paragon of eternal life and of eternal being, another name crowns this series, the mental rose: the w-o-r-d."

Music for Listening to the Third Chapter

Joseph Haydn. *The Creation* (oratorio). Chicago Symphony and Choir, conducted by George Solti. London LDR 72011.

4 🐚 "Before We Make Music, the Music Makes Us"

From Macrocosm to Microcosm

OUR TIMES ARE filled with discoveries, and the media report them constantly. One discovery, however—one of the greatest of our generation—is hardly ever mentioned, the discovery that the world presents itself to us as sound in a way we just recently could not have imagined; and that particularly those realms of the universe that for centuries represented the epitomy of silence and muteness are full of sounds. Rudolf Kippenhahn, director of the Max-Planck Research Institute for Astrophysics in Munich, wrote about this phenomenon:

> At a lecture I gave around 1960, I asked the audience to imagine an instrument capable of transforming all the incoming radiation from space into audible sound. We would hear the constant rushing of the starlight and the radio eruptions of the sun, as well as the rushing of the radio waves whose sources in space were known to us at that time, as they swelled and faded rhythmically with the rising and setting of these steadily radiating objects as they appeared to revolve around the earth with the rest of the firmament. In fact, it would be a pretty boring affair. Today, twenty years later, I must correct that picture. Besides the radiation we knew about back then, the auditory image of space we would receive today would be dominated by newly discovered sources. Now we would hear the heterodyne ticking of the

pulsars—the low humming of the Cancer pulsar, for instance; sources of X-radiation would fire their salvoes, the source MXB 1730-335, for instance, emitting pulses of very high energy from a spherical star cluster, about a dozen pulses with breaks of ten or twenty seconds between each one, to be discontinued then for minutes until a new sequence would be fired off again. There is not only rushing to be heard in space, there is ticking and drumming, humming and crackling. Probably the neutron stars are most responsible for this noise being transferred by our imaginary instrument from space to our ears.

The discovery that space is filled with sound was made with modern radio telescopes. In their "Amateur Radio Astronomer's Notebook," Jeff Lichtman and Robert M. Sickels comment:

> By the science of radio telescopy a whole new dimension of the universe is revealed. The edge of the galaxy becomes a noisy hissing cacaphony of sound, these sounds being produced by quick shifts in molecular and atomic energy levels in gases made hot by newly born stars. The giant planet Jupiter . . . produces its own peculiar noise. Huge rapid sighs like the intense roaring of a distant surf are triggered by Jovian electrical activity very much like the electrical storms on earth, although storms of such intensity as to be worthy of the god whose name the planet bears.
> The sun makes its noises too . . . hisses and crackling sounds when it is in a condition of relative quietude . . . and roars of alarming intensity when it becomes angry and spews giant portions of matter far out into space.

The most interesting producers of sound in space are the pulsars, also referred to as pulsating stars or neutron stars. Although the first of them was discovered only in 1967 by radio astronomers at Cambridge University, we have already learned a lot about these "miniature starlets" whose diameter rarely exceeds ten miles, but whose density is so high that they easily reach and often exceed the mass of comparatively gigantic objects in space. Isaac Asimov has figured out that a human being five feet seven inches tall would weigh around 124 billion tons on the surface of a pulsar. A pulsar hitting the earth's surface would go right through to the center of the earth and come out again on the other side. In all probability there really was such an incident in the geologically recent past: on 30 June 1908, when an area in the Tunguska region of central Siberia was laid waste in a mysterious manner whose cause has never been precisely identified. In no way can these devastations have come from the impact of a gigantic meteorite (as was assumed at first): in spite of years of searching no crater or meteorite fragments were ever found. Scientists are therefore increasingly inclined to believe that the disaster was caused by a pulsar. Were this kind of event to take place today, as Asimov points out, "whichever superpower was struck might launch a retaliatory strike before learning the truth, and the whole Earth might be ravished."

Pulsating stars consist of so-called "degenerated matter." They possess unimaginably strong magnetic fields, and they are constantly encircled by fierce electric storms. Some pulsars sound like bongo drums, others like castanets, still others like the scratching needle of a record player. Most of them are simply ticking and tocking away as they have done for millions of years, some in a strangely rhythmical manner. These "living sounds" often change from one day to the other, even from one hour to the next, growing or diminishing, expanding or contracting as if they were being emitted by a living creature. One of the most interesting pulsars lies in the constellation of Cassiopeia, 500 million light-years away, the remains of a gigantic supernova (exploding star) so shrunken that it can hardly be made out even by the strongest telescopes in the world; but its sounds come in so strongly that even the simple gear of a radio amateur can pick them up. Some pulsars emit their pulses with a frequency so high that the human ear is unable to hear their rhythm. You can hear the rhythm, however, when you tape that interstellar message drummed millions of light-years away and then play the tape at half speed, as Lichtman and Sickels have done.

This, then, is a new addition to our knowledge: The cosmos is filled with sounds and rhythms, from pulsars and quasars, from supernovas, from so-called "red giants" and "white dwarfs," from fleeting and colliding star systems and, of course, from our own sun. In light of this phenomenon, the word *cosmos* (from Greek *kósmos*) regains much of its original meaning of "adornment."

And yet it was not long ago that the cosmos was the epitomy of silence, of utter stillness. No sound seemed to reach us from its endless expanse. At that time, anyone speaking of the "harmony of the spheres," as did Plato in the *Timaeus,* or of the "harmonia mundi" ("harmony of the world"), as did Pythagoras in the sixth century B.C.E. and Johannes Kepler in the seventeenth century C.E., was understood metaphorically at best. Now we are finding out that all this is to be taken literally.

In the prologue to *Faust,* Goethe wrote:

> The Sun intones, in ancient tourney
> With brother-spheres, a rival song,
> Fulfilling its predestined journey,
> With march of thunder moves along.
> Its aspect gives the angels power,

Though none can ever solve its ways;
The lofty works beyond us tower,
Sublime as on the first of days.

Goethe suspected that the sun "intones"; today we know it.

The Roman astronomer Ptolemy titled his work on the cosmos *Harmonia*. The most famous work of Johannes Kepler was entitled *Harmonices mundi libri V* ("Five Books About World Harmony"), as if it were music he had written about rather than planets. Kepler, indeed, felt himself to be an astronomer but also a musician; and there are indications that the latter was more important to him than the former. Pythagoras and Ptolemy both anticipated correlations between the orbits of the planets and the vibrations of a taut string, the so-called monochord.

Kepler was the first to suppose that the orbits of the planets were elliptical. Only in this way did it become apparent how precise the harmonical structure of our solar system is. According to Kepler, God was master of the cosmic sounds, causing the planets to leave their initially inherent circular orbits and to adopt the conspicuously complicated elliptical orbit in order to produce even more beautiful sounds. The fact that the planets move in elliptical orbits is indeed remarkable, but even more remarkable is the fact that from an unlimited wealth of possible orbits they have chosen precisely those which oscillate and sound in the proportions of undivided numbers prevalent in our "earthbound" music.

The overtone scale that is produced when a valveless horn in C is blown or when one listens to the flageolet tones of a viola's C-string corresponds to certain proportions in the planetary orbits.

Here is the overtone scale, which is actually the "natural" tone scale of all music:

Proportions of String Length

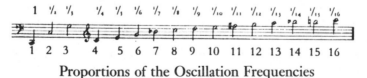

Proportions of the Oscillation Frequencies

What is astounding about this scale are the numbers printed above and below it. They show that the vibration of any tone on this scale will be higher than that of the preceding tone by precisely one whole number. Take an example: The fifth tone on the scale, e, vibrates with a frequency five times as high as the first tone, c. The special proportions on the monochord are in accordance with that: In order to produce the fifth tone, e, only one-fifth of the entire string length is needed; and this continues up to high c′, for instance, which needs only one-sixteenth of the full length of the string. Thus, when we divide a string into twelve equal parts and shorten this string to the points 6, 8, and 9 (thus obtaining the proportions 12:6 = 2:1, 12:8 = 3:2, 12:9 = 4:3), then by shortening the string by one-half we get the octave; by two-thirds, the fifth, by three-fourths, the fourth, and so on. It is to this phenomenon that I refer when I speak in subsequent pages about the "whole numbers" of the overtone scale, the so-called "harmonics." The following table lists the proportions (and *proportion* is just another word for *interval*):

octave	1:2
fifth	2:3
fourth	3:4
major sixth	3:5
major third	4:5
minor third	5:6
minor sixth	5:8
minor seventh	5:9
major second	8:9
major seventh	8:15
minor second	15:16
tritone	32:45

One basic rule is immediately obvious from this list: The lower the proportions of the numbers, the stronger the consonance, the more "harmonious" the sound of the two tones together. The broken line indicates the approximate border between "consonant" and "dissonant" sounds (which, of course, actually is a gradual transition). We shall see that in the proportions of the macrocosm, the microcosm, and our terrestial world, consonant sounds (that is, proportions made up mainly of low whole numbers) are highly prevalent—in fact, the most frequent consonance by far is also the most "harmonious," namely the octave, the proportion 1:2, which has always been used to signify the polarity of the world: *yang* and *yin*, male and female, heaven and earth, etc. In a way, then, this "primal polarity" is "written into the sky."

But it is also "written into our ears." All the sounds and proportions of sound that we find in such overwhelming wealth in the macrocosm, the microcosm, and our human world (and in music!) correspond, as the musicologist Rudolf Haase pointed out, to the natural disposition of our sense of hearing. Our ears prefer consonance, major proportions, relations in low numbers. This is true for the ears of human beings of all races and nations as well as for the ears of birds as well as apes, dogs, whales, dolphins, wolves, and other mammals.

Altogether there are seven basic laws of harmony. They are written into our ears as well as into the macro- and the microcosms, and we shall recognize them throughout this chapter and the following one:

1. the overtone scale
2. the interval proportions
3. the division of the octave into twelve semitones
4. the difference between consonance and dissonance, the consonance growing as the proportion of the numbers gets smaller
5. the difference between major and minor, the major proportion being the most frequent by far
6. the predominance of the 1:2 polarity, the octave
7. the law of the Lambdoma (a column of numbers written in the form of the Greek letter lambda, whose right leg consists of whole numbers going from one to infinity while the left leg contains the fractions of these same whole numbers, so that the coordinates of the open isosceles lambda triangle follow the scale of overtones or undertones). Hans Kayser and Rudolf Haase inquired into the instances of the Lambdoma in different fields and computed these precisely; they found correspondences in physics, acoustics, arithmetic, geometry, crystallography, cybernetics, theology and philosophy. Rudolf Haase even found correspondences in the Chinese *I Ching* and in the genetic code system, thus corroborating the impression that the lambdoma seems to appear just about everywhere.

This is not the place for a detailed mathematical discussion; Hans Kayser and Rudolf Haase, above all, have furnished us with such a presentation in their voluminous life's work, complete with tables, graphs, and computations. Important for our purposes, however, are two things: For one, the fact that the seven laws we mentioned earlier are based on the primal law of whole-number quanta (illustrated by the overtone scale as well as by the quantum theory of theoretical physics). Second, the fact that all seven laws can be relatively easily demonstrated on the monochord, the musical instrument consisting of only one string, that was used as far back as ancient Greece by the Pythagoreans for their experiments and referred to by Plato in his dialogue *Timaeus*, in which he recognized that the soul of the world is a musical scale. Hans Kayser has shown, for instance, that the harmonical proportions of the monochord theoretically could have made it possible to discover those planets not yet known to the Greeks and Romans or to the medieval astronomers: Uranus, Neptune, Pluto, and the swarms of planetoids.

Hans Kayser, who died in Berne, Switzerland, in 1964, was the founder of the scientific study of harmonies that I shall refer to often in the course of this book. One of his best-known works, published in 1946, is titled *Akróasis* (the Greek word for "hearing"—as opposed to *aisthesis*, "viewing"). The world as it really is, argues Kayser, can be better understood through hearing than through viewing. He writes:

> The concept of the harmony of the spheres is as old as the first awakening of mankind to consciousness. First in myth, then in astral symbolism, and as the integrating constituent of nearly the whole of mankind's poetry, this concept became the presupposition for astrology and the first astronomical inquiries of all ancient peoples. Kepler however was the first who gave it that foundation which lifts it out of mere faith and brings it in line with modern scientific thinking. In his main work, the *Harmonice mundi*, a work which Kepler described as his most important and to which throughout his life he devoted his special love, he shows, with a vast amount of material still substantially valid today, that between the mutual velocities of the planets there exists a great number of musical harmonies. He discovered his famous Third Law of Planetary Motion, which is contained in his work, through typical harmonical thinking, the so-called octave reduction. It is significant for Kepler that just this discovery, still considered by us today as the only worthwhile part of the *Harmonice mundi*, is named in his works only as one among many other "harmonies." We do Kepler an injustice, and bar ourselves from the deeper understanding of him and his intention, if we consider his harmonics only as a stimulant, over which we should hurry as fast as possible toward the normal order of the day. . . . for anyone who has read the works of Kepler and allowed his enthusiasm to transport him, Kepler's harmonic proportions are spiritual realities. He knows that here we are not dealing with mere formulations and practical applications, but with the truly shattering experience of *Tat twam asi:* This is you. There are powers above and shapes written in the sky which sound in your own soul, which concern you most vitally, and which belong to the Godhead as much as do you in your innermost self.

Kepler himself wrote: "Give air to the sky, and truly and really music will sound. There is a 'Concentus Intellectualis,' a 'mental harmony,' which gives pleasure and delight to beings of pure spirit and in a certain way even to God Himself, no less than which musical chords give to the human ear."

One of Kayser's particularly interesting reflections refers to the planetoids between Mars and Jupiter. The scientific hypothesis—that they are the remnants of a shattered planet—is corroborated by the teachings of harmonics (because a planet is "needed" in this spot: the planetoids move along the significant orbit of the third of the major chord; unthinkable, that this orbit would have been left empty!). Harmonics can also show the reason why the planet that must have been in this orbit inevitably had to burst. Kayser computed that the orbit of this hypothetical Planet X

> stood within the zone of the split of the two enharmonic degrees between d and d^v; but at the same time it stood in the "most beautiful" position of the whole planetary combination, because it occupied the middle point (the third) of the only major chord occurring here—b flat d f. One is tempted to say that Jupiter, which represents the tone b flat, was "clever enough" to place itself just outside the second enharmonic pair of the two b flats, but in a position which yet, according to its sound, still belongs to the b flat sphere. For anyone in the habit of thinking akroátically, it is beyond all doubt that it was just this splitting of the tones d and d^v which should prove fatal to Planet X, for while it occupied the most "beautiful" location in the planetary space, this was also the most dangerous one.

Kayser continues, however, that "an analysis like this one, of course, is highly unusual in the categories of today's science."

Not only the planetary orbits, but also the proportions within these orbits follow the laws of harmonics, much more so than statistical probability would lead us to expect. Francis Warrain has figured out that of the 78 tones created by the different planetary proportions, 74 belong to the major scale—a truly overwhelming configuration that no "chance" in the world will be able to explain.

Of particular interest is the fact that as the orbits of the planets change (as they do constantly), the angular velocities relative to the sun at the so-called aphelia and perihelia (the two extreme points of the elliptical orbits of the planets) remain nearly constant. These angular velocities are the basis for computing harmonic proportions. Certain minor aberrations aside (about which I shall say more later), the system of planets has been producing the same, mostly harmonic major sounds throughout the ages. It is more than mere metaphoric embellishment when poets (and other sensitive people) again and again over the centuries have sensed an "inner harmony" while looking at the starry sky.

As a matter of fact, this "inner harmony" is really our own sound —for one thing, in the already mentioned sense that all these sounds are "written into" our sense of hearing by predisposition; and for another thing, inasmuch as all the "aspects" arrived at by way of harmonics and mathematics are also astrological aspects. Astrologers have called my attention to the fact that the elements of classical astrology "of course can also be understood harmonically." It is obvious that a conjunction is an octave, an opposition is a fifth, a trigon a fourth, a quintile a minor third, a biquintile a minor sixth, etc. In the final analysis then, the horoscope of a person (or of an event) is a system of chords and sounds. *Man "sounds."* From an astrological viewpoint too, this statement is more than simply poetic metaphor. Whenever people meet, when in the course of their continuous motion their constellations move toward each other only to separate again and to form new aspects, conjunctions, and oppositions, music is created —again, not in the sense of metaphorical embellishment, but in a sense real enough to be transcribed onto music paper. Hence lovers know what they are talking about when they feel they are "in tune with each other," just as each of us can sense "harmony" between ourselves and another person—or "disharmony."

The scholar Thomas Michael Schmidt writes:

> The concept held in antiquity that all terrestial music is only a pale reflection or kind of substitute for the harmony in the sky [thus] becomes true in a concrete sense, because the same mathematical proportions are the basis of both our musical sounds and the movements of the planets. Long before human music was sounded on earth, the mathematical primal images of sounds were emitted in truly cosmic dimensions from the skies. Therefore, the acoustic proportions have a universal character. As organizing principles they regulate the world of the planets, the macrocosm, as well as human music on earth. . . . In this way, the universal validity of tonal proportions reveals its comprehensive cosmic connection.

Here is Kepler once more: "For this reason we should not be surprised that men discovered the beautiful, effective succession of tones in the musical modes when we see that in so doing they did nothing but imitate God's work, thereby playing down to earth the drama of the celestial motions."

"Dicunt astrologi vel musici" are the first words in the work of David Blaesing, a medieval astronomer: "It is said by astrologers or [!] by musicians . . ." And then he refers to the cosmos as if it were music.

Plotinus, the philosopher of Hellenism, wrote: "All music, based upon melody and rhythm, is the earthly representative of heavenly music."

The eminent Austrian scholar Count Hermann Keyserling, sums it up: "Ever since mankind exists, music has been granted a favorite position among the arts. Whether consciously or not, it has been considered an expression and a conveyor of cosmic things."

In recent years it has become possible to make the "song of the planets" audible. Willie Ruff and John Rodgers of Yale University programmed the angular velocities of the planets into a synthesizer. Unlike Pythagoras or Copernicus, they worked not on the basis of circular orbits but of elliptical ones, and they followed Kepler's data precisely. Just as Kepler had computed it, they assigned the contra-G (the low G, situated far to the left end of the normal piano keyboard) to the planet Saturn. On that basis, Kepler's laws define the tones of all other planets, from Saturn to Jupiter, Mars, Earth, and Venus all the way to the one closest to the sun, to Mercury, which is the four-line E sharp, a note that lies almost at the highest end of the piano keyboard.

You can hear all this on a record that Ruff and Rodgers produced. Particularly moving is the "Duo in the minor mode danced by Earth and Venus." Venus "dances" around the three-line E sharp while, a sixth lower, Earth "dallies" between the two-line G sharp and G sharp. In this constellation of tones, Kepler sensed "the endless song of the misery of love on Earth."

To nobody's surprise, the sounds of the planets (as realized by Ruff and Rodgers) correspond with the conceptions traditionally attributed to the different celestial bodies. Mercury, the fast and restless "messenger of the gods," symbol of intelligence and businesslike agility, does indeed have a quick, busy, chirping, "quicksilvery" sound. Aggressively and "ruthlessly," Mars slides up and down across several notes. Jupiter has a majestic tone reminiscent of a church organ, and Saturn produces a low, mysterious droning. The sound spectrum of the six visible planets including Earth covers eight octaves, almost identical with the human hearing range.

After Kepler's death, three further planets (Uranus, Neptune, Pluto) were discovered, and of course their orbits also fit perfectly into Kepler's laws, corroborating them. Since these planets have very low orbital velocities (Pluto's orbit around the sun, for example, takes 248 years), their transposition into sound would be below the human hearing capacity. The orbital ellipses of these outer planets, however, can be made audible to the human ear as rhythms, because rhythms have lower vibrations than tones. Ruff, who is not only a scientist but also a jazz musician, commented: "I knew there just had to be rhythm out there."

All that summarized: The six visible planets with their elliptical orbits form a (the expression was coined by Kepler: Kepler the *musician*) "six-part harmony motet," while the outer three planets add the "rhythm section" (in Ruff's words), in which Pluto, the most distant, beats the cosmic "bass drum."

It is interesting to hear how, in the trilogy of the three "rhythm planets," Uranus and Neptune shift "beats" relative to each other. When Uranus moves slowly, its ratio to Neptune is almost exactly 1:2½, but in times of faster speed the two planets beat their cosmic drums almost in unison. In this manner, a network of interesting polyrhythms is formed, orientated to Pluto's bass drum. There is nothing metronomelike in this cobweb of meters, however, as the bass rhythm also shifts—albeit in cycles of approximately seven minutes, so that rhythmical changes created by these shifts can hardly be perceived. (These changes, by the way, occur as slowly as the shifts we hear in so-called "minimal music.")

On their recording, Ruff and Rodgers realized as sounds the orbits of the planets for a time span of approximately 250 years, beginning in 1571, the year of Kepler's birth. Their work was inspired by Hindemith's opera *The Harmony of the World* (which, in turn, was inspired by the life and work of Johannes Kepler). Ruff himself studied with Hindemith, who had intensive contact with Hans Kayser in Germany; after the Nazis came to power, Hindemith emigrated to the United States, where he became a teacher at Yale.

Gottfried Wilhelm Leibniz, the great seventeenth-century philosopher and mathematician, wrote:

> Music is a hidden arithmetic exercise of the soul, which does not know that it is dealing with numbers, because it does many things by way of unnoticed conceptions which with clear conception it could not do. Those who believe that nothing can happen in the soul of which the soul is not conscious are wrong. For this reason the soul, although not realizing that it is involved in mathematical computation, still senses the effect of this unnoticeable forming of numbers either as a resultant feeling of well-being in the case of harmonies or as discomfort in the case of disharmonies.

"As above, so below" is a basic principle of ancient wisdom. We have been well aware of the structure of sounds "above"—that is, in the cosmos—ever since Pythagoras and Kepler; and modern astronomy and cosmology are constantly discovering new, exciting harmonic relationships far beyond the bounds of our own planetary system. But what about the world "below," the world of genes and cells, of DNA and RNA, of atoms and elementary particles? Do they also contain harmonic structures? More than anywhere else, they would have to exist here, too, if what this book is about makes any sense.

For decades it all seemed very easy: Niels Bohr's model of the atom seemed to postulate certain orbits of the elementary particles around the atomic nucleus. The hypothesis was that these orbits were subject to harmonic laws similar to those guiding the planets around the sun. In reality they obey statistical laws, and there are no orbits in the sense of the planetary ellipses.

There are so-called "shells" in the atom, however, whose function is approximately comparable to the "orbits" in the solar system. The shells fill up with electrons, and these saturation states form a relationship with the atomic number of the particular element in the periodic table (the atomic number corresponds to the charge of the nucleus). Here—in the shells, saturation states, atomic numbers, and nuclear charges, in the number of electrons and protons, and in the spin (this term is explained below)—is where the harmonic proportions exist, and that with such a remarkable density that even a skeptical observer will be astounded. The discoveries leading to this realization were brought together almost simultaneously, by two specialists who thereby verified and complemented each other's work in a fascinating way: the German musicologist Wilfried Krüger and the French nuclear physicist Jean E. Charon.

Krüger discovered an overwhelming treasure of structures at those points in the microworld most decisive for the development of life: in the atoms of oxygen, nitrogen, carbon, and phosphorus, and in RNA and DNA.

With its atomic number 8, oxygen is the element of the octave. The eight electrons of the oxygen atom shell and the eight protons of the oxygen atom nucleus form a major scale, the spins of the particles precisely marking the half tones and whole tones. The spin $-\frac{1}{2}$ is the semitone, the spin $+\frac{1}{2}$ is the full tone; the negative spin lies at the fourth and eighth steps, just where in the C major scale f and c′ indicate the semitones.

The concurrence between microcosm and harmonics becomes even more astonishing when one notes that the model of the nucleus of the oxygen atom with its protons has twelve steps, the exact number of intervals found in the scale formed by the atomic model. In the normal state, seven of these intervals are filled and five empty, just as the intervals are in the musical scale of seven "regular" notes, leaving the other five unused. It does happen in music, especially in the process of modulation (change of key), that these five "irregular" notes are employed; precisely the same thing happens during the various saturation states of the atomic nucleus, although these have only a transitory function—as does modulation in music.

Krüger made similar discoveries in the nuclei of other atoms: the more frequently the more important these atoms are for the development of organic life. In this way, "the electron shell of the carbon atom, saturated according to the rules of nuclear physics and in the steps of the basic theorem, produces the tone scale C-D-E-F-G-A," which is the hexachord of Gregorian chant; in fact, depending on the saturation state of the atom all three Gregorian hexachords exist in carbon, the so-called *hexachordum durum, hexachordum molle,* and *hexachordum naturale.*

The largest atom of DNA, that of phosphorus, has the atomic number 15, which means that it has fifteen protons in its nucleus, forming a fifteen-step scale from g to $f^{\#\prime}$. Here, too, the negative spins precisely mark the semitones.

The entire microcosm is replete with harmonic concurrences. The long strings of nucleic acid in DNA are structured precisely according to the Pythagorean Tetractys, the fourfold subdivision of the octave (octave, fifth, fourth and major second). The Pythagoreans attributed magic power to the Tetractys and called it sacred. This same structure is almost ubiquitous in those mysterious processes whereby inorganic structures are transformed into organic life. The four oxygen atoms, for instance, that surround the phosphorus atom vibrate in the Tetractys! Lama Govinda's word (which was uttered long before Krüger's discoveries) has to be understood literally: "Each atom is constantly singing a song, and each moment this song creates dense or fine forms of greater or lesser materiality."

A key position similar to that of the holy Tetractys is held by the mysterious tritone, the *diabolus in musica:* the augmented fourth or diminished fifth, which is neither consonant nor clearly dissonant, and which in the microcosm produces exactly the same "touch of freedom" as in music—for instance, in bebop. There, it is often felt as a "jumping" fifth; and in the division of the cell nucleus, too, it has a "jumping" function. The energy necessary for the jump comes from incoming photons which, as we shall see below, are the "carriers of communication." The "blessing of the photons," as Krüger put it, comes down "pentecostally in large swarms mainly on the tonal region of the tritone," on F, F sharp and G; and it does so particularly intensely briefly before mitosis (the cell division) when two identical nuclei with identical genetic information are formed. In this process, as in countless other microcosmic processes that Krüger has analyzed carefully, the "flatted fifth" (as jazz musicians call it), still is what it was for the alchemists: the *quinta essentia,* the quintessence. Being open to all sides, it is "seesaw" and "swing," creating freedom and paths into new life. Krüger investigated the parallel position of the tritone in the microcosm and in bebop down to the most minute details.

Franz Schubert experienced the one-line F sharp as a "green note." I have no idea how Schubert could have heard that, but just that note, a tritone (relative to C), forms the key tension in the nitrogen atom during photosynthesis when sunlight is transformed into chlorophyll, into living green. From sunshine grows living matter. The word made flesh. At this juncture, the tritone represents the crucial force, the *quinta essentia*—as do two further proportions, as it happens. These, too, are of particular harmonic importance and have always been considered magical and sacred, by the Pythagoreans, Cabalists, and followers of other secret sciences in the East and West. These are the seven of the major scale and the twelve as the sum of all semitones contained in an octave. And indeed, the magnesium atom, which vibrates at the center of the chlorophyll has the atomic number 12. It is surrounded by four nitrogen atoms with the atomic number 7.

In 1864, five years before Lothar Meyer and Dmitry Mendeleyef discovered the periodic system of elements, the British chemist John Newlands pointed out that elements of the same group appear in musical intervals: "It is recognizable that the numbers of analogous elements generally differ from each other by seven or by one of its multiples. . . . I propose, therefore, to designate this proportion as the 'Law of Octaves'."

Rudolf Haase, who teaches basic harmonic studies at the Vienna Academy for Interpretive Arts and also directs the Hans Kayser Institute in Vienna, has corroborated this law. According to his findings, the entire periodic system is based upon the notes c′, c′′′, d′′′′, and c′′′′′, that is, primarily on higher octaves of the basic tone C.

Haase has pointed out that the "law of constant and multiple proportions" known from chemistry leads to numerical proportions that are harmonics, and remarked that, since it "forms the basis for all chemical formulas, the formula idiom of chemistry can be understood as a giant catalogue of harmonical proportions."

Here we have left the realm of atoms (and atomic particles) and entered that of molecules. Haase has shown that their structure "is based upon a striving for maximum symmetry, which is manifested mainly in groupings commonly designated as 'Platonic bodies'"—that is, the tetrahedron, octahedron, hexahedron, icosahedron, and pentagondodecahedron. There are only these five, all constructed out of regular polygons. The sums of the corners, surfaces, and edges of these five bodies can all be expressed by the following numbers (and these numbers only!): 4 - 6 - 8 - 12 - 20 - 30; in an overtone scale based on C they form the following notes: c′′, g′′, c′′′, g′′′, e′′′′, b′′′′.

After studying hundreds of thousands of chemical compounds, L. Wolf, a German scientist, found that the dominance of the major mode is further corroborated by the coordination numbers (which designate the number of atoms directly adjacent to each other in a molecule). Here we find the same numbers as above with the exception of the 30, the four-line B; interestingly enough, it is the only note among those named above that does not fit in the major triad. Haase, who spent years of research working out these discoveries, notes additionally that these numbers, when transposed to interval proportions, produce only and exclusively the most consonant intervals: octave, fifth, fourth, major sixth, and major third. Here is truly overwhelming evidence for the "harmonic" as well as "harmonious" sounding musical structure of the world.

I mentioned earlier that the findings of the musicologist Wilfried Krüger were supplemented by those of the physicist Jean E. Charon. Before we deal with Charon's work, however, the already mentioned concept of "spin" needs to be explained. Generally in physics, spin is understood as the movement of a body revolving around its own axis. According to the theory of Paul Dirac, the electron spin can adopt only one of two different locations in space, either in the direction of the electron orbit or against it. This is referred to as a spin of $+\frac{1}{2}$ or $-\frac{1}{2}$, or generally as "plus spin" or "minus spin." The most important point for our context is the fact that the spin is always a whole-number multiple of the most important natural constant of the microcosm, of Planck's constant. When I say "whole-number multiple," it is clear (even without going into the details of Krüger's work) that we are dealing with a harmonic phenomenon. As a matter of fact, Max Planck, who was very much interested in music, supposedly was inspired to work out his quantum theory by the well-known phenomenon that the notes in an overtone scale jump from one whole number to the next. That, in the final analysis, is the point of the quantum theory: the "particle energy" in the atom changes not gradually but in "jumps." (Is it not a strange coincidence that Kepler and Planck, the two great scientists who shaped our concept of the macrophysical and microphysical worlds, were both interested equally in music and physics?) Back to the concept of spin: The spin numbers of electrons, protons, and neutrons correspond to the interval proportions on a monochord, always relative to the unit of Planck's constant (and divided by 2π).

Particularly important in this context, as we shall see, is the photon. What are photons? Krüger gave the following answer: "By establishing that time stands still, that 'place' is nowhere and everywhere, and that the mass of a particle moving at the speed of light (such as a photon) is equal to zero, nuclear physics approaches a threshold that mystics have approached, and still approach, from the other direction."

Its "place" is nowhere, its mass is equal to zero, it moves at the speed of light, and it is continuously active and effective—if one asked an unbiased person what "it" is, one might get the answer: a thought.

A crucial impulse for the growing consideration of mind and spirit in theoretical physics came from the (often minimal) deviations of the results in physical experiments from what scientists would have expected on the grounds of the laws of physics. Again and again, physicists and mathematicians have been confronted with these minimal and unpredictable deviations. They began to ask: Where are the energies, the impulses behind these deviations? What is it that keeps slipping through the ever-finer net of our experimental measuring capacities?

In interpreting findings of modern physicists, the French physicist-philosopher Jean E. Charon points out that electrons have a "choice," an option to choose between different "ways of action," and that they actually exercise their option. But this is just what the mind is *per definitionem:* the agent that chooses.

The more recent models of explanation in microphysics and cosmology are totally unthinkable without the concept of option. Physicists no longer attempt to do away with these "possibilities of freedom" or to deny them. They have accepted them and have increasingly realized that accepting the option means accepting a mental and/or psychic element.

No doubt, Charon's ideas are speculative—rejected by many of his colleagues—and yet a continually growing group of physicists—clustered in France around Charon and in the United States around leading research institutes in Pasadena and Princeton (the "Princeton gnostics")—believes that it has found the source of these mental and psychic impulses in the electron and in the photon.

Charon writes: "Inside its micro-universe, the electron encloses a space that is able, first, to store information, second, to make this information available again during each pulsation period of its cycle by way of a sort of 'memory system', and third, to control complex operations by communicating and cooperating with the other electrons of the system."

The electron is a sort of "miniature black hole." Its structure is similar to that of the black holes in outer space and, to a certain degree, to their preliminary form, the heavy pulsars that I have talked about. Like black holes and pulsars, the electron has an extremely high temperature (between 60 million and 650 million degrees Centigrade;

try to imagine such temperatures in the unimaginably minute space of the microworld!) and similarly has an immense density (between one thousand billion and one million grams per cubic centimeter). Like black holes, it is also characterized by curved space and curved time in the sense of Einstein's theory. Thus, the time of electrons (and of black holes) is not identical with our "material time," which leads from the past to the future. It is rather a "mental time" which "runs cyclically," so that everything once stored can be retrieved during any further cycle. For Charon, the electrons are the "prime stores" of memory. They are among the few elementary particles that do not disintegrate; in other words, they exist from the beginning of the cosmos to its end. As Charon writes:

> An electron that was successively part of a tree, a human being, a tiger, and another human being will thus remember for all time the experiences it has collected during these different lives. The electron will maintain within itself all of its experiences as tree, as human being No. 1, as tiger, and as human being No. 2, to whose organisms it belonged at certain times.

The groundwork for these discoveries was laid as early as the twenties by the Swiss physicist Wolfgang Pauli. The "Pauli exclusion principle" holds that atoms are able to "know" and to "remember" whether they have been in contact with a specific atom before and that they "know" the state of other atoms.

The electron's recollections are stored and controlled by its spin, and they are assembled with the help of photons. Each progression of the spin leads to an increase in information. What is most surprising and, in our present context, most wonderful is the fact that these progressions take place in steps comparable to the steps on the string of a monochord.

Photons control not only memory but the process of cognition. As Charon points out, they are messengers: "Here, a photon of the outer shell disappears, thereby making its impulse, its energy, and its spin available to a photon of the electron shell." In this way, the interior photon now possesses the potential that previously belonged to the exterior one. And this phenomenon also takes place in whole-number progressions. It is as if the particles were communicating their "tones" with each other. The language in which they communicate is a language in harmonic progressions, in tones!

In comparison to an electron that has existed as part of an animal or a human being for a long time, an electron that has been in dead matter has a totally different level of information. In a sense, both have gone through different "courses of education," which makes it improbable that a spin exchange (Charon speaks of "communication," "mating," "deeds," "cognition," and "love") will take place between them —which corresponds exactly to normal human behavior. Psychologist Oscar Ichazo writes: "Love is the recognition of the same consciousness in oneself and in the other person." And Charon notes: "In contrast to the views that most organized beings have worked out for themselves, it is their electrons that give or elicit love. The organized being itself is only the 'vehicle' of this love, and even that only in a narrow sector of space and time."

Thus we can vary—and sharpen—Ichazo's statement in the following formulation: Love is the recognition of identical spin states, that is, of identical harmonic states, identical vibrations or, finally, identical harmonies (which is why in everyday language we speak of a "harmonious" relationship between lovers). Hence love is *accord* (from the Latin root *cor*, "heart"!). The more "harmonic" it is in the literal sense, the more "harmonious" it will be figuratively. This also makes it obvious that the processes of love, its "deeds" (caresses, union, orgasm), are steered through harmonic states and at the same time (in a kind of feedback mechanism, as in the control loops of cybernetics) themselves elicit harmonic processes of increasing power and intensity, just as poets of all periods (Shakespeare, for one) have known: Love is music.

By this time we certainly have an idea of the immense act of repression with which conventional science has busied itself. For generations, science has been trying to explain the basic processes of the universe and the microcosm and even those of life itself purely in physical and chemical—that is, material—terms. Time and again, scientists have encountered the dimension of the spiritual, the psychic, the metaphysical, but whenever this has happened they have closed their eyes as if warding off an allergic reaction or as if this dimension did not exist. The result was a kind of ascetic convulsion: thinking and feeling human beings, for whom (as for any other human being) the most important thing in the world is their own thinking and feeling, were trying to explain the world as if thinking and feeling never existed.

The French psychoanalyst Pierre Solié once asked the following question: "Do you believe physicists could have ever discovered the laws of the atom if they themselves did not consist of these atoms?" In analogy to that we can ask: Can one believe that humankind would ever have pointed to the existence of a creative and active, loving and discerning spirit if man himself did not consist of spirit?

That is why the most creative scientists, the most brilliant, the most inspired in all fields (in medicine, physics, biology and chemistry) are the ones who have refused to deny or exclude the existence of mental, spiritual, and metaphysical forces, but rather have included them in their scientific work.

Here is a final word from Max Planck, who founded quantum mechanics and particle physics as they are known today and whom traditional science in its matter-oriented thinking calls upon as a witness—illegitimately, as the following quote will show:

> There is no such thing as matter *an sich!* It is not the visible yet transitory matter that is real, true, and actual but the invisible, immortal spirit. . . . However, since spiritual beings cannot exist through themselves but have to be created, I do not shy away from naming that mysterious creator just as all ancient cultures of the world have named him throughout the millennia: *God!*

Sounds and Music for Listening to the Fourth Chapter

Amateur Radio Astronomer's Notebook. Typescript and cassette tape of pulsar sounds by the American astronomers Jeff Lichtman and Robert M. Sickels (Fort Lauderdale, FL: Privately published), copyright © 1977. A copy is owned by the library at Rutgers—The State University, New Brunswick, NJ 08903.

The Harmony of the World. A Realization for the Ear of Johannes Kepler's Astronomical Data from *Harmonices Mundi* (1619). Realized by Willie Ruff and John Rodgers. Yale University LP 1571 (may be ordered from W. Ruff, School of Music, Yale University, New Haven, CT 06520).

Earth's Magnetic Field. Realizations in computed electronic sound by Charles Dodge, produced at the Columbia University Computer Center. Nonesuch Records H-71250. (Computerized, electronically realized "music," generated by the vibration network between solar winds and the magnetic field of the earth.)

DNA Music. A musical translation of DNA sequences by Dr. David Deamer. Cassette from Science and the Arts, 144 Mayhew Way, Walnut Creek, CA 94596.

5 🐋 The Sound Calls

... stars and elementary particles · plants and marine animals · crystals and leaf forms · the male and female bodies and sexuality · cathedrals and cloisters · the structure of the earth ...

Nada Brahma. The world is sound. It sounds in pulsars and planetary orbits, in the spin of electrons, in the quanta of atoms and the structure of molecules, in the microcosm and in the macrocosm. It also sounds in the sphere between these extremes, in the world in which we live. Here, too, we will discover sound first and foremost in those areas where one would have last and least expected it.

In the animal kingdom, the denizens of the deep have always represented the epitome of silence. Nowadays we know that the ocean, especially the deep sea, is filled with sound. There is whistling and grunting, rattling and snoring and ringing, sawing and creaking and electronic noises, snapping and snipping and crackling, the beating of bass drums and tom-toms and tambourines, screaming and howling, groaning and moaning. And the fish producing these sounds have names like drums and croakers, spot snappers, parrotfish, catfish, white grunts, trunkfishes, tunas, wrasses, black gobies, snapping shrimps, sea robins ... Many of them have antennae and other means of electric transmission. In addition to the auditory waves they produce with their "sound instruments," they permeate the oceans with a network of electric signals.

The scientific research on deep-sea sounds is only in its beginning stages. The predecessors of whales and dolphins, the maritime mammals (the so-called *Cetacea*), were land animals. They were able to conquer the sea (even the great depths where there is no light whatsoever) only by developing the capability to produce sounds, to transmit and receive and interpret them. They do so (like other maritime animals) with the aid of echo effects, and in this way can locate partners, targets, objects, and enemies as well as fathom the depth of the water. Maritime science is still not sure how and with which part of the body many of the animals produce these sounds. One hypothesis is that it is done in the brain, which also presumably receives response signals.

Whales, for instance, can literally talk to one another over distances of hundreds of miles. Computer analysis of these exchanges has shown an information density of between one and ten million bits per half hour of whale song—which is the approximate amount of information contained in the *Odyssey*!

Long before man invented the radio and the transmission of sound by way of electric waves, these animals were "transmitting," without tubes or transistors. Like many other great human inventions, the radio is simply a later technological realization of processes that nature has known and utilized for a long time. In our context, of course, it hardly makes a difference whether we can hear the sounds of these animals directly or whether we have to first "transpose" them from their ultra-short-wave range in order to make them audible to us. Rudolf Haase, among others, has pointed out that the harmonic structure of the world shows itself in each and every kind of wave and radiation, and that transposability is one of its basic principles. Proportions are the point, regardless of the particular vibration or frequency range, and proportions would not appear as such without this possibility of transposition. The music of the cosmos and of nature is unthinkable without it. It would be wrong to assume that transposition exists only in our human, terrestrial music and not in other kinds of music that are made by the cosmos, by the microcosm, and by nature. (Folkways Records has published two records of *Sounds of the Sea*, recorded directly below the water surface as well as in sea depths of up to eighteen hundred feet, off the Florida coast and in the Pacific near Point Lobos, south of San Francisco.)

It was also assumed until recently that plants, like sea creatures, were silent. After all, they grow soundlessly. No form of life is more noiseless than theirs. It was found, however, that there are sounds also in the realm of vegetation. In Israel, Great Britain, and the United States, photo-acoustic spectroscopy has been used to make the sound of a rose audible at the moment when the bud bursts into blossom: it is an organlike droning, reminiscent of the sounds of a Bach toccata or

Messiaen's *Ascension* for organ—in other words, reminiscent of what in traditional organ music is perceived as a "spread" succession of chords.

David Cahen of the Weizman Institute of Science in Rehovot, Israel, and Gordon Kirkbright of the Imperial College in London have investigated the potential of photo-acoustic spectroscopy with particular care. Their work—they call it "listening to cells"—has shown that even a simple corn stalk has a sound. Imagine thousands of stalks growing next to each other in a field, each with its own sound, a waving symphony of sounds. Certainly, no human ear can hear it; and yet the symphony would not exist if there were no sensory system perceiving it. The next time you find yourself in a meadow, try to activate this sensory system within yourself. Look at the millions of blades and flowers and herbs growing there, and try to imagine that each of them has its own sound. It is the song of life *par excellence,* an immense choir, millions and billions of sounds that fuse into a grand polyphony, a harmony beyond human imagination.

Recent research has also shown that plants in a meadow, field, or forest will wither if their vibrations (in other words, their sounds) relate disharmonically to other plants in the vicinity. Flower lovers have always known that certain kinds of plants do not do well in close proximity to certain other kinds, even though they may favor the same types of soil and climate. We now know the reason for this phenomenon. The plants do not go together because their vibrations don't harmonize, because their sounds do not fit together, because they are in disharmony—or, in harmonic terms: because their sounds do not "swing" together in low whole numbers.

It is no wonder, then, that plants can also "hear" and differentiate between various kinds of music. In India, botanist T. C. Singh exposed an Asian strain of the mimosa, *Hydrilla virticillata,* to Indian raga music for several hours per day. In their book *The Secret Life of Plants,* Peter Tompkins and Christopher Bird describe this experiment:

> After a fortnight, to Singh's intense excitement, he discovered that the number of stomata per unit area in the experimental plants was 66 percent higher, the epidermal walls were thicker, the palisade cells were longer and broader than in control plants, sometimes by as much as 50 percent.
>
> Encouraged to further experimentation, Singh requested Gouri Kumari, a lecturer at Annamalai's Music College, to play a raga known as the *"Kara-hara-priya"* to some balsam plants. Kumari, a virtuoso, played for twenty-five minutes each day, on a fretted lutelike instrument usually fitted with seven strings, the *veena* traditionally associated with Saraswati, goddess of wisdom. During the fifth week, the

experimental balsams began to shoot ahead of their unserenaded neighbors and, at the end of December, had produced an average of 72 percent more leaves than the control plants, and had grown 20 percent higher.

The power of sound can also have a destructive effect, as the American biologist Dorothy Retallack discovered. Each day for eight hours, she exposed a number of philodendrons, cornstalks, radishes, and geraniums to the uninterrupted sound of the tone F and an identical group of plants to the same F, but only for three-hour periods followed by extended breaks. After two weeks, all plants in the first greenhouse had died while in the second, as Tompkins and Bird relate, the plants were more vigorous than a third group of control plants, which had not been exposed to any kind of sound.

In the same biology institute in Colorado where Dorothy Retallack works, a team of young biologists piped radio music into two greenhouses with cucurbits; one greenhouse heard music from a Denver rock station, the other heard a classical station. Bird and Tompkins relate that

> the cucurbits were hardly indifferent to the two musical forms: those exposed to Haydn, Beethoven, Brahms, Schubert, and other eighteenth- and nineteenth-century European scores grew *toward* the transistor radio, one of them even twining itself lovingly around it. The other squashes grew away from the rock broadcasts and even tried to climb the slippery walls of their glass cage.

Even more astounding was an experiment that Dorothy Retallack made herself. She planted and kept up three groups of plants, each group consisting of the same kinds of plants, grown on the same soil under identical temperature and watering conditions. The first group was exposed to music by Johann Sebastian Bach; the second one, to sitar music played by the great master of classical Indian music Ravi Shankar; and the third one, to no music at all. As Bird and Tompkins report:

> The plants gave positive evidence of liking Bach, since they leaned an unprecendented thirty-five degrees *toward* the preludes. But even this affirmation was far exceeded by their reaction to Shankar: in their straining to reach the source of the classical Indian music they bent more than halfway to the horizontal, at angles in excess of sixty degrees, the nearest one almost embracing the speaker.
>
> In order not to be swayed by her own special taste for the classical music of both hemispheres Mrs. Retallack, at the behest of hundreds of young people, followed Bach and Shankar with trials of folk and

"country and western" music. Her plants seemed to produce no more reaction than those in the silent chamber. . . . Jazz caused her a real surprise. When her plants heard recordings as varied as Duke Ellington's "Soul Call" and two discs by Louis Armstrong, 55 percent of the plants leaned fifteen to twenty degrees *toward* the speaker, and growth was more abundant than in the silent chamber.

The science of harmonics knows that any form of organic life—a fish, a flower, a leaf, a fruit, a beetle, any creature at all—*is* sound, that in fact even the "most beautiful" forms of the inorganic world, the crystals, *are* sound. This means that their structure is dominated by numbers which can form consonances. "Or, to put it differently, research in the field of harmonics proves that in nature an important role is played by those quantities which in man can be transformed into qualities" (Rudolf Haase). Hans Kayser described the "correspondences between the spectra of leaves and those of tones" in detail:

If all the notes of an octave are graphically displayed with their particular angles (the same octave operation, by the way, which Johannes Kepler used in his famous work *De Harmonice Mundi*), the result will be the shape of a primal leaf. Which simply means that the interval of the octave, and with it the very possibility of playing and perceiving music, bears within itself the shape of a leaf. Imagine what that means, that a plant is capable of executing within its blossom a precise division into three parts as well as into five parts. Other than supposing the activity of a logically operating mind one has to assume that in the soul of the plant certain creative prototypes are at work, here in the shape of the third, there in that of a fifth, which—just as in music—structure the shape of the leaf as intervals.

In his work *Harmonia Plantarum*, Kayser reproduces a table showing that practically all plants that he and other scientists were able to examine have harmonic shapes and proportions—in the calyx, the leaf bud, the stamen, the ovary, the fruit, the stem, and the configuration of leaves. The table contains plants as diverse as chestnut, ash, pumpkin, rose, blind nettle, valerian, plantain, woodruff, sage, blackberry, and lime tree.

Many of the things we find to be "beautiful" in nature, in art, and in the human body follow the laws of the golden section. The following is a dictionary definition: "Golden section: a proportion (as one involving a line divided into two segments or the length and width of a rectangle and their sum) in which the ratio of the whole to the larger part is the same as the ratio of the larger part to the smaller. Or: a:b=b:(a-b)."

That sounds rather dry, but it starts to get lively as soon as one imagines that the golden section is a phenomenon involving the sixth, an interval of particular importance in music as well as in the cosmos. The proportions of the golden section vascillate around the major (3:5) and minor (5:8) sixths and around the so-called ecmelic intervals (8:13, 13:21, etc.), which can all be interpreted as variations of the sixths. Let us take a closer look at the laws of the golden section in application to the human body.

In his work *Harmonologia Musica*, published in 1702, the organist and musicologist Andreas Werckmeister wrote:

> Assuming that the world at large is structured like a *macrocosm*, then man as *microcosm* must have a relationship to it. Therefore, Pythagoras and Plato said that the soul of the human being is a harmony; this is not only supported and proven by many scholars, but one has also made the experience that a well-proportioned human body with its limbs displays the *proportiones musicae* (musical proportions).

Thomas Michael Schmidt describes the "well-proportioned" body as follows:

> The navel divides the entire body length in the proportions of the golden section. . . . The nipples divide the entire width of the human body with stretched arms in the proportions of the golden section. The loin divides the distance from the ground to the nipples in the proportions of the golden section. . . . The knee divides the entire leg in the proportions of the golden section. . . . The eyebrows divide the head in the proportions of the golden section. . . . The elbow joint divides the entire arm including the hand in the proportions of the golden section. . . .
>
> Inasmuch as the human body is structured by the golden section, by musical proportions, that is, one can call it a sounding work of art, because its shape is dominated by the most perfect mathematical proportions. Thus it is entirely correct to say that at least in terms of his anatomy man is meant to be perfect.

To be sure, similar proportions can also be found in the bodies of animals (and in the entire organic world), but nowhere do they exist as clearly and plentifully as in the human body. Schmidt continues:

> After what has been said, it is hardly surprising to find that the proportions of the human body correspond with the mathematical proportions of the planetary orbits. . . . For each proportion of the human body corresponding to a musical interval, there is a corresponding proportion between two or three planetary orbits. Thus, the

two apparently very distant fields of musical tones and the movements of the planets find a directly palpable expression in the human body. The link between man and cosmos are the musical proportions, which in this way represent a universal organizing principle in the truest sense of the word.

Since the healthy human body is structured according to the laws of harmonics, the idea of healing human suffering and disease through music arose at an early stage. Early in the sixteenth century, Agrippa von Nettesheim, a Dutch physician, wrote: "A person who is ill no longer is in harmony with the universe. He can find this harmony, however, and get well again if he orientates his movements to the motions of the stars."

Johannes Kepler wrote: "Many doctors are used to healing their patients with beautiful music. How can music have an effect in the body of another person? In such a way that the soul of man as well as that of many animals understands the harmony, takes pleasure and delight in it, and thus makes the body more vigorous, so that the heavenly force comes down to earth through harmony and serene music." Modern music therapy supports this insight fully.

Hans Kayser has also interpreted human sexuality—the driving force behind all organic life—as a musical phenomenon. As far back as in the late Middle Ages, musicians spoke of the "gender" of chords and scales, major ones being associated more with "male" traits and minor ones more with "female" traits. Even though this division into major and minor modes is prevalent mainly in European-dominated forms of music, we must allow ourselves to refer to it just as in certain contexts we refer to Indian or African music. Major and minor "feelings," in any case, exist in most music cultures. It can be said in general that the proportions that we are dealing with here from the viewpoint of harmonics are common to all cultures. In the final analysis, they are based on the disposition of the human ear. Haase has pointed out that even in ancient China there was a knowledge of chromaticism, of the number twelve as the sum of all intervals, and of the circle of fifths. The music of India, too, knows diatonicism and a clear dominance of the major mode.

Hans Kayser writes:

The gender of a chord is determined by its third: the major third makes it a major chord, the minor third, a minor chord. The third, in turn, is determined by the fifth vibration, or by one-fifth of the string length calculated from a base unit. This number "five," however, is of relevance in the realm of plants not only inasmuch as the petals of a large number of blossoms are grouped in fives, but also as an aspect of morphology since the "five" as a morphological constant appears in plants but not in minerals.

In a different context, Kayser notes:

> The five as a rationing image does not appear in the internal structure of crystal axes. As a constant of form, the five makes its first appearance in plants. In terms of harmonics, it is the tone that determines the gender, the mode. This emphasis on the third and its split into the major and minor thirds has to be regarded as at least one of the heretofore unknown prototypical reasons why sexuality first begins to play a role in plants.

When scientists at Vienna's Institute for the Science of Harmonics, headed by Rudolf Haase, compared the shapes of male and female skulls and faces, they found that in women the minor proportions, minor thirds and sixths, are dominant, whereas in males it is the corresponding major intervals.

Even more noteworthy is the fact that the female body is dominated particularly clearly and more frequently than the male body by minor proportions. What has been called the "primal proportion of femininity," the triangle formed in the female body between the breasts and the point where the thighs meet, corresponds to a minor third-sixth chord statistically much more often than does the corresponding triangle in the male body. As a metaphor, it may have been sensed and proclaimed often enough by poets and lovers, but it is a mathematical reality: this triangle, this primal proportion, is music.

Let's listen to our own language in this context, too. The violin player talks of the "body" of his violin. For hundreds of years, there has been a striking similarity (of which many guitarists are conscious and which many poets have described) between the *body* of the guitar (the expression can't be accidental) and the female body. We say that a "tone is *produced*" or "*generated*" in the instrument's *body*, which is *stimulated*. A guitarist or a violinist uses these words when explaining to his student how the sound is made. With almost the same words, however, one can describe the act of love. In both cases, *bodies* are *stimulated* in the act of *generating* something or someone new.

Many cultures of the world perceive guitarlike instruments as female, and flutes (especially end-blown ones) as male. Lord Krishna blows the flute (the musical penis symbol *par excellence*) while making love to Radha. The ancient Greek deity Pan (also a primal symbol of maleness) was flute player and lover at the same time. For the Aztecs and Incas, a flute player symbolized the lover and the procreator. In order to make this plain to everyone, the Incas of Peru created miniature statues depicting a lover who (like India's Krishna) plays on his flute during the act of love.

In Hinduism and Buddhism, on the other hand—in the temples of Angkor Wat in Cambodia, for example—the guitar-playing Apsaras, the "maidens of the celestials," serve as a symbol of highly eroticized femininity. When one actually views these Apsara statues and reliefs in the Angkor jungle, where they are overgrown by the *fromagiers*, the "cheese trees" (so called because their roots overrun whatever they touch like strips of melted cheese), and literally embraced by tropical vines, one gets the feeling that here two bodies are holding each other, adding to and surpassing each other: the female body of the Apsara and the (also female) body of the guitarlike instruments that the maidens carry and play. Very much in the sense of the Tantric art of love, both together are elevated metaphors of that ravishing "sexuality of the blessed ones" that these "angels" of Indian mythology promise to the inhabitants of celestial worlds.

To be sure, there also are works of art depicting love and music as one in our Christian culture, even though these characteristics are usually very much more hidden and filtered. You can find them in Florence, for instance, in the adoring angel musicians created by Luca della Robbia for the church of Santa Maria del Fiore. Nowhere in European art, however, has music become visual art in such a grand manner as in the works of the Venetian school of the fourteenth and early fifteenth century, featuring such artists as Paolo and Lorenzo Veneziano, Carpaccio, Stefano di San Agnese, Nicolo di Pietro, Giovanni Bellini, and Jacobello del Fiore. Especially moving is the *Coronation of the Virgin in Paradise* of Jacobello del Fiore, in which the blessed ones form entire orchestras and choirs and making music is Paradise itself. Whatever is depicted in the works of old Venice, even the presentation of Jesus in the temple or the martyrdom of Saint Sebastian, cannot be taking place without guitars and lutes, flutes and *trombas*, cymbals and violins and harps, large and small organs and mouth organs.

Fittingly enough, at this same time—or, more precisely, a little later on—stereophonics, even quadro- and multiphonics, were discovered. When the Venetians devised the multiple choir, featuring soloists, instrumentalists, choirs, and contra-choirs echoing and answering one another, the various parts and divisions of the music would cascade down from the galleries, balconies, and balustrades of the church to pour over the listeners below in a kind of super-stereo.

Even before music sounded in the churches, however, their architecture itself was sound. More and more, precise mathematical correspondences between architecture and music are being discovered, as between the Baroque church of Vierzehnheiligen in Bavaria and certain passages in Johann Sebastian Bach's *Well-Tempered Clavier*. Or (as Marius Schneider discovered) between the seventy-two double columns in the cloister of the monastery of San Cugat in the Spanish region of Catalonia and the Gregorian hymn to Cucuphatus, named for the martyr to whom the monastery is dedicated. Or in the capitals of the Romanesque cloisters in Gerona and Cluny which can be "read" as if they were rhythms, "as a hidden, encoded music notation."

As Paul von Naredi-Rainer of Vienna and other scientists have shown, many of the world's most beautiful structures are built in exact harmonic proportions, such as the temples on the Acropolis in Athens, the temple of Paestum in southern Italy, the Great Pyramid at Giza, Egypt, the cathedral at Chartres in France, and many more.

Sensitive architects have always known (consciously or unconsciously) that the length, width, and height of a room must be related to each other in the whole-number proportions of the overtone scale if the inhabitants are to feel comfortable in them. It is noteworthy that these relationships are currently being rediscovered. This, too, is an expression of the growing awareness of harmonics in the present generation.

Once the architectural masterpieces of mankind have been examined systematically for their "musical" basic character, these monuments will begin to sound to our rational ears as they have sounded to our subconscious ears for centuries. Then we will realize that they never would have been felt to embody the height of architectonic splendor had they not been "sound" from the beginning, sound that corresponded precisely to the musical masterpieces of their own historical period: Romanesque capitals to Gregorian chant, the Baroque churches to the fugues and preludes of the Baroque composers, or the Taj Mahal to the great music of India during the Mogul period.

If planetary orbits, leaves and bodies, churches and cloisters obey the laws of harmonics, then these laws must also apply to the earth itself. It too is a harmonic entity. Let us hear Hans Kayser on this subject:

> One of the strangest phenomena of geology is the shell-like structure of the earth's interior. The earth does not consist of a thin, hard "skin" around a liquid main mass, as we once believed, but rather is composed of layers of varying density, which are rather clearly separate from each other. This was discovered through observation of the way the shock waves of earthquakes spread. Inside the earth,

various zones were discovered that break these waves in various ways. If one compares the spatial proportions of these zones with the string lengths of the primary major chord of the overtone scale . . . , one finds a triad structure inside the earth, whereby the measurements of the earth layers, in strange correspondence with those of the chord degree, and with the hard outer layer of the earth falling into the seventh octave, thus becoming understandable morphologically as condensation or concentration. . . . The earth: a giant chord! It is an image that may have little to say to the rational mind, but which speaks all the more clearly to the heart!

Hans Kayser took particular care in his investigations of the harmonic structure of rock crystal, which he found in abundance in the mountains of Switzerland where he lived. He described his findings:

> The different zones of a crystal can be expressed by numbers that in turn can be translated into notes, since they are of harmonic origin. The following sample notation (fig. 2) presents the tone material of some zones of certain crystals. . . . All the samples included here are transposed to C. In reality, each crystal has its own key, but one would have to decide on the crystallographic "chamber pitch," that is, one would have to define one particular axis-proportion as the A to which all other proportions would be referred. Anyone, however, who plays these sample notations on an instrument will hear how individual—in fact, how "modern"—the surface scaling of each of the various crystals is. Often utterly magnificent sequences of notes are the result. Who knows what surprises we might encounter if we would take the trouble to notate all these themes and chords. We would certainly have a collection of musical structures ranging from the simplest and most monumental to the most differentiated and interesting, an inexhaustible source of themes for counterpoint and polyphony.

Harmonic correspondences are correspondences in two senses: they are quantitative, since they can be computed, and qualitative, since they can be heard. Yet the fact that a differentiation exists between "qualitative" and "quantitative" implies that "deviations" must exist. In a way, they seem to "creep" into the gap between quality and quantity. There is an abundance of them, minimal "deviations" between the computed, wanted result and the *de facto* measured data.

In order not to get bogged down in mathematical computations, this book will not go into these "deviations" in detail. In fact this is legitimate, because our ear "corrects" these "deviations" when hearing them. Our tempered tuning, which would not work at all if the individual tones were not deliberately, minutely "out of tune," could otherwise not be accepted as being "in tune."

Rudolf Haase has pointed out that this phenomenon has been known

since the Baroque period as "corrective hearing." The "ranges of corrective hearing" are quite large. Adjustments can be made for up to forty percent of the particular half-tone step. It is obvious that, if there are "ranges of corrective hearing" in music, they also must exist in nature. After all, it would be absolutely absurd to expect of nature a degree of precision not expected of music (which also is "nature").

We have to realize clearly that the phenomenon of "deviations" is nothing but a corroboration of the harmonic character of the universe. If music is unthinkable without "deviations," then it follows logically that the "music" of the universe (i.e., of the macrocosm, the microcosm, and our terrestial world) is unthinkable without corresponding "deviations." If the universe "is" music—if the world is sound, if what *Nada Brahma* expresses is true—then all those fields we have been talking about, the orbits of the planets and the structure of atoms, the shapes of leaves and bodies, must have precisely those "ranges of corrective hearing" that also exist in music. And in fact they do exist, and that, to a degree that is comparable to that found in music. Since the times of Johannes Kepler, for example, the aphelion and perihelion of most planetary orbits have changed, but only by those very minute differences that can be "heard correctively." This example makes clear that, had they not changed, it would be impossible to speak of living "music." Something similar is expressed by the fact that over and over again (in the structure of molecules and atoms, for instance) we find individual "tones" that do not fit in the particular harmonical structure, a major triad, for instance. Our own terrestrial, physically audible music would be a boring affair if it did not contain tones "alien" to the scale, if there were nothing but pure triads moving up and down in cadence. In this way, too, the "deviations" support the harmonic (i.e., musical) structure of things. They support *Nada Brahma*.

A "deviation" even occurs, as Euclid pointed out, between the golden section and the precise harmonic proportion by the minimal difference of .007, which, of course, is within the "range of corrective hearing."

The "deviations" become more and more frequent as the music of nature gets closer and closer to human music, most of all in the song of birds, which is one of the main reasons why the sounds of the birds can be directly perceived by human beings as music. Experts have shown that the "laws" of bird music correspond to those of human music. Some birds—very much like humans—make "modern concert music"; in their music the "deviations" are frequent, as in the song of the blackbird, the "quintessential composer" among birds. The blackbird, writes Haase, sings highly complex melodies that are almost atonal. In this connection it is significant that certain notations of the blackbird's song from the nineteenth century display a degree of complexity that was reached in human music only much later, as, for example, in the opera *Salome* by Richard Strauss.

Ever since the advent of the quartz watch and the atomic clock, we know that not even the most precise cosmic processes, which only thirty years ago served as corrective for humankind's system of time measurement, take place without "deviations." The hypothesis of Jean E. Charon and of several American physicists that "deviations" from precomputed processes show the influence of spirit and psyche is in no way contradictory to our understanding that they show the influence of the "spirit" of music.

The "aesthetic principle" formulated by the German art historian Theodor Lipp states that "in the fine arts and in music minimal deviations from the precise proportions are necessary so that they can be perceived as particularly beautiful and stimulating." This principle, however, must be broadened. It refers not only to art and music, but to the entire cosmos.

Basically, the whole universe behaves the way we human beings behave every day in relationship to measurement and time. When asked for the time, we look at our watch, see that it is 11:56, and answer; "It is twelve." Or we say, "It is a quarter after ten," when our watch shows 10:13. Or a road sign indicates a distance to a particular goal as "four miles," while in reality the exact distance is several hundred yards more or less. We human beings also tend to favor whole-number proportions, just as nature does, from the macrocosm to the microcosm, with ourselves right in the middle!

We need only take one more step to reach the comforting realization that in fact the entire universe holds the same attitude as we humans to precision and punctuality: a strained one. The idea of absolute precision is one of those ideas of Western rationalism that produces its own absurdity. It is an idea of separation, of isolation and abstraction. A person living in unison with nature also lives in unison with what we have called its "deviations," with its imprecision and unpunctuality.

The American psychologist George Leonard writes:

> At the root of all power and motion, there is music and rhythm, the play of patterned frequencies against the matrix of time. More than 2,500 years ago, the philosopher Pythagoras told his followers that a

stone is frozen music, an intuition fully validated by modern science; we now know that every particle in the physical universe takes its characteristics from the pitch and pattern and overtones of its particular frequencies, its singing. And the same thing is true of all radiation, all forces great and small, all information. Before we make music, music makes us. . . . The way music works is also the way the world of objects and events works. . . . The deep structure of music is the same as the deep structure of everything else.

Wassily Kandinsky, the great Russian expressionist painter, whose *Blaue Reiter Almanac* spoke of a "thorough bass" and a "Harmonology of Painting," remarked: *"The world sounds. It is a cosmos of spiritually effective beings."*

This book keeps making the statement that the world is sound. Not: The world is vibration. Of course, one could say that as well—it is true, and everybody says so. But it isn't precise enough. From the standpoint of physics, there are billions of different possible vibrations. But the cosmos—the universe—chooses from these billions of possibilities with overwhelming preference for those few thousand vibrations that make harmonic sense (and in the final analysis, that means: musical sense): the proportions of the overtone scale, the major scale (and less frequently the minor scale), the Lambdoma (see p. 62), and certain church music scales and Indian ragas.

This is true of almost all proportions in the cosmos—planetary orbits, DNA genes, the shapes of leaves and crystals, the proportions in the periodic table, body forms, the quanta of the atomic nucleus, the spins of the electrons and all the other proportions about which we are talking in this book.

Against odds of one to one million, more often than not the universe tends to select the harmonic vibrations—those that sound—from an infinite number of possible vibrations. Even using the generous (and certainly anything but "scientific") interpretation of the term *chance* as adopted by positivistic science, these odds certainly cannot be classified as "chance."

In order to make the word *sounds* totally clear in this context, we have to realize that "sound" definitely exists in scientific thinking as an abstraction. We experience it this way too. Without its being played physically, we can hear a tune we particularly like by listening in the mind, with our "inner ear." Similarly, a composer hears a sound (a tone or a chord) while writing it down without using an instrument. Before playing a piece, musicians read the score. There it is already sound. They hear it sounding in their "inner ear." Only then do they "feed" it into their instrument. In precisely this sense, the universe continually "feeds" sounds into each one of its "instruments," from atoms and the genes all the way to planets and the pulsars.

Perhaps you remember the demonstration of "Chladni's figures," with which schoolteachers used to awe their pupils: Sand grains and dust particles loosely spread out on a glass plate quickly take on the most beautiful and symmetrical forms when a violin bow is drawn over the edge of the plate. It always seemed as if the sound "called" the particles "to order." As youngsters we could not do much with this phenomenon. Now, however, we know that what happened there is happening everywhere. The sound that gives order and beauty to the world is everywhere. Confronted with its power and might, the "particles" of the universe, the planets and stars, are only particles of dust that the sound "calls" to order and to beauty. It calls stars and elementary particles, crystals and leaf shapes, plants and the bodies of human beings and animals (and their sexuality), the architectural forms and geological structure of the interior of the earth, the elements and their periodic table, the spin of the particles, the structure of the atoms and the molecules and nucleic acids and many other things that we haven't yet discovered—for most research in this field is only at its beginning. And yet we know enough to be able to conclude: Sound calls the world. The world calls in sounds. The world *is* sound. *Nada Brahma.*

Sounds and Music for Listening to the Fifth Chapter

Sounds of the Sea. Folkways Records, Science Series, FPX 121.
Sounds of Sea Animals. Folkways Records, Science Series, FPX 125.
Songs of the Humpback Whale. Capitol St 620.
Olivier Messiaen. *L'Ascension.* Meditations for Organ. Unicorn DKP 9015.
Ravi Shankar. (See p. 172.)
Claudio Monteverdi. *Messa e Salmi.* Pantheon 68209.
———. *Mass à quatre voix avec trombones.* Harmonia Mundi 221.

6 ≈ Sound is More Certain than Time and Matter

IN THIS CENTURY, entire worlds of seemingly certain knowledge have crumbled. Time and matter were once the foundation, precisely measurable, weighable, computable, the most certain things we had. Our understanding of the world was founded on them, all processes of perception were based on them. Today, theoretical physics is confronted with the ruins of what once were time and matter.

Ever since Einstein—since his special theory of relativity (1905) and his general theory of relativity (1916)—we are aware of the illusory, "crutchlike" character of time. Now we know there are events that seem to be taking place simultaneously from one vantage point, while from other viewpoints they appear as successive phenomena, progressing from the past over the present into the future. The concept of time in modern physics is remarkably similar to the "eternal presence" that flows in many different directions, a concept inherent to the philosophy of Hinduism for thousands of years.

Let us imagine that we are observing a distant spiral nebula out in the depths of space (a routine observation in modern astronomy)—say, somewhere in the region of Cassiopeia, five hundred million light-years away. What happens when we think we see Cassiopeia? What do we see? Obviously something that was there 500 million years ago. Maybe Cassiopeia doesn't even exist any more. But quite obviously we are looking at it "now." Without a doubt, we are looking backwards, from the present into the past; and both are "now."

The farthest known systems in outer space are five billion light-years away. When we observe them we are observing something "now" that existed before the earth was even formed.

This train of thought shows that space can turn into time and time can turn into space. A light-year is the distance that light travels in one year. In one second, light travels 186,000 miles; in one minute, it travels 186,000 × 60 miles. In one hour, this sum multiplied by 60; in one day, that sum multiplied by 24; in one year, this sum again multiplied by 365—in all, the unimaginable distance of six trillion miles. Thus the light-year is a working metaphor for a distance whose spatial extension, even more than its temporal aspect, is beyond all "normal" imagination. We will find that most terms in physics are "metaphors," including those that play a central role in the present chapter: time and matter.

Obviously, space and time are related to each other also in the smaller dimensions of our earth. We simply fail to notice it. Here's a simple example: The longer the string (the larger the spatial aspect), the lower the resulting tone when the string is plucked, that is, the slower the vibrations of the string (which means: the smaller the temporal aspect). On the other hand, the shorter the string (the smaller the spatial aspect), the higher the tone, that is, the faster the vibrations (which means: the larger the temporal aspect). The resulting rule was formulated by Hans Kayser: "As the spatial aspect, the string length, diminishes, the temporal aspect, the number of vibrations, increases, and vice versa."

The modes of time (past, present, and future) can seamlessly turn into spatial concepts. Under certain circumstances temporal concepts can define things normally expressed as spatial concepts—distance, extension, or length.

For all practical purposes, there is no difference between space and time in certain computations in theoretical physics. The words *space* and *time* have lost their separate meanings. It is of no relevance to their mathematics whether the two concepts are used interchangeably, treated as equal or as a unit, or are kept strictly separate in the conventional way.

The great nineteenth-century mathematician Bernhard Riemann already tended to mathematically change time into space. In the course of the years, it became more and more untenable that the one dimension of time and the three dimensions of space perceived by our senses should be sufficient as the base of a realistic picture of the world. As it became increasingly reasonable to assume that our world has at least four, if not many more dimensions, the most diverse theories were proposed, based, for instance, on two temporal and three spatial dimensions (by the British physicists Arthur Eddington and Adrian Dobbs), or on the assumption that time is nothing but a misinterpreted spatial dimension. In mathematical terms, worlds with five, six, or more dimensions function flawlessly; in fact, some physicists have pointed out that their mathematics work better than those of the system of three dimensions that our optical and tactile senses perceive. In this regard, P. D. Ouspensky reminded us in *Tertium Organum* that it is impossible to find a mathematical foundation for our system of three-dimensionality:

> How shall we understand that mathematics does not feel dimensions —that it is impossible to express mathematically the difference between dimensions? It is possible to understand and explain it by one thing only—namely, that this difference does not exist. . . . [In this way we see] that no realities whatever correspond to our concepts of dimensions. . . . The representation of dimensions by powers is perfectly arbitrary.

When trying to make the "illusory" nature of our concept of space and time understandable, it has become customary to postulate the existence of two-dimensional beings as a sort of "mental bridge." While we cannot imagine a world with *more* than three dimensions, we can approach it to a certain degree by picturing a world with *less* than three dimensions. Imagine, then, a creature that lives on one plane only, say, on a tabletop. It knows only two dimensions, height and width. For such a creature, as Ouspensky points out, "a circle or a square, rotating around its center, on account of its double motion will be an inexplicable and incommensurable phenomenon, like the phenomenon of life for a modern physicist." When a multicolored cube is passed through the surface upon which the two-dimensional creature lives,

> the plane being will perceive the entire cube and its motion as a change in color of lines lying in the plane. Thus, if a blue line replaces a red one, then the plane being will regard the red line as a past event. He will not be in a position to realize the idea that the red line is still existing somewhere. . . . For the being living on a plane, everything above and below . . . will be existing in time, in the past and in the future . . . Therefore, though not conceiving the form of his universe, and regarding it as infinite in all directions, the plane being will nevertheless involuntarily think of the past as situated somewhere at

one side *of all,* and of the future as somewhere at the other side of this totality. In such manner will the plane being conceive of the *idea of time.* We see that this idea arises because the two-dimensional being senses only two out of three dimensions of space; the third dimension he senses only after its effects become manifest upon the plane, and therefore he regards it as something different from the first two dimensions of space, *calling it time.*

We know that the phenomena of motion or the manifestations of energy are involved with the expenditure of time, and we see how, with the gradual transcendence of the lower space by the higher, motion disappears, being converted into the properties of immobile solids; i.e., the expenditure of time disappears—and the necessity for time. To the two-dimensional being time is necessary for the understanding of the most simple phenomena—an angle, a hill, a ditch. For us time is not necessary for the understanding of such phenomena, but is necessary for the explanation of the phenomena of motion and physical phenomena. In a space still higher, our phenomena of motion and physical phenomena would probably be regarded independently of time, as properties of immobile solids; and biological phenomena —birth, growth, reproduction, death—would be regarded as phenomena of motion.

Thus we see how the idea of time recedes with the expansion of consciousness.

We see its complete conditionality.

We see that by time are designated the characteristics of a space relatively higher than a given space—i.e., the characteristics of the perceptions of a consciousness relatively higher than a given consciousness. . . .

In other words, the growth of the space-sense is proceeding at the expense of the time-sense. Or one may say that the time-sense is an imperfect space-sense (i.e., an imperfect power of representation which, being perfected, translates itself into the space-sense, i.e., into the power of representation in forms).

If, taking as a foundation the principles elucidated here, we attempt to represent to ourselves the universe very abstractedly, it is clear that this will be quite other than the universe which we are accustomed to imagine to ourselves. *Everything* will exist in it *always.*

This will be the universe of the *Eternal Now* of Hindu philosophy —a universe in which will be neither *before* nor *after.*

"To put it differently," writes Lama Govinda, "we do not live *in* time, but time lives *within us.* . . . Space is externalized, objectivated time, time projected outward. Time . . . is internalized, subjectivated space. . . . Time and space are related to each other as the inside and the outside of the same thing."

A similar view is held by the German philosopher Jean Gebser: "The body . . . is nothing but solidified, coagulated, thickened, materialized time." Gebser postulates the "integral man" who has become "free of time."

When interpreting certain scattering processes in quantum mechanics, it can happen that a particle will be moving forward in time in one process, while in the immediately adjacent process it will be moving backwards in time. In fact, time may progress forward for a particle interpreted as a positron, and backwards for the same particle interpreted as an electron. Both interpretations are physically conclusive and both are mathematically "correct."

Only ten years ago, physicists thought that such phenomena were limited to the field of quantum physics, with its unimaginably small dimensions. In the meantime, however, they have computed that certain situations are thinkable (must be thinkable from a logical point of view) wherein processes of the microworld also appear in macrophysics. In fact, Ilya Prigogine, a Soviet-born physicist living in Belgium, was awarded the 1977 Nobel Prize not least for this very discovery.

Werner Heisenberg has shown that field equations for electromagnetic fields can be solved mathematically not only for events in the past but also for future events. In many respects, all these words—*past, present, future, cause,* and *effect*—have taken on a ring of absurdity, much like the closed control loops of cybernetics in our excursion into logic (see pp. 43ff.)

The interpretation of time as a spatial dimension that our senses are unable to perceive opens possibilities for explaining countless psychic phenomena so well-documented that even skeptical scientists do not doubt them (such as precognition, prophecy, clairvoyance, and *déjà vu*). One example is the frequently observed fact that in the event of a forest fire or an earthquake, animals leave the danger zone before the actual disaster takes place—a particularly impressive sight at the eruption of Mount Saint Helens in the state of Washington in 1980, or during a wave of forest fires in northern Germany in 1973. Very few animals lost their lives in these disasters; most of them had fled as if they had sensed what was about to happen. Only the human beings stayed at the scene. Quite obviously, animals (and surely also, as Jean Gebser supposes, "archaic" man of prehistoric times) have a gift that among us rational and "mental" human beings is limited to a few especially blessed (or cursed?) individuals—the gift of being able to perceive time as a spatial dimension, simply as a distance stretching before us that we can "see." This is the sense in which time and again great clairvoyants of all ages have described their special gift as seeing into a distance opening up in front of them—as distance and as space. As I have mentioned, the mathematical realization of this concept offers no problems; it is "correct."

I have structured the present chapter in such a way that the concepts of time and matter of both modern physics and the thinking of Asia merge together, patchwork fashion, into one. Lama Govinda writes:

> When speaking of the perception of space in meditation, we are dealing with a wholly different dimension . . . where temporal succession becomes simultaneity, where spatial parallelity becomes a fusion of one into the other, where fusion becomes a living continuum beyond existence and nonexistence in the merger of space and time.

As much as seven hundred years before theoretical physics, the famous Japanese Zen master Dogen realized: "Most people believe that time passes. In reality, it stays where it is. The concept of the passing of time is false, because man, limited to experiencing time only as passing, does not understand that it stays where it is." And D. T. Suzuki, the contemporary communicator of Buddhism, comments: "In the spiritual world, there is no such thing as past, present, and future." Einstein meant precisely the same thing when he stated: "For a believing physicist like myself, the separation between past, present, and future has the value of a mere, albeit stubborn illusion."

It is clear that there is no contradiction between the interpretation of time by modern physics, on the one hand, and by Buddhism and mysticism, on the other. In fact, the further physics progresses the more similar these two conceptions become. We shall return to this point later on.

Most of us would agree that when time becomes endless, it becomes eternity. In the thinking of most people, time as succession of past, present, and future is nothing but a section of eternity. Yet does not such an interpretation represent the—unconscious—attempt to dispel eternity as much as possible from our human life and consciousness, into an endlessly distant past on the one hand and into a just-as-endlessly distant future on the other? The point here is not to reflect upon the psychological implications of such an attempt—as interesting as that might be—but to remind ourselves that over the centuries the spiritual wisdom of both East and West has known that eternity is *now:* in *this* moment. Suzuki: "Eternity is the absolute present." Saichi, one of the masters of Japanese Pure Land Buddhism, said: "Being reborn means this present moment."

The same knowledge has also existed in European mysticism, because Buddhism and Christian mysticism actually speak "merely two dialects of the same language," as Erich Fromm put it. A key word in the thinking of the great thirteenth-century German mystic Meister Eckehart was "Now." This "Now" means both the present moment and eternity, because "the now-moment in which God made the first human being, and the now-moment in which the last human being will disappear, and the now-moment in which I am speaking are all one in God, in whom there is only *one* now." The power of the soul "knows no yesterday or day before, no morrow or day after (for in eternity there is no yesterday or morrow): therein it is the present now; the happenings of a thousand years ago, a thousand years to come, are there in the present and the antipodes the same as here."

The same is meant by a modern "mystic," the twentieth-century writer Franz Kafka: "Only our concept of time makes us call the Last Judgment by that name, actually it is martial law."

Characteristic of martial law is that the deed, the apprehension, the judgment, and its execution fall together so narrowly that the time between them no longer exists.

Projecting the "Last Judgment" into the future (especially into an unimaginably distant future) is literally what the word means, a projection in the sense of psychoanalysis. The fault always lies with the other person. He is responsible. In this case, we enshroud the future with a fog as densely as possible. Nothing is "foggier" than eternity, which is so far removed from us that we can rest assured that nothing can happen to us.

An ancient Zen *mondo* tells of the knowledge that eternity is "now"; this *mondo* has been handed down to us in the most diverse forms and is attributed to various Zen masters, which indicates that it has become common wisdom:

> It is springtime. The Zen master and his pupil work in the garden. There, a flock of birds in the sky!
> The pupil says to the master: "Now it will turn warm, the birds are coming back."
> The master answers: "The birds have been here from the beginning."

You can feel that Buddhism—Zen in particular—and European mysticism essentially are of one mind. As Professor Gorbach of the University of Copenhagen writes:

> Basically, mystics throughout time have expressed the same thing; in fact, they are in such agreement that often they use the same words and images. Certain scriptural passages from ancient India, thousands

of years before our civilization began, are almost identical with those written by European monks during the late Middle Ages; and even creations of modern poets are reminiscent of ancient scriptures. The reason for this agreement is that they all share a common experience that is as clear and convincing as what the average person perceives in his material world. There is no room for dreams and fantasy here. The mystic is dealing with an experience that shapes his whole life.

All these quotations—do they not express a certain glimpse of freedom? We are all slaves of time, of its inescapable motion. "The birds have been here from the beginning." The man who said that is free of the tyranny of time.

At this juncture, a phenomenon from the days of the French Revolution may be highly illuminating. According to several unanimous eyewitness reports, on the evening of the first day of fighting in July 1789, revolutionaries in various sectors of Paris destroyed the church clocks, independently of one another and without prior arrangement. Spontaneously, they became aware of the clocks as symbols for the tyranny to which they had been subjected. In this truly "clairvoyant" moment, time and tyranny became synonymous for them. Now, everyone had his own time. Just as in Salvadore Dali's paintings, there is no need for clock hands. Time is *now*. "The birds have been here from the beginning."

Freedom from time, as Jean Gebser once put it, is freedom *per se*. Clocks have to do with lack of freedom. Just consider how quickly medieval Europe covered itself with a network of clocks as soon as that became technologically feasible. This was done so eagerly and unnoticeably that the chroniclers could hardly keep up with the process. Thus we do not even know exactly who invented the first mechanical clock for a church tower. Perhaps it was Pacificus, the archdeacon of Verona (d. 846); perhaps it was Gerbert of Aurilac (c. 950–1003), who constructed the famous clock in Magdeburg in 966 and who later became famous himself as Pope Sylvester II; perhaps it was the abbot Wilhelm of Hirschau (d. 1091). This knowledge has been lost in the fog of history. The only thing we know for sure is the fact that it was the clergy who saw to it that the mechanical clock became a functioning timepiece.

After Paris got its first public clock around the year 1300 and Milan got one in 1306, followed by Caen, Padua, Nuremberg, Strasbourg and other cities, the fourteenth century became the "century of the mechanical clock." Before the close of the fifteenth century, it was almost a matter of course all over Europe that even the smallest church had a clock in its steeple, even when several other churches were built close by. Each of these clocks had its own hourly toll, insisting on time every sixty minutes. Soon there were clocks striking every thirty and every fifteen minutes, so that even those who could not see the face of the clocks were constantly reminded of the admonishing finger of time and its tyranny. Hardly a stroke of the bell sounded but that it was answered (a few seconds or minutes earlier or later) by some other church within hearing range, intensifying the general insistence on time. The chiming of the clocks in the cities was carried into the suburbs and from there across the land into the villages, and from one village to the other. From Sicily to Scandinavia and from Great Britain to Poland and Russia, Europe had donned a gigantic hood of church-clocks and bells. In the improbable case that some sleeping citizen was not aware of the time, night watchmen in the cities wandered through the streets reminding everyone with their dreary singsong: "Ten o'clock and all's well." No other culture has anything comparable. The call of the *muezzin* a few times a day from the mosques in the Islamic world is nothing in comparison with the constant reminder in the cities and villages of Europe. And here we should bear in mind that it was the monks and priests, the institutions of Christianity, who cast the net of time along with their teachings over the continent, as if the clocks could help them (which they did) to keep countrymen, citizenry, and nobility under close scrutiny, in a never-ending, flagrant insult of their Lord and God whom they profess to be "free of time": "A thousand years in they sight are but as yesterday when it is past, and as a watch in the night" (Psalm 90:4).

Most philosophers of time differentiate between "lived" time and "measured" time, between "subjective" and "objective" time. Measured time is considered to be steadfast and precise, the same time and obligatory for all people. Lived time is the personal time of each single individual, passing by much too fast during moments of bliss and much too slowly in the hour of suffering. According to what we know today, however, anyone who takes the theory of relativity and the principle of uncertainty to their logical conclusions must judge the value of these two kinds of time almost in total contradiction to what was upheld just two or three generations ago: Lived time, which only recently was called "relative," now seems much more dependable than the kind of time that just as recently was considered to be "objective" and that has been relativized so much that little of it is left to be "objectivized." At least we can feel our personal, "lived" time, whereas the physicists have to admit that "objective" time cannot even be measured dependably and that nothing certain can be said about it.

Even the ancient Greeks must have been "unconsciously conscious" of the difference between measured and lived time. They had two gods of time: Chronos and Kairos. Chronos, the archfather, was the god of absolute, "eternal" time. For Kairos, however, the youngest son of Zeus, time simply meant the favorable moment, the "right time." Penelope Shuttle and Peter Redgrove have shown that Kairos has a more female approach to time while Chronos has more male elements. They found the male element to be rigid, proud of its "objective" measurement of time, and the female element to be relative, "waxing or waning," just as women are subject to natural cycles: "In the female consciousness, time is subject to the Kairos and less to the Chronos of the male consciousness, although both can be experienced by the same person."

The "most lived" of all times is the female cycle. The woman lives it each month. More than anything else, this cycle is her "inner" clock. In fact, certain scholars are of the opinion that primeval man first experienced time through the female cycle. That was the actual primal meter—and there we have it: the Greek word *metra* originally meant "uterus." It was *the* measure, there was no other one. *Metre,* the Ionic original form, has no plural, that is, no different measures. *Mater* ("mother") is related to this word. Almost all words expressing "measure" (including this word itself) come from this root: mensuration, immense, dimension, meter, diameter, parameter, thermometer, meteor, and so forth, across all languages, even in Sanskrit. There, *matri* is the mother and *matra* is the measure. Even though it is almost unimaginable for modern rationalistic man, let us try to become aware that the "germ cell" for all these different words is in *metra,* the uterus. It brought forth—measure! It *was*—measure. By coming forth from the uterus, man emerges from measure to become *mater*-ial!

Rationalistic Western civilization has suppressed its Kairos. Its time is taken with clocks and watches, with (take note of the word) *chrono*meters. Its time comes from archfather Chronos, the patriarch. It is male, patriarchical, rational, and functional. In the more archaic cultures, however, as in those of the African continent, even today the time of Kairos is more important than clock time, which is "primal time" only for male-dominated thinking.

Meanwhile, we have discovered the ironic (and even somewhat "Ionic") fact that modern particle physics, although unthinkable without measurements and clocks (i.e., without Chronos), is no longer quite as far from Kairos as it previously appeared to be. As we said, for Kairos time is the right moment, the favorable hour, the good opportunity, sensitivity to the right measure and the fitting relationship. And that is just what time is for quantum theory and Heisenberg's principle of uncertainty. For photons and electrons and for quarks and leptons, time exists only as "good opportunity" or as "right moment," but certainly not as clocked time and even less as the supposed "primal time" of Chronos.

To make Kairos the son of Zeus, indeed his youngest son, and to attribute measured time to the archfather Chronos—from a logical point of view as well as in terms of physics and the history of evolution, this must be counterfeit, a reversal of the way things really proceeded. For doesn't the actual sensation of time begin by someone perceiving the right moment? First came the measure set by the uterus, the female time; first came lived time, the right moment. Only then came the measured time of Chronos, the patriarch, who according to the ancient Greeks mated expressly with Ananke, the goddess of coercion in the sense of "necessity" but also that of violence and suppression. One can well imagine that he must have loved her! (Haven't we seen that time loves tyranny?) The fact that the descendants of Chronos "murdered" Kairos so effectively that today he is virtually unknown by anyone but classical philologists is a truly "oedipal" crime whose analysis is long overdue. The whole scheme, as I have said, is counterfeit, and it is obvious at what point in time it must have been made: during the era of transition from the original matriarchal society to patriarchal society. There is an aspect of Ionic-Greek humor in this forgery, as if someone were sitting behind it trying to hide his roguish Odyssean grin—just like Ulysses and his men in one of their bits of knavery (and indeed it is a forgery that could have been devised only by males). I could propose a headline for the story: "The Greek's Prank with Time."

Now to matter. Under the influence of modern physics, matter has become almost more radically frayed than time. And yet it used to be so for Western society: There is nothing more certain than this chair on which I sit, this desk at which I work, this typewriter on which I hammer all night long. . . . Now, however, the nuclear physicists verify what Buddha and the sages of Asia have said all along: Matter is emptiness. Material is "not."

Let us begin this section on matter with a quote from *The Silent Pulse* by George Leonard, a book that I recommend highly to anyone wanting to know more about the present context:

> The electron microscope allows us these perceptions of the body, a beautiful and terrible place, seemingly as spacious as the sea. . . . As the magnification increases, the flesh does begin to dissolve. Muscle

fiber now takes on a fully crystalline aspect. We can *see* that it is made of long, spiral molecules in orderly array. And all these molecules are swaying like wheat in the wind, connected with one another and held in place by invisible waves that pulse many trillions of times a second.

What are the molecules made of? As we move closer, we see atoms, tiny shadowy balls dancing around their fixed locations in the molecules, sometimes changing position with their partners in perfect rhythm. And now we focus on one of the atoms; its interior is lightly veiled by a cloud of electrons. We come closer, increasing the magnification. The shell dissolves and we go on inside to find . . . *nothing*.

Somewhere within that emptiness, we know, is a nucleus. We scan the space, and there it is, a tiny dot. At last, we have discovered something hard and solid, a reference point. But no—as we move closer to the nucleus, it too begins to dissolve. It too is nothing more than an oscillating field, waves of rhythm. Inside the nucleus are other organized fields: protons, neutrons, even smaller "particles." Each of these, upon our approach, also dissolves into pure rhythm.

Scientists continue to seek the basic building blocks of the physical world. These days, they are looking for quarks, strange subatomic entities, having qualities which they describe with such words as upness, downness, charm, strangeness, truth, beauty, color, and flavor. But no matter. If we could get close enough to these wondrous quarks, they too would melt away. They too would have to give up all pretense of solidity. Even their speed and position would be unclear, leaving them only relationship and pattern of vibration.

Of what is the body made? It is made of emptiness and rhythm. At the ultimate heart of the body, at the heart of the world, there is no solidity. Once again, there is only the dance.

Lao-tzu once said: What makes a wheel a wheel is the emptiness between the spokes. In this sense, what makes an atom an atom, is the emptiness between the elementary particles. An atom, enlarged to the size of the Empire State Building, would have a nucleus about as big as a grain of salt. This, then, is how we have to imagine matter—so empty: a grain of salt whirling through the Empire State Building at a speed of approximately thirty-six thousand miles per hour. Or the other way around: A human being, compressed to those parts which can truly be called "matter," would be invisible to the naked eye; he would be the size of an atom. One more metaphor as an aid to the imagination—this one borrowed from Isaac Asimov: If one wanted to fill out the entire volume of one atom with nuclei, one would have to have a thousand trillion atomic nuclei.

Upon closer inspection, however, the "nucleus" itself dissolves into smaller and smaller particles, into more and more "empty" dimensions!

For half a century, this has been going on: Whenever a "final," smallest, "indivisible" nuclear particle is discovered, it doesn't take more than a couple of years before an even smaller one is found.

In the beginning was the atom (from Greek *átomos*, which means "the indivisible" but also, interestingly enough, "that which is sacred to the gods," in this latter sense originally understood not materially but harmonically as the smallest musically meaningful interval, 45:46). Then came electrons, neutrons, and protons (from the Greek word for "the first," because this too was believed to be the "first" and smallest of all particles), and then a breathtaking series of smaller and smaller particles all the way to the photons and quarks, hadrons and leptons, gluons, tions and myons, and more recently on to the weakons, the Z zeros, the rishons, the tohus and vohus. The last three particles were discovered by physicists in Israel in 1980. Two are named for the biblical phrase "tohu va-vohu" (Genesis 1:2), meaning "without form and void," that is, the state of the world before God put it into order. In Hebrew, *rishon* is what *proton* is in Greek: the most original, very first entity.

In the meantime, more than two hundred such entities have been discovered. Many physicists are aware of the fact that the word "elementary particle" can only be used in an ironic sense. Indeed, nothing is less "elementary" than what we are accustomed to call "elementary particles." Many of these not very "elementary" particles exist for minute fractions of a second before they disintegrate into even smaller particles or into waves or energy. As we mentioned, they move from past to future as well as backward, from the future to the past. What used to belong to the realm of folktales and myths really exists after all: a life moving backward, from that which is to come to that which has already been. What has been "tomorrow," will be "yesterday."

Since each of these particles has its antiparticle, we also know that there is "antimatter" and, thus, an "antiworld." In it, each particle has the opposite charge of its counterpart in our "real" (impossible, not to put this word in quotation marks) world. Scientists have already succeeded in producing antimatter, even though only for fractions of a second and in smallest amounts. Physicists are now asking the question: "Where is the antimatter that must have come into existence together with matter at the beginning of the universe? Maybe there are entire galaxies consisting of nothing else but antimatter" (Isaac Asimov).

Fritjof Capra, author of *The Tao of Physics*, has made the following remarks: "The creation and destruction of material particles is one of the most impressive consequences of the equivalence of mass and energy. . . . The classical contrast between the solid particles and the space surrounding them is completely overcome. . . . Particles are merely local condensations of the field; concentrations of energy dissolving into the underlying field."

As early as the second decade of the twentieth century, one of the founders of modern nuclear physics, Niels Bohr, was among the first to understand the implications of the disintegration of matter "into nothing": "For a parallel to the lesson of atomic theory . . . [we must turn] to those kinds of epistemological problems with which already thinkers like the Buddha and Lao-tzu have been confronted."

Let us remember that the concept of zero was first developed by Hindu mathematicians, as early as the sixth century. From the mathematics of India, the zero was adopted in Arabia; and there European mathematicians "discovered" it and adopted it. Without zero, all Western mathematics (the foundation of modern physics) would have been impossible. The preoccupation of Hindu philosophy with the "void," with "nothing," was the original impetus, for the Hindu scientists derived their mathematical concept of zero from the philosophical and spiritual understanding of "nothing." This is the source of the rule in differential calculus that the result of zero divided by zero can be any number—zero, one, or infinity. Because the "nothing" created everything. Just as it does in modern physics.

As early as the fourteenth century, Zen seers developed the formula "Shikisokuseku": "Matter is void" and "Void is matter."

Capra has pointed out that the two foundation stones of twentieth-century physics, quantum theory and the theory of relativity, force us to look at the world much as a Hindu, a Buddhist, or a Taoist would see it. Capra quotes a famous sutra attributed to Buddha himself: "Form is emptiness, and emptiness is indeed form. Emptiness is not different from form; form is not different from emptiness. What is form that is emptiness; what is emptiness that is form."

There has been tension—often even hostility—between the natural sciences and the institutions of the Christian church for centuries. Galileo, Bruno, Kepler, and other great scientists were persecuted, incarcerated, burned at the stake; Darwin and Einstein were discriminated and fought against. Between the natural sciences and the concept of the world in Asia, however, there is basic concurrence. Thousands of years before Einstein formulated his theories concerning time and before the discoveries of quantum physics about matter, the Buddha said the same things, only in different words. In fact, even before the Buddha, the philosophy of Hinduism referred to space as *akasha* (from the Sanskrit root *kash*, "to shine, to appear"). And every student of

Hindu and Buddhist thought is familiar with the term *shunyata*—the void, a void that is fuller than wealth, which again leads us to the dictum: "Void is plentitude" and "Plentitude is void."

On trips to Asia, many modern physicists have experienced the parallels between their own findings and those of Asian spirituality. When Niels Bohr was in China in 1937, he was impressed by the notion of complementaries as an essential part of the Chinese worldview. And when he returned home to Copenhagen, he added the Chinese *yin-yang* symbol to his family coat of arms.

Capra has shown that the findings of the theory of relativity and those of quantum mechanics sound as if they were Zen koans, the seemingly absurd meditation tasks given by Zen masters to their pupils. He feels that quantum theory may be the ultimate koan of our times.

The British physicist James Hopwood Jeans has concluded:

> There is broad agreement today, bordering on unanimity in the avenue of physics, that the stream of knowledge is flowing toward a non-mechanistic reality; the universe is beginning to look more like a mighty idea than like a machine. The spirit no longer seems to be a casual trespasser in the territory of matter. We are starting to presume that we should rather welcome it as creator and rector in the field of matter.

In 1964, the Swiss physicist J. S. Bell pointed out that "no theory of reality compatible with the quantum theory can proceed from the assumption that spatially separate events are independent of each other." Anyone raised in the spiritual tradition of Asia will stop short in amazement here, because this tenet—which has acquired worldwide acceptance in theoretical physics as "Bell's theorem"—means exactly the same as that which the sages of Asia have always known: Nothing in the cosmos, how ever wide its boundaries may be, is separate from anything else. "Everything is one." "Tat twam asi."

Let me present another quote from the works of George Leonard:

> For quantum theory really to work, to put it into everyday language, each electron has to "know" what all the other electrons in the universe are doing in order to "know" what it's to do. It's as if at every point in every electromagnetic field there were a tiny supercomputer that was constantly figuring out everything that's going on in the universe. . . . In such a universe, information about the whole of it is available at its every point.
>
> These implications of quantum theory resonate with the deepest intuition of the ages, the direct experience of the most revered spiritual masters, and the thought of such philosophers as Leibniz and Spinoza and Whitehead.

Ilya Prigogine has remarked that Darwin's theory of evolution was an early step in this direction, implying as it does that all forms of life are connected with each other. "The expanding universe implies that all things in the cosmos are interconnected." Exactly the same thing was said by the Chinese Zen master Ch'an-sha Ching-ts'en in the ninth century: "The whole universe is your eye. The whole universe is your source of light. The whole universe is within your own source of light. In the whole universe, there is nobody who is not your own self."

Here one is reminded once more of the famous pearl of Lord Indra, which reflects all other pearls in the world and which at the same time is contained in every other pearl in the world. For the ancient Brahmans, it was a symbol of the universe. Wise men in India use it as a meditation task: Penetrate the absurdity of Indra's pearl; it reflects all the pearls in the world and yet lies within every other pearl. Grasp this!

To the rationalist, the pearl may be a metaphor (physicists also have only metaphors!), but the metaphor corresponds precisely with the theories of quantum mechanics and the more recent findings of particle physics, which has developed theorems like the following: "Each particle consists of all particles." Or: "Each particle helps produce other particles, which in turn produce the particle itself." These read as though they were Buddhist sutras, but in fact they are theorems of modern theoretical physics.

The actual point of Heisenberg's principle of uncertainty is something the Buddha and the Zen masters have always been certain about, the fact that only our perception of things makes them what they are. A particle is a wave if I want to look at it as a wave. It is matter if I want to look at it as matter. The particle may be on the moon, but when I consider it as a wave, it is a wave. If someone else up on the moon were (simultaneously) to consider it as matter, it would be matter. If I look at it as a positron, it is a positron. If I look at it as an electron, it is an electron (and the direction of time is reversed). My observation is thus able to reverse time, past into future and vice versa, positive into negative and vice versa. That is the actual point of the principle of uncertainty. Whatever we may say about the world, we ourselves are in the middle of it. We cannot leave it. We are "in" things, in the smallest particles, in the "core of the pearl."

Heisenberg's principle of uncertainty is more than half a century old and yet is still acknowledged only by physicists. The rest of us look upon it as something exotic, like a message from a distant star, although it should long ago have revolutionized our entire attitude toward the world. Only then could our thinking really be called "modern." As long as we do not understand the message of the new physics, our way of thinking is antiquated, premodern, a school of thought from the nineteenth century. One example is traditional medicine. Without consideration of the principle of uncertainty, it becomes a "medicine of uncertainty"—which, in fact, it is.

With his principle, Heisenberg discovered a fundamental concept that is valid not only in microphysics. Let me repeat: Observe a particle as a wave, and it is a wave. Observe it as matter, and it is matter. So the principle of certainty is a principle of the point of view. If we were not so deceptively sure of the "objectivity" of our point of view, we humans would have noticed long ago that we have been living with the principle of uncertainty from the beginning of our evolution. Almost all of us have had the following experience: You see things from your point of view, and no doubt, you consider your viewpoint correct. Someone else, however—your father or your friend or your lover —looks at the problem from a different angle and comes to the opposite conclusion, which for that person is just as undoubtedly correct as yours is to you.

Thus it is our point of view, the way we look at reality, that makes reality the way it is. In the nineteenth century, most people in the Western world were aware of the idea of "the survival of the fittest." The nations of the small continent of Europe had subjugated the greater part of the world and were ruthlessly exploiting it. Year after year, the process of exploitation was making headway. Nations were exploiting nations, capitalists were exploiting workers, workers were exploiting their wives, families were exploiting their children. Education was directed from the first—not just by the schools—at establishing those patriarchal and authoritarian structures in society that helped legitimate the general process of exploitation. Industrialization and capitalism led to fantastic profit margins. It all worked marvelously, and it was obviously all based on exploitation. Exploitation was inevitable. Everyone is everyone else's enemy. Everybody fights against everybody else. The more ruthless the struggle is, the more rapid the progress. Darwin's theory of the survival of the fittest and the interpretation of the evolutionary theory that many of us were taught in school fit perfectly into this picture. There was a need for this kind of theoretical foundation and so science furnished it.

In the meantime it has become clear that the concept of evolution by struggle, destruction, exploitation, and the survival of the fittest is a matter of point of view. That idea stood in precise correspondence to the way the people in Europe (especially in Britain) thought and behaved at that time. Today many scientists realize that what the old biology explained as parasitic exploitation was in fact symbiotic cooperation. We have to understand that parasitic types of relationships are not characteristic of nature. The opposite is true: symbiotic aid is part of the idea of evolution. We know that the majority of all living creatures have "understood," each in its own way, that all living things are connected with each other and that the death of a partner (even of an enemy) or the extinction of a race (again, even of an enemy) also means danger for all other partners or races, danger for the entire system of life. We have learned that those predatory relationships that our grandfathers (and even our fathers) tried to teach us as "typical in nature" are exceptions; that, in comparison to the billions of cooperative and symbiotic relationships in nature, there are not very many "murderous" ones; and that we have noticed the "murderous" ones precisely because they are so rare. Now we realize that human beings distorted the partner roles that are naturally dominant in creation, turned them into those of a predatory relationship as justification for their own behavior. They projected themselves onto nature—and those who overly "project" need therapy.

Nineteenth-century science "celebrated" the "survival of the fittest," because deep down it wanted to celebrate "the fittest"—the human being. The new biology, by contrast, "celebrates" the bonds between all living creatures, because now more important than the "celebration" of the human being is the survival of life (including human life) on this planet.

I have cited this example in such detail not only because it illustrates the new consciousness with which this book deals, but also because it shows so clearly that the phenomena prevalent in particle physics are not limited to the microcosm. Not only in physics, but also in other sciences (in biology, for instance) is "certainty" relative to the point of view or the level of consciousness.

If we could only acknowledge that this holds true even for the areas of religion and spirituality, we would become more tolerant. Westerners pray to one God as the Christian God, to Jesus Christ, the Lord Almighty. The Arabs pray to one God as Allah of Islam, the Lord Almighty. The Indians pray to Brahma as Lord Brahma, the Creator and Lord Almighty. Whatever the religion, it is always the almighty God (or an almighty principle, or the almighty nothingness). There is no way of deciding who is right. All are right. In every culture there are people who have experienced beyond a doubt that they are right.

Is this a relativistic point of view? Is it even a denial of the divine principle? Is it not rather the opposite? The absolute certainty that the believers are right in not only *one* of those religions and cultures but in *all* of them? We do not deny a particle if we look at it as a wave here and as matter there. The particle *exists*. And yet it is dependent on us.

God *exists* in the same sense. But He also is dependent on us. The great mystics of all cultures have known it as long as mankind can remember: He is within us.

The discovery of the laser beam led to the development of holography, a kind of photography with laser waves. Surprisingly, a "picture" produced by holography cannot be divided. If it is divided, it "jumps" back to form the full picture. Divisions or detail sections cannot be produced. Even a smaller format shows the *holos,* the whole (from the Greek word *'olos,* "whole"), although somewhat less brilliant. Theoretically, one could go on dividing down to microscopic dimensions; a detail section would never be produced. The picture remains itself, even if the picture itself should become an elementary particle. Which means that in each elementary particle there is the whole, the entire universe. Physicists working with holography could easily subscribe to the Buddha's realization that "everything is one."

From this angle, too, we have reached a point that became visible in the first part of the chapter when we talked about time. Physicists today are asking whether the so-called psi-phenomena of parapsychology might not be seen as "natural" from the vantage point of quantum mechanics—phenomena such as precognition, materialization, dematerialization, and telekinesis. If everything is one, even the most distant things must be Here and Now.

In an article on physics and parapsychology, Wolfgang Büchel writes:

> Even though the psi-phenomena apparently do not fit into the present categories of physics, certain analogies between parapsychology and modern physics are unmistakable. . . . Leading quantum physicists such as Jordan or Pauli have reached a point where they no longer deny psi-phenomena *a priori* as something impossible, but rather take an unbiased look at the question of their reality. They are truly interested in the epistemological and philosophical questions posed by these phenomena. The fact that clairvoyance and precognition cross the categorial barriers of space and time, in any case, can no longer be accepted as sufficient reason to deny the possibility that the psi-phenomena may fit into a future body of physical categories.

To sum up: That which only recently appeared as the most unshakable and certain—time and matter—has become illusory. Instead, we have been given (and I use the word "given" quite deliberately) a new, more certain realization: that the cosmos and the earth, organic and inorganic things, plants and animals and human beings are sound. Of course, you may say that they are vibrations; but in the overwhelming majority of cases they are vibrations in whole-number relationships. Vibrations in whole-number relationships, however, sound—whether within the human hearing range or above or below it.

In the second chapter, we became familiar with this ancient Zen koan:

> If you blot out sense and sound—
>   what do you hear?

Now we can vary the koan as follows:

> If you blot out time and matter—
>   what do you hear?

That is the actual question. We will do better (and have a higher chance of success) to try to solve it as a koan than to expect the solution from intellectual considerations. Take a look at the passage quoted from Chuang-tzu on the epigraph page at the front of this book.

7 ✺ Harmony as the Goal of the Universe

ANYONE WHO IS even slightly familiar with the theory of harmony knows that every dissonance tends toward becoming a harmony. If it is true that the harmonic relationships in music reflect the harmonic and mathematical relationships in the planetary system as well as in the cosmos, the microcosm, the biosphere, and all the other fields we have talked about, then this rule must be valid also outside of music: All dissonances gravitate toward becoming harmonies. It would fill the pages of a thick book to carry out this thesis in all the different fields. Hence this chapter will limit itself to a small body of evidence.

Let us begin with music itself. Its history could be written from the viewpoint that music consists of the continuous discovery of new harmonies, of novel consonances and harmonic possibilities. In the beginning phase of man's perception of music, only monophonic melody lines were felt to be "euphonious." The first step toward developing harmonies was the discovery of the octave. In the Western world, this step was taken during the era of Hellenism. Its fundamentally new aspect was the possibility of connecting a tone of the melody line with another one and to experience this connection as harmonious. The next steps (still in late Hellenism and the early Middle Ages) were the discoveries of the fifth and fourth intervals. Throughout the Middle Ages, the third was considered to be a dissonant (even—according to medieval musicians—satanic) interval. The first natural thirds (and, by the way, also the first natural sixths, the reversed third) appear around the year 1300, mostly in love songs, for instance in Guillaume de Machaut's "Mirror of Narcissus," as well as in the songs of the troubadours of Provence in southern France. They were then considered avant-garde and gave rise to heated discussions. Today we hear the third as the epitome of conservative euphony.

In the course of the fifteenth century, the major scale won general recognition, first as the C modus, derived from the system of the old church scales, which contained all five "natural" consonances. Even today, the prominence of the major mode as opposed to the minor one usually is explained by the greater wealth of consonances in the major scales.

Starting with Johann Sebastian Bach, the entire development of Western music can be interpreted as an increasingly intense (and successful) search for consonances in those intervals and chords previously considered to be "unharmonious" and "dissonant." Again and again in this development, the line we drew in chapter 4 between the more consonant and the more dissonant sounds was crossed—even by Bach himself, with his fondness for chromaticism. In the nineteenth century, finally, only the intervals of the second and the seventh (above all the minor second and the major seventh) remained as "intervals of displeasure." Debussy found chromatic "consonance" even in these, particularly in the most critical of these intervals, the minor second. And the especially sticky tritone, the "flatted fifth," has become indispensable perhaps since the late Beethoven, but certainly since Wagner. In his *Craft of Musical Composition,* Hindemith attributed a key position to it. The fact that it also holds a similar position in jazz, particularly since bebop, has already been mentioned. Modern concert music had reached a point in the 1950s, where composers felt that dissonances could be achieved only by so-called clusters (the simultaneous sounding of all tones across the entire keyboard). In a few years' time even these were turned into "euphonies" of sorts, for instance by the Polish composer Krzysztof Penderecki, his German colleague Bernd-Alois Zimmerman and especially by György Ligeti of Hungary in his compositions for organ. Ligeti's work *Volumina* is a truly touching example of the irridescent beauty achievable by a series of minor seconds. Ligeti said about *Volumina:*

> Chordism, configuration and polyphony have been obscured and suppressed, but underneath the sound surface of the composition they remain secretly effective as if they were deep below a water surface.

... Figures without faces are created as in paintings by Chirico, immense expanses and distances, an architecture consisting of scaffolding only. . . . Everything else disappears in the wide empty spaces, in the "Volumina" of the musical form.

Ever since the beginning of modern concert music, the question has been asked why, in all cultures where music plays a role (that is, in all cultures), the great musical creations limit themselves to a comparatively small arsenal of tones. In experiments made at the University of Illinois in Chicago, Richard Norton found the extent of the reservoir of tones that the human ear can clearly differentiate:

We found that, depending on the length of tone, on the time elapsed between hearing different tones and on the state of mental fatigue of the listeners, musicians and non-musicians alike were able to hear far more than one thousand "just noticeable differences" (JND's, as the experts in acoustics put it) between the lowest and the highest audible tones. Precise experimentation resulted in 1,378 "just noticeable differences" between these musically "raw tones."

The conclusion to be drawn from this simple but somewhat fatiguing experiment is that the human ear is an astounding sense organ whose potential has never been realized in music. Thinking of the music in the Western world as well as in all other cultures, we realize that all of us, musicians and music lovers, are rather idle people when it comes to making music, considering the giant potential which the ear, in fact, has. Even the modern piano has only 88 keys which seem to be entirely satisfactory to both composers and listeners. What are eighty-eight tones (more or less) out of more than thirteen hundred? After thousands of years of human history, do we have to admit, with a certain amount of embarrassment, that we use only five per cent of the available tones when we make music? Why have we limited ourselves to the twelve tones of the chromatic scale, which we keep duplicating in so-called octaves in order to create that object, full of meaning and emotions, which we call music?

One of the answers to this question (as I have mentioned) lies in the hearing disposition of the human ear. The ear "prefers" whole-number relationships. Another (similar) answer results when we relate the "music" discussed in chapters 4 and 5 (the "music" of the macrocosm and of the microcosm) to our human music. We are aware by now that music is more than music. It is cosmos and atomic microstructure, earth and stream, plant and leaf shape, human and animal body, to such an extent that the French-American composer and musicologist Dane Rudhyar was able to write: "The physical world of human experience resembles a gigantic sounding board." Everywhere on this board, this instrument with its truly cosmic dimensions, there are the same harmonic proportions. Precisely these proportions are the foundation of "music" in the narrower sense (the audible music of our human cultures) and define the arsenal of its tones. Whenever these tones are not struck exactly, they are "heard correctly" in the sense laid out at the end of chapter 5. Those areas not open to "corrective hearing" are excluded. That is the reason, Rudolf Haase has suggested, why the so-called quarter tones, which fall precisely into the gaps between the "areas of corrective hearing," have never been able to prevail in music.

What is tonality? Richard Norton answered: "Tonality is the decision against the chaos of tones created by those thirteen-hundred JND's we discovered in the acoustics lab."

That means, music is unthinkable without an act of choice. From the wealth of "possible" tones, from that which Norton calls the "chaos of tones," only few tones are chosen in order to prevent chaos, exactly those tones that exist also in the cosmos and in the organic forms of nature. It is the same act of choice that we heard about in chapter 4 as a prerogative of mind and spirit.

This "act of choice" can also be referred to, with an expression taken from nuclear physics, as "quantizing." We (nature, spirit, mind) choose in quanta. This, too, becomes apparent on the monochord and in the overtone scale. When the finger slides upward on the string, a preference of certain tones is sounded: "Nature itself makes a choice. The tones jump from one to the other, so to speak. They are not part of a continuum but rather in a series of quanta." Kayser points out that the same thing happens on a valveless horn. "It is very difficult for the player to produce pure intermediate tones. In reality, the tones jump from the basic tone to the octave, then to the fifth, then again to the octave, etc." Thus nature does not do "what we want but what it wants. I can slide up or down with my finger as carefully as I want to, if it strikes a spot where the string 'doesn't want it,' the effort is in vain. Thus it is obvious that nature makes a choice or, to put it another way, that it 'creates norms.'"

Kayser also points out that Max Planck, the founder of quantum mechanics in modern theoretical physics, did extensive research on the monochord and problems of acoustics. In an essay published in 1893 entitled "Die natürliche Stimmung in der modernen Vokalmusik" (Natural Tuning in Modern Vocal Music), Planck wrote:

> According to the postulate of quantization, the discrete intrinsic values of energy lead to certain discrete intrinsic values of the period

of vibration. This happens in the same way on a tense string fastened at both ends. The difference between them is that on the string the quantization is conditional on an exterior factor, the length of the string, while here it is conditional on the quantum of energy resulting from the differential equation itself.

Wilfried Krüger (to round out the picture) even succeeded in finding a basis for tempered tuning in nuclear physics. The question as to which of the different possible tunings is the correct one has a long history. It has become customary to look down upon the "equal temperament" as something "artificial" and "violent" and "mathematically constructed." The basic idea of tempered tuning, however, lies in the division of the tonal space into identical subspaces. This corresponds to Planck's quantum mechanics, according to which effects can be produced only as a multiple of a smallest unit no longer open to further division. Thus, the "quantum mechanics" of the microcosm correspond to the "quantum harmonics" of equal temperament. "The tonal space, in actuality, is an atomic space."

Only through tempered tuning was the miracle of modulation possible. Only through it are transpositions easily executed (and we have already learned that the possibility of transposition exists everywhere in the universe). Above all, though, only after the introduction of equal temperament in the seventeenth century began that true musical explosion, that immense boom of music in the Western world that numbers among the greatest phenomena in the cultural history of humankind.

It is important to realize that the tendency toward harmony, immanent in music, in a way is nothing else but a reflection of the same tendency outside of music, in almost all fields. As George Leonard notes: "In 1665 the Dutch scientist Christian Huygens noticed that two pendulum clocks, mounted side by side on a wall, would swing together in precise rhythm. They would hold their mutual beat, in fact, far beyond their capacity to be matched in mechanical accuracy. It was as if they 'wanted' to keep the same time."

Science has taught us that this phenomenon is universal. Two oscillators pulsating in the same field in almost identical rhythm will tend to "lock in," with the result that eventually their vibrations will become precisely synchronous. This phenomenon is referred to as "mutual phase-locking" or "entrainment." Entrainment is universal in nature. In fact, it is so ubiquitous that we hardly notice it, "as with the air we breathe," as Leonard put it. It is a physical phenomenon, but it also is more than that, because it informs us about the tendency of everything that vibrates—in other words, everything—to swing together, to lock in. It informs us about the tendency of the universe to share rhythms, that is, to vibrate in harmony. Leonard continues:

> To get the feel of entrainment, you might try playing with the "vertical" and "horizontal" knobs of an old television set. Every set contains horizontal and vertical oscillators that position the scanning electronic dot that forms the picture. These oscillators must match the signal coming from the station very precisely; otherwise the picture will move sideways or vertically. When you turn the knobs, you're adjusting the frequency of your set's oscillators to match the frequency of the station's oscillators. Fortunately, you don't have to create a perfect match. When the frequencies come close to one another, they suddenly lock, as if they "want" to pulse together. . . .
> Living things are like television sets in that they contain oscillators. In fact, we might say that living things *are* oscillators; that is, they pulse or change rhythmically. . . . There is an electrifying moment in the film "The Incredible Machine" in which two individual muscle cells from the heart are seen through a microscope. Each is pulsing with its own separate rhythm. Then they move closer together. Even before they touch, there is a sudden shift in the rhythm, and they are pulsing together, perfectly synchronized.

The Boston scientist William Condon has shown that this "harmonization" or "entrainment" also takes place when two people have a good conversation. All of a sudden, their brain waves will oscillate synchronously. In fact, Condon was able to show that the brain waves of students listening to their professor's lecture will largely oscillate "in harmony" with those of the lecturer. Only when this takes place do those present perceive the atmosphere in the lecture hall as "good."

George Leonard found an especially impressive example of such entrainment in the relationship between preachers and their audiences, particularly in the sermons and addresses of prominent pastors, as for instance Martin Luther King, Jr. A sermon is perceived as "successful," "electrifying," or "exciting" only when the brain waves of the members of the audience vibrate synchronously with those of the preacher.

Similar observations were made between mothers and their children, husbands and wives—in short, in the most diverse groups of individuals for whom harmony is a goal.

Another scientist, Paul Byers of Columbia University, documented on film and analyzed human interaction in greatly varying cultures —those of Americans, Eskimos, African Bushmen and New Guinea Aborigines. In each case, he found rhythm sharing. Byers wrote:

"Synchronized heartbeats have been reported between psychiatrist and patient. Female college roommates sometimes find their menstrual cycles synchronized."

As Leonard points out:

> In music, the miracle of entrainment is made explicit. The performer's every gesture, every micromovement, must be perfectly entrained with the pulse of the music, or else the performance falls apart. Watch the members of a chamber group—how they move as one, become as one, a single field. We have become accustomed to such miracles: the extraordinary faculty of jazz musicians to "predict" precise pitch and pattern during improvisation. . . . The miracle springs not so much from individual virtuosity . . . as from the ability of a large group of human beings . . . to sense, feel, and move as one.

This tendency to feel and move as one can also be observed among large flocks of birds or schools of fish. The flock or school is constantly changing, and yet it remains miraculously well ordered, its form still "harmonious." For decades, Western functionalistic-mechanistic thinking led science to assume that large flocks must have a "leader." Today we know that "alpha animals" exist only when two or three birds or fish fly or swim together. When the number of fish or birds becomes larger, the group itself becomes a "being." Professor Brian L. Partridge of the University of Miami, a specialist in the behavior of animals in large groups, wrote that "in a certain sense, the entire school is the leader, each individual being part of the followers." The group is "more like a single organism than an accumulation of individuals. . . . In all probability, it is as if each member of the school knows where the others are going to move. . . . The fact that they never collide fits this hypothesis." The commands come from the group as a whole, not from a single animal. In this sense, the group is the "being"; and in this way people close to nature have always seen large flocks of birds, as one "being" moving in the sky in constant change and yet "keeping in form."

It is highly interesting in this context that collisions are, in fact, very rare occurrences in nature. Compared with the frequency of collisions among human beings, they are surprisingly infrequent, even in much denser populations, as in the bustle of an anthill, a termite nest or a beehive, in compact cultures of bacteria, in the blood vessels of humans or other mammals, or in compact flocks of birds, which are able to change direction all at once even while flying at high speeds. So rare is the occurrence of collision that we may conclude that "collision" is largely a human phenomenon. We have "unlearned" to feel (that is, we do not listen to) the "harmonization" and "entrainment" of our own "flocks" or "schools." Possibly this has to do with the fact that in many instances human behavior is largely controlled by the rational left-brain hemisphere.

Resonance phenomena, entrainment, and related phenomena have been discovered in the most diverse fields, in architecture, in electronics and acoustics, in psychology and psychotherapy, in biology and chemistry, in medicine and pharmacology, in physics and astronomy.

Entering into harmonic relationships is the goal not only of music. It is the goal of atoms and molecules, of planetary orbits, of cells and hearts, of brain waves and movements, of flocks of birds and schools of fish and—in principle—of human beings. All of them (or better: the cosmos, the entire creation) have harmony as their final goal. They are all moving to realize *Nada Brahma*.

The phenomena of entrainment and synchronicity discussed in the present and in the fifth chapter can also be understood in terms of rhythm. Rhythm is "harmony in time." Rhythm and harmony complement each other. The inclination toward rhythm contains the inclination toward harmony.

Gunther Hildebrandt of the Institute for Ergophysiology at the University of Marburg writes: "The human organism is not only constructed according to harmonic principles but also functions with them." Similarly, Haase explains: "It has been found that the rhythmics of the human organism function utterly harmonically—that is, the frequencies of pulse, breathing, blood circulation, etc., as well as their combined activities. We can observe that these rhythms are strictly coordinated, primarily in terms of the numbers one through four, which are able to form the intervals octave (1:2), fifth (2:3), fourth (3:4), twelfth (1:3), and double octave (1:4)."

As Haase points out, interrupting these rhythms with their whole-number proportions causes illness in the human body. "Particularly in cancer cases we observe a total irregularity of all rhythms. Apparently the cancer cell causes a withdrawal from the temporal harmony of the body functions."

Haase, too, refers to rhythm as "temporal harmony." In the final analysis, it is a matter of interpretation whether we experience the numerical proportions that are found in so many phenomena of the organic and inorganic world as harmony or as rhythm. Harmony *is* rhythm *is* harmony *is* rhythm.

Rudolf Haase's description of cancer as a state of "rhythmic chaos" touches upon another important point. The cancer phenomenon ought to be seen against the background of the fact that any individual cancer is only part of a much more encompassing cancerous disease that we encounter throughout the modern world, in society, urbanization, economy, ecology, politics, in the military arms race, the medical system, and dozens of other fields. Cancerous growth is a state of mind. Since it takes place in the head, it causes new processes of cancerous proliferation in all areas influenced by human consciousness. Anyone who has seen Lagos, São Paulo, Mexico City, Calcutta, or Tokyo is familiar with the phenomenon of cancerous urban growth, for example. Yet this is a problem that is limited neither to the Third World nor to large cities. Examples can be found in smaller communities as well —say, an American town such as . . . but I hesitate to write the name of the town I was thinking of, because there are people living there, human beings, to whom I would be saying: You are living in the middle of a cancerous ulcer. For we have the same attitude toward cancerlike growth in public life as toward the physical disease: we try not to talk about it.

On any transcontinental flight you can see how the cancerlike spread of cities and suburbs, of industrial parks and projects has seized the earth like an epidemic. It is like a scabby white crust creeping over what remains of our green land.

Even more obvious are cancer phenomena in the field of economics. World economy in the 1970s and 1980s has literally been dominated by them. That is why the tried-and-true economic systems have failed and why, in almost all cases, the prognoses of even the most experienced experts and scholars in economics and politics have turned out to be wrong. Processes that according to our conventional causal concepts should exclude each other are coupling together to produce novel combinations such as growing industrial investments plus simultaneous mass unemployment. Or declining capital flow along with growing inflation. Or simultaneous economic growth and recession. Precisely this is the nature of malign proliferation: it can be neither controlled nor predicted. It simply grows wild.

Cancerous growth is a problem also in the political and administrative apparatus, as anyone will recognize who has read about the giant bureaucracies in the capitals of the West (and the East!), from the Pentagon in Washington, D.C., to the Common Market Center in Brussels to the KGB Headquarters in Moscow. Departments constantly create new departments, subdepartments keep splitting into ever new offices and special divisions that question one another's existence, go to war with one another, cancel one another out so that not even the chiefs of staff really understand the administrative structure of their outfit —which in turn drives them to invent new structures, departments, divisions and—"cells." All we have to do is exchange a few words, and the description of the bureaucratic cancer turns into a description of cancerous growth in the human body.

The same is true about administration in industry. In large companies, you often find that the central administration is opposed by the administrative apparatuses of the company's various subdivisions. In this situation, communication would seem to be of utmost importance. In reality, however, communication is replaced by a flood of paper, by forms to be filled out. Often enough, division chiefs, department heads, administrative personnel, and secretaries spend more of their time filling out forms than doing their actual work—forms that frequently disappear in somebody's files as quickly as they are completed. Computer-written documents and graphs, whose language and system most people fail to understand, wander from one desk to another as if they possessed a life of their own, as if they were ghosts. Insiders exchange knowing glances: Just write anything, it doesn't matter; don't worry, we don't understand it either. And they all know that the really important processes, which most of them want to keep going in spite of everything, are self-controlled, and that with a little bit of common sense you somehow make it. What I have described here is precisely the struggle between the uncontrolled wild growth and the core of health that is characteristic of the clinical picture of cancer.

Almost anyone who is part of contemporary professional life is familiar with such processes of cancerous growth. The disease of cancer exists not only in the human body. It exists everywhere. Which means it is impossible to overcome it as long as we fight against it *only* in the human body. Let us remember our description of cybernetic networks. There is an entire network of causes for cancer that goes far beyond the field of medicine into the sphere of consciousness. The school of medicine that is stuck in the causal thinking of the nineteenth century (the belief that there is one and only one cause for any particular illness) is unable to solve the problem, as we know by now. We need to concentrate on the network—not only the network of cancerous cells in the human body but also the cancerous network in our consciousness. The formation of chaotic rhythms.

I previously quoted the poet Novalis: "Every disease is a musical problem." The realization that cancer has to do with malfunctions of rhythm, resonance, vibration, and harmonic "tuning" is not only an aesthetic-philosophical finding. It is a discovery in line with the state of the art in modern cybernetics.

"Harmony as the Goal of the Universe": the seven words that form the title of this chapter have to do with a teleological (from Greek *télos*, "goal") idea, with the idea of finality. Harmony is the goal. In order to reach this goal, harmony has to grow. We began our deliberations in chapter 4 with the harmonic structure of our planetary system as discovered by Johannes Kepler. Already that context made clear that structure is a goal. Whatever theory one adheres to about the genesis of our solar system, one thing is obvious: The planets, whether they were pulled in by the sun or cast into space from the prime mass of the sun or "bred in the primal cosmic broth," cannot possibly have been revolving around the sun in harmonic orbits from the beginning. They must have "found" these orbits after millions or billions of years. Which means, the harmony of the orbits was a (finally reached) goal. This is what is so extraordinary—that in spite of the billions of possibilities, the goal was reached with such remarkable determination.

Let us return to the discipline from which the word *harmony* takes its primary meaning, to music. We have seen that harmonies had to be "discovered." This took hundreds of years during which different musical and harmonic systems were found, kept for a while, and discarded, until (around the time of Bach) the system was reached that today is largely considered to be the valid "occidental" system. From this point of view it can be seen as "goal." Almost all cultures and peoples tend to adopt it as a whole or at least in part as soon as their musicians become familiar with it. It is often said that this is an undesirable process of "Westernization" or even "Americanization" in the wake of American pop music. At first glance this may be so, but at the core of the matter there is something quite different. The musicians (and the ears) of the world experience the teleological nature of the Western system of harmony. They have no problem doing this, because the crucial characteristics of this system are embedded like "germ cells" in all music of all people.

Let's look at the word *germ* for a moment. There is nothing harmonic in germs, seeds, or sprouts. The plant has first to develop before its harmonic beauty reveals itself to our eyes, in the leaf shapes and in the blossoms. The growing process of a plant from germ to fruition is a constant reminder that harmony is a goal to be reached.

Part of the idea of a goal is consistency. One reaches a goal, and then one stays there, at least long enough to decide on a new goal. In the periodic table of elements, those elements are least consistent and stable that have a surplus of protons and neutrons. Harmonically, this "surplus" means that the particular elements possess particles that do not (or only very fragmentarily) fit into the harmonic overall structure of the system. It is as if they have too many "particle tones" that are "alien to the scale" and "alien to the major triad." Therefore they decay in radioactive processes, aiming for a different, more stable state. Their state becomes "more stable" when it becomes "more harmonic." The less harmonic these elements are (for instance, plutonium, uranium, actinium, thorium), the more radioactive they will be, which also means, the more dangerous they are for man. The smaller the "harmony" of the atomic structure, the greater the danger for life. This is similar to what we discovered about cancer. By the end of the present chapter we will see what truly astonishing consequences the idea of harmonic finality can have. Before continuing with this train of thought, however, we must consider the opposite force: entropy.

In opposition to harmonization as the goal of the universe stands the second law of thermodynamics. In brief, it states that what develops is not harmony (structure, order, differentiation) but quite the opposite, disorder and chaos: entropy. Entropy therefore seems to characterize the final state toward which the universe is developing, its death in the lowest energy state possible, its "caloric death" and sinking into an undifferentiated "caloric soup."

More and more frequently, however, science has been confronted with the question why—if entropy develops so irresistibly—the final state of general chaos was not reached long ago. In fact, certain theoretical models suggest that it should have been reached millions of years ago. Biologists in particular have become outspoken opponents of thermodynamics. For a long time—indeed, until Prigogine solved the problem—it was difficult to combine the findings of evolution (the "simple" fact that life exists and is in a continual process of differentiation and development) with entropy.

In the work of Jean E. Charon, an important role is played by so-called negentropy. Entropy, as we said, means the disintegration of order and differentiation. Negentropy, however, negative entropy, is the cosmic force opposed to entropy. It holds the promise of increasing order and differentiation, of a constant development not only of life but of the entire universe, of the microcosm as well as the macrocosm.

For Charon the electron is to the microcosm what the black hole is to astrophysics. Both the electron and the black hole are characterized by totally curved space and by curved time. This means that the time of electrons and of black holes is opposite to our "material" time, which moves on a straight line from past to present to future. This, in turn, may imply that if entropy grows in the "material" world, then in the world of electrons (and black holes) precisely the opposite force might grow, the force of negentropy. This, then, could be the place where order and differentiation are on the increase, where the principle of development toward a higher state is valid (which, in the final analysis, is a development toward a higher state of consciousness).

Until recently it was believed that the development of negentropy was characteristic of life. No doubt negentropy is a principle in the cell, in genes and DNA molecules. Now, however, there seems to be evidence that this expansion is a much more encompassing principle, a principle of electrons and photons. In no way can it be limited to the sphere of life. Charon writes:

> Only when one has understood and accepted this standpoint, one begins to realize how the spiritual standard of the *entire* cosmos is progressively on the upgrade. This takes place by the primal matter passing through many successive "life experiences." For more or less extended time periods, the primal matter will be part of mineral matter, then of living or even of thinking creatures. All the information stored in the course of these successive life-experiences cannot be lost.

The evolutionary tendency of electrons is analogous to that of human beings. Whatever our cultural and educational background may be, all of us feel that our lives become "better" the more we devote it to the service of cognition and love. In this sense, we have been "programmed" by evolution. To be sure, I should not have used the word "analogous." There is no "analogy" when you look at things precisely. We *are* our electrons. Charon: "My thinking *is* the thinking of my electrons. It is not merely analogy but identity."

The electronic "prime matrix" (the space within an electron) can be imagined as a honeycomb. Each cell of the honeycomb is either "empty" or contains a photon—with the characteristic inclination to reach higher spin states. The fact that electrons, as microcosmic particles, are smaller in size than we can imagine does not speak against their unimaginably large capacity for information storage. Consider how dense matter is inside an electron. We have learned that it is similar to the density of black holes, that is, to the mass of the sun concentrated in an object about 3.5 to 6 miles wide. Also consider their temperature—millions or even billions of degrees. Besides, nothing is really imaginable. The honeycomb is just an auxiliary concept. No structure is conceivable in curved space that would make any sense in the spatial context of our human three-dimensional space. The honeycomb cells would have to be packed much more densely, in a manner more complex and complicated than would ever be possible in a beehive. One more reason for the immense information storage capacity of the electron is the fact that photons have zero mass. In other words, the number of photons in an electron is almost unlimited since the mass of the electron is so incredibly dense.

Think of the number of electrons we have talked about. A simple computation made by Charon shows that even in this moment, toward the end of the twentieth century, each one of us, with each breath we take, exhales or inhales a few dozen of the same electrons that Julius Caesar expelled with his last sigh at the moment of his assassination in 44 B.C.E. Our assumption that an electron stores everything that has taken place since the beginning of the universe does not just apply to some random electrons way out in the depth of cosmic space. A few of these "oldest" electrons are in each one of us. And each one of us, therefore—the repetition is intentional—has electrons that have been part of Jesus or the Buddha or other great saints and seers in history, electrons that are charged with their photon information, their photon cognition, their photon love. In each one of us, on the other hand, are also electrons that have been in (and are thus programmed by) people like Hitler and Stalin, Himmler and Eichmann and other arch-criminals of mankind. Indeed, even from this vantage point we seem to be headed toward the realization of the seers and wise men of Asia and Egypt that everything is in us—the same realization that is suggested by modern theoretical physics, holography, and the other phenomena we have discussed.

To stretch our imagination even further: Each particle—each of the millions of "matrix boxes"—has its own spin, and all these spins vibrate together in the whole-number proportions of the overtone scale. This, then, is the prime model of mind and spirit, the prime model of "cognition," "reflection," "deed," and "love": an enormous chord, a chord that is "tuned" to the "keynote" of Max Planck's energy quantum.

Negentropy, the counterforce of entropy, increases not only because the spin matrices of the electrons become more and more differentiated through "cognition," "reflection," "deed," and "love." It also increases insofar as the number of black holes (and also, following certain theories, the number of electrons in the cosmos) constantly increases. For a long time now, astronomers have felt that the black holes with their temporal progression running counter to entropy are becoming more and more numerous in the course of the history of the universe. Their appearance is one characteristic indicating a late stage of development. In fact, according to one cosmological theory, everything in the vicinity of a black hole—close enough to be attracted by it—will disappear from this world forever, only to reappear in a "counterworld." Thus, a black hole can be seen as an embryo of a new universe. A universe of negentropy? Of spirit?

The following cosmological model now moves into the range of the possible: Each spin state can be interpreted as a tone of an overtone scale. Each spin contains all prior whole-number spins, as each tone of an overtone scale contains all other tones. According to the cosmological model of the "complex theory of relativity," it is conceivable that only at the end of time (Charon has computed that this state will come in approximately 20 billion years) will *all* spins have reached their highest spin state. And just that is the process of differentiation and development: the higher the spin, the higher the state of consciousness. To be sure, there are particles of the highest category even today, but they are rare. In this way, we have found a new interpretation of evolution: The further it progresses, the more spins will reach the highest point of their development. The endpoint of evolution will be achieved when all spins have reached this highest level. What the French philosopher and anthropologist Pierre Teilhard de Chardin called the "Omega point," the attainment of the highest cosmic consciousness—could it be understood as a harmonic process? As "climbing up" the overtone scale? Note the question marks. It is too early to postulate all this, but we must ask the question, since certain findings of particle physics point in exactly that direction.

Again and again, I have used the expression *harmonic*. Originally, we all understood it in the context of harmonics in music, of the laws of overtones. But have we not come to a point now (if we weren't already there at the end of chapter 4) where we must differentiate the term *harmonic?* The entire cosmos, reaching to the depths of pulsars and black holes, the subatomic world down to the electrons and photons, the world in which we live, leaves of plants, animal and human bodies, and minerals—is all that supposed to be structured according to the laws of the musical theory of harmony and to swing by them? Must we not assume that things are exactly the other way around, that harmonics in music were formed according to the structural laws of our world, of the macrocosm and the microcosm? Do expressions like *harmonic* or *overtone scale* not have a narrowing effect, limiting things too much to the field of music? No doubt the word *harmonic* has to be understood, in the sense of this chapter, not merely as the fact that the world is structured according to the musical theory of harmony, but rather as an increase in harmony in the entire cosmos. This is to take the word *harmony* in its widest sense, encompassing the "harmonious" relationships that are desirable between all human beings as well as musical "harmonics" or the "harmonics" of the spin of particles. This understanding makes "harmony" (for example, that between humans) a task for all of us. The more we obey this command, the more decisively will we be on our way to the "goal" that is the theme of this chapter, to a "finale" (another musical expression) of truly cosmic-musical dimensions.

More than once in this book, we have referred to the age-old wisdom of Asia that "Everything is One." Or, as it is stated in the Upanishads: "The spirit down here in man and the spirit up there in the sun in reality are only one spirit, and there is no other one." The harmonic structure of the universe—in the final analysis, what is expressed by the words *Nada Brahma*—may well be the most striking and convincing indicator for the unity of the world that we inquiring human beings, with our limited perception, can find. Beyond that, there is only one path, the path pointed out by the seers of the East and of mysticism: to experience the unity itself, to hear *Nada Brahma* itself.

"When you blot out sense and sound, what do you hear?" You hear primal sound, you hear *Nada Brahma*. At some point in time, somewhere along the path to the goal you will hear it. We have found that *Nada Brahma* is there, even from the viewpoint of Western rationalistic science. Doesn't there have to be some sort of sensory apparatus that is able to perceive all these sounds permeating the universe? For what other reason would they exist? Music is inevitably made for ears, even if it is meant for ears beyond the two fleshy extensions on either side of the human head. Our "ears" (note the quotation marks) *must* transcend their limits, because the "music" we have been talking about is also transcendent. "He that hath ears to hear, let him hear" (Matthew 11:15).

8 ✍ Sound in the Belly

On "Male" and "Female" Sound, Amen and OM

Nada Brahma: The world is sound. Like the Indian word *nada,* the English *sound* has a wide range of meanings. It encompasses everything audible, even noises. *Sound* became an important word in music through jazz. Rock musicians and fans later adopted the term, even though most of the young people listening to rock and pop are unaware of its derivation from jazz.

In the vocabulary of jazz and rock, *sound* is used in a slightly changed meaning. A jazz musician has to have a sound, his own personal sound by which the listener can, after a few bars, identify him. How different is the sound ideal of classical European music: Basically and with a few grains of salt, there is *one* obligatory sound ideal within each style of classical music for *all* musicians of an orchestra. In jazz, however, each player has to have his own unmistakable, individual sound if his music is to have real meaning. Wynton Marsalis, for example—a trumpeter of worldwide renown both in classical and in jazz music—has said: "To be good in jazz, you have to be an individualist—which isn't necessarily so in classical music."

This point becomes even clearer when "sound" is applied to a group, a rock or pop formation. In jazz, it is the individual who has his personal sound. In rock, the group (the collective) has its own unmistakable sound (or, to be more realistic, should have one).

In a way, these two sound ideals, that of the Old World and that of the New World, have different "genders" of meaning. Old-world sound seems to be more male-oriented, it grows, rises, searches you out, penetrates you. . . . New-world sound, on the other hand, has more female traits. The sound of a rock group, for instance, is a body that incorporates a musical process and in which the listener himself is incorporated. There are sounds in rock that can be said to be "as large as a cathedral." When hearing them, the listener "stands inside them." Whatever a rock group with a truly original, individual sound plays is basically a variation on that one sound. To drive the point home, old-world "male" sound presents a melody to the listener; but the melody presents the listener with the "female" sound. In this way, a mantra is much more a "female" sound than a "male" sound. Like the "cathedral" of rock sound, it provides a space in which the meditator lives and that he carries with him wherever he may go. Thus the "sound," the *nada*, that is the subject of this book is more the "female" than the "male" one.

It is informative to take a look at the etymology of the word *sound*. *Sound* is related to the word *tone*. This becomes clear through its French cognate, *son*, which, via the linguistically frequent phenomenon of an exchange of *t* for *s*, is derived from the Latin *tonus* and the Greek *tónos*, also the source of the English *tone*. *Sound*, in other words, is the anglicized form of *son*. *Song*, of course, also belongs to the etymological periphery of *sound*; so does the Sanskrit word *sangit (samgita)* which denoted the original unity of language, dance, and music (similar to the Greek concept of *musikē*). Linguist Arnold Wadler even supposes that *tonos, tone, son, sound, song,* and *sangit* are part of a still larger linguistic context that also includes the word *sun*.

What is interesting is that the word *sound* refers not only to audible things but also to everything that is whole, unimpaired, firm, and healthy. Your health is *sound*. Is it *sound* because you are "within the *sound*"? Because *you* sound? To *sing* is a *sound* thing to do, not only in the superficial sense that a singing person most likely is a healthy person, but rather in the most basic, original sense our language can have, in the sharing of primal roots of words.

In our discussion of the singing technique of Tibetan monks and Central Asian shamans, we saw that the sound originates in the belly and spreads from there throughout the body. This idea of the belly as a center of musical (and spiritual and creative) power seems foreign to Western man. Not so in Asia. An American or a European may love someone "from the depth of one's heart." Someone on Bali or in Japan, however, loves his or her partner "from the depth of one's belly"—and both cultures have figures of speech to that effect. A Japanese who commits suicide will not stab himself in the heart but will rather commit *hara-kiri. Hara* means "belly." In the history of Japanese art, the concept of *hara-gei* plays a role. The Japanese musicologist Shoichi Yui explains:

> *Hara-gei* literally means "thinking of the belly and communicating with others from the belly." Any Japanese understands the expression "thinking of the belly" in connection with art. Europeans and Americans, however, find it difficult to conceive that *hara,* the belly, could have anything to do with art. In Western philosophy and literature, the heart is used instead of the belly. Obviously it makes a big difference, however, if art comes from the higher chest region, the place of the heart, or from the depth of the belly. In this sense it is fair to say that among Western artists it is primarily the jazz musicians who are creative from the belly.

This observation becomes recognizable when you listen to a jazz improvisation, concentrating on its source in the body of the musician. Obviously, it comes from those regions where the singing of the Tibetan monks originates, from the belly. This is particularly clear in the case of the great "sound creators" of jazz, especially the "horn" players, musicians like tenor saxophonist Ben Webster, trumpet player Cootie Williams, alto saxophonist Johnny Hodges, or bass clarinetist Eric Dolphy. They all play from the belly. This enables them to put as much expression into a single note as if it were an entire melody. Strangely enough, Rudolf Steiner, the founder of anthroposophy, anticipated this phenomenon. In one of his early lectures, he said: "Present musical perception more and more tends to . . . question, in a way, the single tone as to whether it already is a melody as such." As early as 1920, Steiner anticipated a new experience of sound that, more than ever before in music, would entail "the possibility of getting into the depth of the tone."

Musicians in Asia—Japanese shakuhachi flutists, for instance —know something that in the West primarily jazz musicians know: The sound from the belly is the true sound. Perry Robinson, the American jazz clarinetist who in the 1970s tried to recreate his instrument's former prominence and brilliance, once said: "The clari-net is not loud enough. That's one of the reasons why it has disappeared from the scene. But you can change that. You have to think big and play from the belly. Then you get a tone as big as if you were blowing a tenor sax."

"Man lives through his head," Bertolt Brecht wrote in his *Threepenny Opera.* Today, more and more people in the European-American half of the world have come to the conclusion that living *only* through the head has made our lives poorer. In the Asian way of thinking, the center of human existence is in the belly. The energy rises up from there. When a yoga teacher asks his pupils to "center themselves," he wants them to become aware of the belly, to place the center of gravity in the belly region. The Japanese, with their sense of precision, have located this region two to three fingerbreadths below the navel. It is also the point of origin of meditation.

Asian teachers of meditation have long admonished us: The core of Western weakness lies in the fact that we have displaced our center too far upward—into the chest and the head. That's why we tip over so easily—literally as well as figuratively. Yoga teachers often make the following experiment with their pupils: They ask them to stand up in the way Westerners usually stand. Then the teacher gives them a slight push—and they lose their balance. After that, the teacher asks the students to take all concentration and gravity out of the chest and head regions and place them in the belly. When the teacher gives them a push now, they remain standing, like a tree deeply rooted in the ground. Nothing can make them tip over. If you rest in *hara,* you are unshakable. If you are centered in your chest region or even in your head, however, you will be unstable, unsure, and impressionable. "Shoulders back and chest out!"—this familiar army command exposes weakness (as does most military thinking). The real purpose behind the sergeant's command is to allow him to do with his men what he wants. That's how he likes them: pliable, without the power of *hara* (which would give them a strength surpassing his own, not only physically, but also psychically, spiritually, and morally).

A displacement of the center of gravity from bottom to top can also be discovered in the development from the Asian mantra "OM" to the Christian mantra "Amen." The science of linguistics reveals that the Christian *Amen* gradually grew from the primal mantra *OM.* If you pronounce the two words loudly and slowly, you will be able to feel that the *OM* vibrates much more deeply than the *Amen.* The *OM* vibrates in the belly region and in its surroundings, that is, also in the pubic region which, in the language of yoga, is called the "sacred region" and which naturally is supposed to vibrate at least as much as everything else, perhaps even more.

If you say *OM* in the correct way, leading the sound from the head through the chest down into the belly, then the entire body will start to vibrate. The *M* in particular, spoken forcefully, can make the body vibrate for a long time. In fact, the body will continue to vibrate when the mantra (beginning again with *O*) is "threaded" into the head once more and led down again. At that point, not only chest, stomach, and belly will be vibrating, but also the head and (if you have practiced enough) even your arms and legs. Related to this technique of saying and singing *OM* is the multivoice singing technique of Tibetan monks. If you say and sing *OM* in this way, you also begin to understand how the Hebrew and Christian *Amen* developed from the *OM*. *Amen*—that is nothing else but an extended and more nasal *OM*. *Amen*—however you may pronounce it, it primarily makes the head, throat, and chest vibrate—those regions, in other words, through which Western man primarily lives, thinks, and feels. Changes in sound as a result of the migration of certain words through different languages are often much more than just a change in sound.

The change of sound from *OM* to *Amen* reveals two totally different kinds of existence. *Amen* is a subdivided *OM*, partitioned into *O* and *M*, with each of these parts being further embellished. This happened when *OM* migrated west, first to Israel and then into the Christian world of Europe. Along this route it was subdivided into its component parts—just as everything that comes to the West is divided and taken apart, analyzed and dissected. It all seems like the opening move of a truly royal game of chess, like an overture for everything that was yet to come, when one realizes that this process of taking apart and subdividing was heralded thousands of years ago—back when *OM* became *Amen*.

This change becomes even more apparent when we consider which vowels have always been associated with which planets. The *O* is attributed to Venus, the *A* to Jupiter, the *E* to Mercury (and, to complete the line, the *I* to Mars and the *U* to Saturn). Thus, in the *OM* there is the influence of Venus: love, warmth, communion, oneness. In the *A* and the *E* of *Amen* is the influence of Jupiter and Mercury: success, activity, extroversion; reason, thinking, business. Indeed, the change from *OM* to *Amen* in this way becomes a formula for what separates the East from the West.

It is both a process of thought and of sound and music. The former is clarified by the latter. Listen to the *OM* sung by Tibetan monks and immediately after that to an *Amen* from Western Christian music (perhaps the most powerful one, that from Handel's *Messiah*). You will realize how on the path from one to the other (an intermediate station would be the *Amen* of Gregorian chant) a continual rise in differentiation has been accompanied by a continual loss of "unity" and "oneness." The process continued until not only *OM* became its victim but also (at least for the majority of modern, rationalistic Westerners) *Amen*, which itself was brought forth by this very process, so that both *OM* and *Amen* now have to be rediscovered. That, too, is part of the change of consciousness that is our theme.

More than once (most impressively perhaps in the change from *OM* to *Amen*), we have found that the sound we mean is not simply a sound that becomes audible and then disappears. *Sound* stands for primal sound. Sound is expression and symbol, an audible representative of the inaudible *nada*.

> When you blot out sense and sound,
>   what do you hear?

The echo of what you then hear is the sound from *hara*.

Of all the great musicians of classical music, I know none whose sound could make this point so impressively audible as Pablo Casals, that wonderful and wise cellist. Even jazz musicians, who in their own field are literally surrounded by great sound creators, speak of him with breathless admiration. The Austrian tenor saxophonist Hans Koller once said in an interview: "Actually, we tenor players have it easy. All you have to do is listen to the great tenor players of the jazz tradition. They all really have their own wonderful sound. There is only one musician in Europe I know of who could be compared to them: Pablo Casals."

On a radio program in the early 1960s, Koller played a recording of the unaccompanied solo improvisation "Picasso" by the tenor saxophonist Coleman Hawkins, immediately followed by a recording of Casals' sound in Bach's Suite in C minor for unaccompanied cello. The concurrence was astounding, but an additional phenomenon also became clear. It is easy in the case of a wind instrument to envision the sound as coming from the player's belly, because a column of air moves directly through his body into the instrument. In the case of a string instrument, however, there is only a "spiritual" column. In fact, that column is the crucial one. Even if there is an actual column of air, the spiritual one is stronger. It was like meeting an old friend after many years when I read the following sentences in a book by the German psychologist and musician Silvia Ostertag:

> When I heard Pablo Casals play for the first time, something strange took place inside me. It was at a master class in Zermatt, Switzerland. In each of the lessons, there were also participants who were there only as auditors. I was one of them, one of many. Casals was teaching, and I still remember the moment when he took his bow and played a tone, one single tone. It certainly wasn't the case that I had been asleep up to that point, but in the moment when this tone was sounded, I felt as if I were waking up, violently and yet tenderly. . . .

It was as if this tone had reached an inner ear that hadn't existed before. It seemed as if this tone had gone through all heights and had struck me in my innermost self, a part of myself which I had been unaware of. And yet, this innermost self was more familiar to me than anything I knew of myself; otherwise I would not call it my innermost self.

When the sound of the tone had died away, I found myself unsure for a moment whether Casals had really played it or whether the room had just become really quiet. If I wanted to describe it . . . , it was a tone in which all tones were sounded and in which at the same time was all silence. . . .

It was many years ago that I heard Casals for the first time. Not only have I never forgotten that tone, but ever since that experience I have been trying to become the kind of person who, through my hearing and my deeds, would open my entire life for the sake of this "tone." . . . Back then I experienced something that transcended the horizon of our rational understanding, something inconceivable, unconditional, something eternal . . . the tone in which all tones were sounded—the tone that contained all silence.

MUSIC FOR LISTENING TO THE EIGHTH CHAPTER

Ben Webster. *Ben Webster Meets Don Byas*. Verve/MPS 827920.

——*Ben and Sweets*. With Harry Edison. Odyssey PC 37036.

Coleman Hawkins. *The Essential Coleman Hawkins*. Includes "Picasso." Verve V-8568.

Johnny Hodges. *Blues Pyramid*. Verve V 6-8635.

Cootie Williams and Rex Stewart. *Big Challenge*. Hall 602 E.

Erich Dolphy. *Out to Lunch*. Blue Note BST 84163.

George Frederic Handel. *The Messiah*. Leonard Bernstein, New York Philharmonic Orchestra, Westminster Choir. CBS MY 38481. (Many other recordings available as well.)

The Music of Tibet: The Tantric Rituals ("OM"). (See p. 50.)

Hommage à Pablo Casals. Schubert, Beethoven, Haydn, Bach, etc. CBS M5X-32768.

9 🐌   Temple in the Ear

On Listening, Silence—and Wakefulness

DEALING WITH SOUND means dealing with listening. Experiments have shown that no other sense can register impulses as minimal as those that the ear can register. The amplitude of the vibrations of our eardrum lies in the area of 10^{-9}. That is smaller than the wave length of visible light and even less than the diameter of a hydrogen atom. The smallest stimuli our ear can just barely perceive, on the other hand, have to be amplified by a factor of 10^6 in order to reach the level of the highest volume perceivable, by a factor in the million range. Were we to amplify the smallest impulses our eyes can register by the same factor, we would be blinded instantly.

Hans Kayser points out the astonishing fact that our ears are the only human sense organ that is able to perceive numerical *quantity* as well as numerical *value:*

> The ears not only recognize exact numerical proportions, that is, numerical quantities like 1:2 as an octave, 2:3 as a fifth, 3:4 as a fourth, etc.; at the same time they hear . . . values that they perceive as C, G, F, and so on. So the tone value fuses two elements into one unit: the element of sensing—the tone, that is—with the element of thinking, of numerical value. And this happens in such an exact manner that the value of the tone can be checked precisely against the value of the number, and the value of the number against the value of the tone.

Among all our human senses we only have *one* organ that is capable of this fusion: the ears. In this way sensation controls deliberation—or to put it differently: Our soul is thus capable of deciding on the correctness or incorrectness of an intellectual quantity. Conversely, the phenomenon of tone value also gives us the opportunity to develop proportions and numerical values in the realm of the psyche.

It is important that we appreciate fully this special faculty of our ears not only to judge but also to measure. Even an unmusical person can *hear* whether an octave is correct or not; his ear can measure whether the higher tone really swings with a frequency twice that of the lower one; but nobody can *see* that a color emits a light frequency twice that of another one. The same precision is reflected in the way our language deals with our sense of hearing (just as our language becomes imprecise when it comes to our eyes, as we will see). We are able to identify a certain sound frequency as a "C," a "D," or an "E," thus fixing an exact mathematical measure. There is nothing comparable in color. We can identify "yellow" or "blue" or "red," but that says nothing about the frequency *number*. Our eyes give us only approximate data. There is a multitude of different *tones* (and already we have to adopt a word from the field of hearing) of yellow or blue or red, and yet it is impossible to be precise when describing colors. Even when we differentiate between various shades of blue—navy blue, aquamarine, azure, dark blue, or, if we bring in a good many descriptive words, perhaps another half dozen kinds of blue—we achieve nothing near the preciseness that we attain in the field of hearing by simply saying "F" or "G" or "B."

Most musicians have discovered that a highly trained ear can "beat" the tuning fork. "Leave your tuning fork at home tomorrow," the famous German conductor Hans Rosbaud once said to a member of a choir he was accompanying with his Südwestfunk Radio Symphony Orchestra. "Your tuning fork is incorrect." The singer took offense at his remark, but when we checked the fork afterward, we found that Rosbaud had been right. Again, it is inconceivable that our eyes could ever "measure" with similar precision.

And yet we have only talked about one of the two wonderful faculties of our ears, the mathematical one, the fact that we can hear numbers. However, the ears have also always been viewed as the "gateway to the soul." In addition to their measuring ability, there is their ability to sense. The most wonderful thing is how these two faculties are coupled together. In fact, it seems that in this coupling lies the greatest capacity of our ears: their ability to transfer, with unbelievable precision, mathematical quantities into sense perceptions, conscious into subconscious, measurable things into unmeasurable ones, abstract concepts into matters of soul—and vice versa, of course. In fact, simply by virtue of their existence, our ears constantly demand that these two fields, which appear to our other senses to be so totally different from each other, be related to each other. Even more: They make it irrefutably clear that there is such a relationship.

In comparison to that, our eyes are "vague," more "approximate." The person who mainly lives through his eyes not only leads a reduced life in terms of his spiritual qualities. He also leads a less "precise" life than an "ear person." The impreciseness in contemporary existence —and that also means: the danger of it—becomes directly obvious when you realize that modern man is mainly an "eye person"! As Jacques Lusseyran notes:

> Our eyes run over the surfaces of things. All they require are a few scattered points, since they can bridge the gap in a flash. They "half see" much more than they see, and they never test anything. They are satisfied with the appearances in whose glowing guise the world slides by, while its substance remains veiled.

Consider such common expressions as "It *appears* to me" or "it *looks* as though . . ." or "I *imagine*"—all expressions from the field of optics. That is the field that our language turns to in order to formulate the possibility of illusion, error, and self-deceit. At least our language unmasks the shining halo placed over our eyes by occidental man as deceptively "glittering" and "glimmering." It simply cannot be an accident that these last two words also come from the sphere of optics. After months of research in many languages, I was unable to find a single expression or figure of speech denoting something vague, imprecise, or illusory coming from the field of acoustics. And if there is such an expression, it would fade before the overwhelming majority of the corresponding "optical" terms and figures of speech.

We all know the expression *optical illusion*. There are dozens of such illusions. You can find descriptions of them in any textbook on physiology. The parallel expression *acoustical illusion*, however, does not exist. This is so because, in fact, there are only very few acoustic illusions, that is, because our ear informs us more correctly about reality.

Even physiologists are not aware of the most profound optical illusion, though—of the illusion concerning the dimensionality of our world. In chapter 6, we considered the fact that, according to modern physics, the world has more than the standard three dimensions of length, width, and height. Our eyes, our tactile faculties, and our capability to move in space inform us incorrectly about the world. We live in a world that is different from the way it appears, in a multidimensional world. Outside of its function as a locating aid, our sense of hearing is the sense that is independent of dimensions. Our ears can hear, whether the world has three, four, or even more dimensions. Their ability to hear spatially—stereophonically, for instance—is an additional feature not inherent in the process of hearing. Is this independence of the dimensionality of the world the very factor that contributes to our ears' high degree of precision and competence?

We have often heard and read in recent years how modern man of the television age has become a predominantly "seeing" being. Hardly anyone who makes that kind of statement takes the trouble to ask: What do we see? And: Do we really *see* what we see? In reality, do we not see images and replicas? And do we not take them for reality? We confuse the image of the world provided to us by the media with the world itself. That is why studies of young people often note their loss of touch with reality, and psychologists observe a diminished openness to new experiences on the part of the elderly. By "loss of touch with reality" I mean, for example, the children who murdered one of their playmates in the basement of their building and told the psychologists who examined them: "They do it just like that on TV!" These children no longer knew the difference between reality and television. In fact, television *is* "their" reality. And by "diminished openness to new experiences" I mean: the daily dose of atrocities delivered to your home, from El Salvador, from Afghanistan, from Guatemala, from South Africa, from Vietnam, from Cambodia, from Ethiopia and the North African Sahel: the inflation of horror. The greater the daily dose of horror, the less impact it has on people. That is what the German writer Botho Strauss calls "the separation of the human from the humane, the termination of sense perception."

Listening becomes important in this situation. It has always been important, but now it is even more so. More than ever before, television has shown how superior our sense of hearing is to our eyesight. Child psychologists have recognized that a fairy tale seen on television is nothing but entertainment, at best. It does not trigger anything. Whatever happens is taking place on the screen and took place before that in the studio. The child is viewing nothing more than information about an event that has already taken place somewhere else. The "outer" image makes the "inner" one superfluous. The "outer" image may be more colorful, with more action, more alluring (and above all: more robust), but for exactly that reason it is able to take the place of the "inner" image. By contrast, if you tell your child a fairy tale, the child has to transpose the tale into "inner" images in order to understand it. These "inner" images are the ones that produce experience and enrichment; the "outer" ones "transport" only information and short-lived stimulation.

Whenever a movie is made from a novel, critics almost invariably find the book much better than the film, no matter how good the film may be. This criticism always seems to imply that in principle it should be possible to produce a movie adaptation that is at least as good as the literary work of art, if not better. But that is *not* possible, because perception by ear (and reading is an internalized kind of hearing) is so much more differentiated and complex than perception by sight. That is why anything presented to the eyes has to be more blunt, less subtle than something presented to our hearing.

Ever since we left the treetops, since our ancestors climbed down to the ground to sleep in gullies and caves, our ears have been the primary sense organ of survival, more than any other organ. That is the way it is programmed by evolution. When we are asleep we close our eyes and mouth, our tactile senses are (almost) totally shut down, but our ears remain open.

As a matter of fact, our ears are open before we are born. Even in the womb our ears are more important than our other senses. Our consciousness begins with them. The child in the womb hears its mother's heartbeat—and, later, sounds from the outside world—which means that before we perceive the world with any other sense, we hear it.

Before we enter this world—and throughout our entire life, even when, in the hour of our departure, all our other senses begin to fail us—we hear. We *cannot* close our ears. And in fact, the incantation that is repeated again and again in the *Tibetan Book of the Dead* —"Listen, ye of noble birth"—means that there is listening also in the hereafter. In other words, it is actually our ears that carry us from the prenatal state into our existence on earth as well as from here into the state after death—more so, at least, than any other sense. And that means (a similar statement could not be made with comparable exclusiveness about the other senses): In no other sensory activity "are" we so much as we "are" in the act of listening. To hear is to be! Is that the real reason why we can never, ever close our ears so long as we live? Because to hear = to be? And because we would lose touch with the prime reason of our existence if we were to cease hearing? That is why we cannot close our ears as we can close our eyes.

And yet millions of people are letting this most noble sense become atrophied. They hardly listen any longer. In the age of digital recordings and compact discs, it is unbelievable that the majority of humankind is satisfied with the impoverished sound that bleats from their television sets. Most people don't even realize how pitiful this tone quality is. Their eyes fill in what their ears cannot receive. Or—what is even worse and also even more common—they use their ears only when their eyes are not sufficient. The ears are demoted to the role of an auxiliary organ. At that point it is almost a reflex: The function of the ears is activated only when the information provided by the eyes is absolutely inadequate.

Consider radio. If, as Marshall McLuhan stated, "the medium is the message," then the actual message of radio is: Listen! That is what we radio people are actually doing: in everything we present, we ask people again and again to open their ears, to perceive the world more by ear.

A wonderful ancient Christian legend states that Mary conceived Jesus through her ears. Why through her ears? Because it is the most pure of our sense organs, the one which has the most direct connection with being, with our primal origin, the primal sound, and the primal tension.

Some of my older readers may still remember how radio got started in the 1920s: You'd sit in front of your little crystal receiver set—it didn't even have tubes yet, let alone transistors—with your primitive headsets on, delighted when you were able to identify music as music with all the squawking and scratching static. It was even more sublime if you picked up some station from a distant country—snatches of Italian or Spanish words . . . That is how my listening experience began. It was like a great adventure, an expedition into a strange land: an expedition by ear! The next morning I would talk about it at the breakfast table, my voice trembling with excitement. "You sound like the radio yourself when you talk about it," my father used to say. There is an entire generation that, as Austrian writer Stefan Zweig described it, found out about the world by listening to the radio, by hearing—and that in a state which Zweig called "drunkenness." It is well worth remembering all this, because we discover thereby how much our hearing sensitivity has deteriorated since then.

The move from radio to television, which we all witnessed either in our own generation or in that of our parents, is a step backward, as if humankind, having already reached the state of an agrarian economy, had regressed to a nomadic existence. I have chosen this ironic comparison deliberately, and for good reason. It has been said about the eyes that they are "constantly on the move," as if looking for prey, roving like nomads. Nothing comparable can be said of the ears. A person can have "piercing eyes" but certainly not "piercing ears" or any other attribute which could give the ears a puncturing quality. The epitomy of visual acuity are the eyes of an eagle: from up high the eagle spies its prey and in that instant anticipates seizing it in its claws and piercing it with its beak. It is a single act: spotting and seizing. Not only for the eagle but for the eyes. For human eyes too. And it certainly is no accident that the eagle is such a widespread national symbol, in the seals and emblems of power-conscious nations.

Wherever descriptive attributes are supposed to refer to the ears, however, they come from words meaning "receiving" or "opening up." The ear is similar to a mussel or a conch, which are also used as symbols for the female sex organ: both receive.

The person who gives first priority to the ears among the senses, who is primarily a hearing and a listening individual, this person—we may logically conclude—will be much less aggressive than someone who perceives the world primarily and initially through the eyes. For that reason, the modern television culture is a breeding ground for aggressiveness. Day after day, in millions of middle-class living rooms, aggressions are being bred—with all the "nest warmth" that is necessary for breeding.

In his own distinct style, the great meditation teacher Bhagwan Shree Rajneesh has found a beautiful expression for this ailment, this hypertrophy of the eyes. He sees it as a "madness" that he calls "Kodakomania":

> Eighty percent of your energy is devoted to the eyes. The other senses suffer very much, because there is only twenty percent left for them. The eyes have become an Adolf Hitler. You have lost the democracy of your senses. . . . Don't get too interested in pictures, otherwise you will lose more and more the ability to perceive reality.

Consider something else: Which senses are important for the act of love? Well, for one thing, all of them. But try to establish an order of priority. The eyes are particularly important in the beginning when everything is still uncertain. After that hearing becomes important, and then feeling. And then you can observe something strange: The more intense our love gets, the more often we tend to close our eyes. We feel and hear. What do we feel? What do we hear? The answer is very important: What we feel, particularly and especially when touching our partner, is first and foremost our own overwhelming desire. But we hear—our partner. With our ears we "keep track" of where our partner is along the path of love: Whether he or she is moving quickly or slowly, intensely or receptively, is following us or is ahead of us, or whether both are at the same point on the path . . . This, then, is the ear, the bridge of love to the other person. The bridge may be breathtakingly high, the river underneath may be roaring and wild, but we don't need our eyes. In fact, it seems like a paradox: The higher and wider the bridge is, the wilder the stream underneath, the more intensely we keep our eyes shut. It is illuminating that women go over the "sound bridge" of love more frequently and more intensely than men. Why this is so is the theme of the following passage.

The dimension of the eye is more male, that of the ear is more female, both literally and figuratively. The American psychologists Robert May and Anneliese Korner studied sex differences in newborn infants. They found that male babies react more to visual stimuli, whereas female babies react more easily to stimuli received through the ears. This is true not only for humans, but also for young monkeys and rats, and this difference between the sexes remains intact even in adult men and women.

Accordingly, mothers communicate with their baby daughters much more easily, and statistically more frequently, by making sounds for them and by imitating the baby's sounds, while they attract a male baby's attention by showing him motions with objects or hands. Since sounds are more important for girls than for boys, girls also begin earlier to produce sounds and (as we know statistically) to speak. The word *statistical* is important, because obviously both boys and girls react to both acoustic and visual stimuli. The point is, however, that more girls react sooner, more easily, and more frequently with their sense of hearing, while more boys react with their sense of sight. The "male" element contained in the predominance of the visual and the "female" element contained in the preference for perception by ear could find no clearer expression than in this research, which is supported by findings in psychology and anthropology both in the United States and in Europe. The point gains even more weight through the fact that the above tendency remains intact when children become adults. Camilla Persson Benbow and Julian C. Stanley of Johns Hopkins University corroborated this in tests made over the course of many years: "Men usually perform better in the visual-spatial field, women in language. Both are comparatively weak in that field where the other one is particularly strong." The tests leading to this finding were countertested so carefully that it is certain that these differences are not acquired but inborn. Her stronger perception by ear gives the female from the outset a comparatively more receptive (and probably also more linguistically-oriented) talent.

Interestingly enough, in the Chinese tradition the ear is *yin*, the eye *yang*. *Yin* is more female, *yang* more male. The Chinese *yin-yang* symbol shows that both work together, that they belong together inseparably. We do not have a choice between the ear and the eye, just as we cannot choose between exclusively male and female traits, between only *yang* and only *yin*. Important is that from the Chinese point of view we modern Westerners are traditionally considered to be too *yang*-oriented. We would have to learn to emphasize more the *yin* elements that we have neglected (and often suppressed) for centuries. As (primarily) listening people, we would be able to relearn it.

Everything said in this chapter would be oversimplified, were it to be understood as the grotesque alternative between only hearing and only seeing. We have to do both. What is important is that the preferences become clear: The "ear person" is inevitably more receptive, while the "eye person" is just as inevitably more aggressive.

Anyone somewhat familiar with the physiology of the eye knows that projection is inherent in vision. We cannot see without projecting. Consider what the word *projection* means in psychology: projecting one's own anxieties, fears, problems, and aggressions on another person. And immediately we understand why psychology chose the visual expression *projection* for this phenomenon, and why this word has withstood the test of time better than could be expected. The expression is simply correct. It is correct as well in relaying impreciseness and the potential for illusion and error. The fact that projection is not limited to our daily dealings with other individuals has long been common knowledge. Nations can also project their own anxieties and their own aggressiveness on rivaling nations. In the international sphere, too, we find the potential of illusion and error inherent in the process of projection. The only difference is that here it is dangerous; in fact, it has become a threat to the existence of our civilization. We can all appreciate the potential danger of projection in a world whose main characteristic is that the so-called "West" and the so-called "East" keep thrusting their respective anxieties and aggressions on each other in an endless chain of projections. In this chain, each projected image is inevitably more imprecise, more vague, and thus more confusing and dangerous than the preceding one (just as in a series of optical projections each projection is more imprecise than the one preceding it), until you end up with images that are totally washed out, unclear, without well-defined contours. Which is an exact description of the "images," the information provided to us by the media, images that our politicians use as a basis for their decision-making.

No doubt, it is mainly eye (and male) persons who direct our political life. One has to be an eye person in order to develop the idea that wars can be avoided by more and more arms—an idea behind which the imprecise-speculative, the vague and approximate, traits of the eye person are coupled with his aggressiveness. For the more precise ear person, however, it is plausible without further explanation that to stockpile arms means to arm for war, and that the war will be all the more destructive, the more arms are piled up. Just think how many words politicians must resort to—how truly speculative (from the Latin *speculari*, "to look out, to spy") all the deliberations are with which the ruling eye-people are trying to divert our weakened glance from the simple, conclusive realization that arms lead to war.

The glorification of the eye in Western literature and poetry—a glorification that has shaped all of us emotionally since our childhood days—by no means stands in contrast to our finding but rather supports it. We needed this idealized eye image as basic justification for the overemphasis on the visual element that has been prevalent in the entire cultural and mental development of the Western world. Of course, *all* of our senses are laudable, in the best and most beautiful words of our poets and artists. The point, however (to say it again) are the preferences and proportions—or rather the lack thereof.

Our proportions are off also because our visual senses have formed a strange alliance with our tactile senses. We try to "come to grips" with a problem (as if that were possible), we try to "grasp" a train of thought, we have to "get" it or "get a hold" on it. Actually, our tactile senses find a much more natural partner in our sense of hearing, as is made obvious by a look at the way blind people perceive the world. They experience the world with their sense of hearing *and* touch, one supporting the other. Jacques Lusseyran, a blind university professor from France, once described how he had experienced the world as a child: "When I had eyes, my fingers used to be stiff, half dead at the ends of my hands, good only for picking up things." After he lost his eyesight at an early age, however, Lusseyran began to feel things differently: The objects

> are alive, even the stones. What is more they vibrate and tremble. My fingers felt the pulsation distinctly. . . . If my fingers pressed the roundness of an apple, each one with a different weight, very soon I could not tell whether it was the apple or my fingers which were heavy. . . . As I became part of the apple, the apple became part of me. And that was how I came to understand the existence of things.

Lusseyran's words show the natural alliance between our senses of seeing and touching. They also show to what degree the predominance of our eyes in reality makes us "blind." Our fingers are "only good for picking up things." In the dimension of the tactile senses that Lusseyran talks about, however, there is a touch that does not remain on the "grabbing" surface of things but rather creates a union with the objects.

The range of tactile possibilities is almost as wide as that of the visual or of the acoustic. At one end there is "gripping" and "getting a hold on," at the other end there is the touch of lovers becoming one. Modern man primarily plays on one end of the tactile keyboard, on that end where it can be of service to the eye. From this viewpoint, too, we are letting our sensory apparatus become stunted. We are like novice musicians who have mastered one or two octaves, at best, but certainly not the entire range of the keyboard. Playing the full range of our tactile senses is a capability limited, among seeing people, almost totally to those in love when the body of the beloved partner becomes the instrument in sexual union. In the modern Western world, it is the lovers and the blind who are still in active command of the entire "orchestral" range of the tactile.

We have talked about the "inadequacies" contained in the development from radio to television, from perception primarily by the ear to the preference for the eye. There is a movement in the opposite direction, however, and this book is one example of it. It is a countermovement whose growth we can witness month by month. More and more people want to—and will—experience the world as sound again. They are doing so not by listening to the good old radio, to snatches of words or music and Morse code from faraway lands, but in an even more adventurous way: by listening to the sounds of those worlds that once represented the epitome of silence: the cosmos, the deep sea, plants, emptiness, the void . . . silence and meditation . . .

It is amazing that until now nobody has pointed out that the original title of one of the world's most important spiritual books, the *Tibetan Book of the Dead*, contains the word *hearing*. The Tibetan title of the book is *Bardo Thödol*, which means "Liberation by Hearing in the Intermediate State [i.e., the state immediately following death]." As I mentioned earlier, almost all counsel given in this book to the deceased begin with the words "Ye of noble birth, listen!" At another point, the text states: "When the reader speaks this, he should move his lips close to the ear of the dying person, carefully repeating and clearly impressing it upon him, thus avoiding that his thoughts may wander off for even a moment."

Louise Goepfert-March, one of the German translators of the *Tibetan Book of the Dead*, writes:

The first step is learning to hear, wanting to hear, releasing the chaos within oneself, releasing it in the way one releases the body in physical death. This step means that one no longer wants to interfere, to change things, . . . to quarrel, to express an opinion, to translate what was heard into everyday mechanical language . . . [It] means that one rests easy next to the giant army of onrushing associations of thoughts, feelings, and physical things. The ability to hear is a difficult thing, even if most Westerners do not want to believe that.

If it is true that our generation has rediscovered the sound character of the universe, then it is necessary to develop a better sensory apparatus for listening. Listening begins with being silent. With tranquility. Poets have written about the "music of silence," about the "organ of tranquility." If you want to experience sound, you first have to have learned to experience silence. Martin Buber writes: "Where there is no silence, necessity rules like a voice of arbitrariness. Protect me, silence!"

This is an exercise. If possible, do it NOW. After reading this passage. Certainly, you can also do it tomorrow, but if you do it now, you can take the next step—repetition—tomorrow.

Perhaps you can sit in the lotus position. Try it. For everything I will write now, the attempt is already worth much, because the attempt is the way. As we have said, "thewayisthewayistheway." Since we can do no more than be on the way, since we cannot get beyond the way, the way is the point. However one translates tao *or the Japanese* do, *its primal meaning is "the way."*

If you are unable to sit in the lotus position, try to approximate it. It is important that the knees are below the navel. Sit upright, but not with "shoulders back and chest out!" Rather put energy into your belly, without strain. You are sitting in hara . . . Become quiet . . . Breathe as your breath flows. Not in a shallow, superficial manner, but also not overly deeply. Simply let your breath wander through your belly. Don't puff the breath inside yourself, let it wander inside. This has to take place in your consciousness, but not in your thinking. Your breath is what connects you most intensely with the world and with being, in a constant process of exchange, in a constant process of giving and taking. No looking, no talking can make this exchange process happen more intensely than breathing. Since the exchange takes place in every breath you take, it is more than just an exchange. It's a process of identification. Of "being one." Breathe consciously, and you will experience it: You are one with the world.

First, listen to your breath . . . Do this for seven or eight minutes . . . After a while, listen through *your breath . . . You will hear the room where you are sitting. Do not deliberately decide you want to hear it. If you listen long enough, you will hear that the room has a sound—and you can hear it.*

Now listen through the room . . . Perhaps there is a bell tolling in the distance . . . steps . . . a car . . . birds singing . . . music from someone's radio . . . Do not receive any of those things negatively. Listen through them. Room, bells tolling, steps, car, birds—everything is a veil. Behind that is silence. It opens up, wider and wider. "Open spaces—nothing holy." You can hear that: wideness opening up.

Later, perhaps you hear the pounding of blood through your veins. Or you may become attentive again to the coming and going of your breath. Thoughts will come, but you do not "hear" them. You listen through them. Even if you have no use for them right now, never have a hostile attitude toward your thoughts. Regard them as good friends—which they really are. Good friends may drop in anytime. They will notice it by themselves if they are not wanted just now—and then they will leave.

After a while (maybe only after weeks of practicing) you will notice that nothing is as loud as silence. There is such a thing as the droning of silence. Listen through that, too. With ears as large as sails on an ocean. You are your ears. The ocean is existence. You are sailing on it, with and through your ears. It is delightful to do that. Like sailing on a balmy summer day. Then, if you blot out sense and sound—

What do you hear?
What do you hear?

This is a Zen exercise. Zen exercises should be practiced twice a day. Twenty minutes each time. Don't say, "I can't do that." Just do it. Anyone can do it. Millions of people do it. And since they simply do it without talking about it, outsiders have no idea that millions are already meditating.

If you do it, it will change your life. More than love can change it.

The effect of meditation, says John Blofeld, is "the attainment of increasingly profound intuitive insights into the nature of reality." These insights, he continues,

> invariably result in a deepening of wisdom, of joy in life and greater understanding of life's meaning. Other goals, perhaps to be regarded as incidental to this one, are the prolongation or restoration of youthful vigor, excellent health, and longevity extending to upwards of a hundred years of age that is attended by good health and happiness to the very end.

Longevity in itself might not seem altogether desirable but, in this case, it is likely to go together not only with radiant health but also with a joyous tranquility that will make every moment of life worth living by banishing negative reactions commonly aroused by boredom, frustration, bereavement, loss, anxiety, and fear. Incidentally, a person who is freed from these reactions is likely to be loved and esteemed, if only because he has no sorrows to inflict upon others who feel they have enough of their own sorrows to bear. Besides, he is sure to develop into a merry person, free from envy and dislike, and therefore much sought after as a friend.

I have no doubt that all of these objectives are well within the bounds of possibility. In many a remote hermitage rising from the slopes of one or other of China's innumerable sacred mountains, I used to come upon Taoist recluses extraordinarily merry, healthy and active for their years, able to perform surprising feats of athletic prowess and often skilled as well in such arts as healing, calligraphy, poetic composition, music, painting, defensive combat, or miniature landscape gardening. There was a peacefulness and joyousness about them; merely to be with them for a few days restored one's faith in life's value and opened up new possibilities of happiness. All of these proceeded from a wisdom that comes from inner stillness.

In his *Sonnets to Orpheus*, Rainer Maria Rilke evokes "creatures of stillness," animals that are silent in order to be able to hear. Rilke says that we ought to find a place for them in our own sensory apparatus. He coined the unforgettable image of a "temple in the ear" (which I have used as the title of this chapter).

You have to create this "temple in the ear" for yourself. And it really has to be a temple, a temple within yourself that you keep pure. You *are* this temple.

Once again: No one can hear sounds in such a way that one experiences them as the true nature of the universe, if one has not learned to listen to silence and to experience silence. You cannot learn this in a couple of minutes. The great meditators spend their lives doing it, and through it they find a richer, more fulfilled, more wakeful life.

Part of Zen is wakefulness. A shock will do it. That's why Zen tends to shock. When you are talking with a Zen master, it often happens that he will suddenly clap his hands. These people can clap their hands as I have never before heard anyone clap their hands. It is as if a shot were being fired. You start—and for the rest of the conversation you remain "struck" by the shot. You are wide awake.

Or the *roshi*, the Zen master, may suddenly start to laugh, just when you were thinking that the whole conversation was getting incredibly serious. Anyone who has heard this Zen laughter finds most other human laughter "ridiculous."

The most shocking Zen statement is: "If you meet the Buddha, beat Him to death!" Beat the Buddha to death? The Buddha's position in Buddhism is quite different from that of Christ in Christianity, of course, but the Buddha is loved by the adherents of Buddhism with every fiber of their hearts (or better: of their bellies, their *hara*!). So just transfer this challenge into the Christian concept: When you meet Jesus, beat Him to death! And feel the shock. Zen *wants* to shock. Even Meister Eckehart considered the question "Why we have to become free even of God." This is why: If the Buddha (or Jesus, or God) disturbs you in meditation, in solitude, silence, and becoming one, then beat Him to death!

The Chinese sage Li Pu We once said: "All men need an exercise of the spirit to be able to hear correctly. Those who do not have this exercise have to acquire it by learning. Neither in the old days nor in our times has it ever happened that someone could hear correctly without learning it."

Once more: Part of Zen is wakefulness. Part of listening to silence is wakefulness. If you are not totally awake, all you will hear is the absence of noise, the absence of all those sounds you hear when it is not quiet—which means: you'll hear merely something negative.

The biblical story of the creation of the world contains the following sentence "And the Lord God caused a deep sleep to fall upon Adam, and he slept" (Genesis 2:21). Generally this is read to mean that the man was put to sleep (almost like an early form of anesthesia) so that God could "surgically remove" the rib from which He created the woman. Subsequently Adam woke and saw—Eve. However, we have learned from the works of C. G. Jung, Walter F. Otto, Heinrich Zimmer, and other interpreters of myths to take the myths by their word. Nowhere in the Bible does it say: Adam woke.

So: Adam continued to sleep. And we are still asleep. In other words: Man was awake once, when he still was androgynous, in that state of oneness that is described in so many legends and myths worldwide. Plato's *Symposium*, for instance, and the Bible itself, both obviously use sources of a much older origin. The myth was so old that the author of the Book of Genesis did not fully understand it. That is why he reports (following the primal myth): "So God created man in his own image, in the image of God created he him; male and female created he them" (Genesis 1:27). But he misunderstands this sentence as the creation of two sexually different beings, even though quite obviously what is meant is oneness. God created one androgynous being. That also is the reason for the oft-cited contradictory arrangement of verses in Genesis: The story of the creation of Eve from Adam's rib is related not in the first but only in the second chapter because it comes from a different—patriarchal—source.

The division of the "primal race" (to use Plato's term) into man and woman is the actual, the very first "original sin." It is an expression, perhaps their most elementary one, of all the other polarities between whose poles "sleeping" man is harnessed. Man is awake (Zen would say, wakened) only when he has overcome the polarity, when his oneness is restored.

In the Hebrew Bible, the passage quoted above from Genesis 2 contains the word *tardemah*, which comes from *radam*, "to be congested." The meaning "sleep" entered at a later point. Thus God—this original meaning is still present—"congested" Adam. The translation "deep sleep" is entirely correct, but the Septuagint, the early Greek version of the Hebrew scriptures, chose the word *ékstasis* at this point, which means "stepping outside oneself" and is the same as our word *ecstasy:* "And God put Adam into ecstasy." One might say this was a translation error, but at that level errors are not made (just as the early Hebrew scribe who wrote down the Genesis myth imprecisely did not commit an error in this sense). As the historian Leopold von Ranke put it, "Nineteen centuries cannot misunderstand." Therefore, I prefer to talk about "changing gears in consciousness." More than a millennium and a half after the time of the New Testament, the Protestant (and Puritan!) translators of the Bible switched back. Of course, they preferred "deep sleep" to the "ecstasy" of the Greeks.

Obviously, in the thinking of the Hellenistic world the concept of the separation of humankind into men and women required ecstasy, so much so that the Greek translators felt they had to correct the original. The "ecstasy" that they used as a translation of *tardemah* finds its shadow (reflection, relic) in the ecstasy of the union of love, which tries to reverse the polarity, even though for a short time only.

In the *Symposium,* Plato speaks of the "immense power and strength of the primeval race," when it was still a union of male and female. He continues: "Ever since those days, the love between them is inborn in mankind in order to restore the original nature, in the attempt to make one out of two and to make human nature a union again." And somewhat later: "The reason for the striving for a union and amalgamation with the beloved one lies in the fact that exactly that was our original nature where we still formed an unsevered union. The longing and striving for this union is called love." Love, then, is a distant memory of the original oneness of humankind. A memory that constantly has to be refreshed, in a state of desperate resolution, so as not to lose it altogether.

True oneness is different. We have many descriptions of the state of enlightenment, and even though it is obvious that all of them can only be approximations, it surely can be said that there is no more precise description than this one: oneness in wakefulness. No longer split up in "deep sleep," in the Hebrew *tardemah;* no longer in need of *ʾékstasis* and its constant renewal; to be permeable in wakefulness.

That is the wakefulness that is the goal of Zen, a state in which silence becomes the droning organ of the cosmos, truly the loudest sound of the *uni-verse* (literally, "turning into one, creating oneness"), the organ of *Nada Brahma*. It is the wakefulness in which the answer is given to our question: Who hears all those sounds we have talked about, since obviously no normal human ear will ever hear them? Where are the senses for whose benefit evolution or God—which is the same thing—has created these sounds?

10 🐚 Nada Brahma: What do the Musicians Say?

On Indian Music, Jazz, Rock, Minimal Music— Including an Excursion on Hermann Hesse

Nada Brahma: We have put the question to cosmology and physics, to morphology and biology, to mythology and harmonics. Now we are going to question those who are particularly touched by the statement that the world is sound: the musicians.

In this respect, too, something extraordinary has happened in the present generation. During those same years when we became aware of the sound character of the universe, we also gained a new attitude toward music. We discovered (or rediscovered) kinds of music that correspond to this sound character of the universe in a most fascinating way.

The new consciousness of music unfolds itself in two ways. For one thing, the Western world has discovered the music of Asia, of India in particular. The other thing is that the Western world has come up with a new kind of music that—for the first time in about a thousand years, that is, since the time of Gregorian chant—parallels the consciousness of Asian music and yet is completely contemporary and Western, and that neither is nor wants to be influenced by the horrible dictum of Theodor Adorno, that the inhumanity of the arts has to surpass the inhumanity of the world.

To begin with, some of the great masters of the classical music of India (the sarod player Ali Akbar Khan, the sitar player Ravi Shankar, the singer Pandit Pran Nath, the tabla player Alla Rakha, and many more) have become "stars" on the American and European music scene, filling concert halls just as Daniel Barenboim or Pinchas Zukerman do. That fact alone casts an impressive light on this change in consciousness, since barely fifteen or twenty years ago Asian music—and especially Indian music—struck Western ears as no more than an unbearable, monotonous lamentation.

More important than the "stars," however, are the hundreds of musicians from India who have settled in the Western world, not only in New York and Los Angeles but also in Santa Fe and Chicago, Berlin and Paris, London and Amsterdam, and even in small provincial towns, from where they exert their influence on our musical life. At present it is scarcely more difficult in the Western world to find a good Indian tabla or sitar player than it is to find a good cellist or French horn player.

At parties in certain circles, you are almost as likely to hear records of Indian music as the latest rock album. The young generation has acquired a feeling for Indian, Arabic, Balinese, or traditional Japanese music, as if it were rooted in their own culture—which, in fact, it is.

Alain Daniélou, for years the head of the UNESCO Institute for Comparative Musicology, realized a decade ago that "the West has saved Indian music for India. Just when classical Indian music threatened to perish in India, it was discovered in the Western world. As a consequence, the people in India have gained a new consciousness of their own musical tradition."

Musicians from India residing in the Western world primarily make their living through giving music lessons. Just consider: suddenly there are thousands of young Western people learning to play Indian music on Indian instruments! Of course, they not only learn about music and instruments. That is impossible. As Ravi Shankar puts it: "You cannot learn about Indian music without entering into the Indian way of thinking. Both belong together. One does not work without the other."

Precisely that is the reason why most of these young people learn Indian music. They have been impressed by the spirituality of India. They want to feel it more deeply; and they know that music is the path.

As early as 1921, long before the contemporary wave of Asian spirituality and music started its voyage around the world, Count Hermann Keyserling pointed out that "Indian music encompasses an immensely wide world. When listening to it, one experiences nothing in particular, nothing one can put one's hands on, and yet one feels alive in a most intense way. By following its different tones, one actually listens to oneself."

In his autobiography, Ravi Shankar writes:

Our tradition teaches us that sound is God—*Nada Brahma*. That is, musical sound and the musical experience are steps to the realization of the self. We view music as a kind of spiritual discipline that raises one's inner being to divine peacefulness and bliss. We are taught that one of the fundamental goals a Hindu works toward in his lifetime is a knowledge of the true meaning of the universe—its unchanging, eternal essence—and this is realized first by a complete knowledge of one's self and one's own nature. The highest aim of our music is to reveal the essence of the universe it reflects, and the *ragas* are among the means by which this essence can be apprehended. Thus, through music, one can reach God.

Elsewhere in the same book, Shankar comments:

There is no dearth of beautiful stories relating how great musicians and saint-musicians such as Baiju Bavare, Swami Haridas, or Mian Tan Sen performed miracles by singing certain *ragas*. It is said that some could light fires or the oil lamps by singing one *raga*, or bring rain, melt stones, cause flowers to blossom, and attract ferocious wild animals—even snakes and tigers—to a peaceful, quiet circle in a forest around a singing musician. To us, in this modern, mechanical, materialistic age, all this seems like a collection of fables, but I sincerely believe that these stories are all true and that they were all feasible, especially when one considers that these great musicians were not just singers or performers, but also great yogis, whose minds had complete control of their bodies. They knew all the secrets of *Tantra, hatha yoga*, and different forms of occult power, and they were pure, ascetic, and saintly persons. That has been the wonderful tradition of our music.

The German musicologist Gerhard Nestler explains:

One-line music with an indefinite pitch and with its wide range of intermediate tones and overtones has a wider base of expression than polyphonic music with its definite pitch and its interval structure, than conventional Western music, that is. In the final analysis, such music is unhearable. What we hear is its symbol. The symbol is the tones that man chooses from the wealth of tones provided by the universe. Such music grows out of the polar tension between the audible and the inaudible.

More than any other music, this music is characterized by the fact that it is excepted from an eternal music. It stands in the place of the inaudible. It is *anahata nad*, as opposed to *ahata nad*. *Anahata* means "unstruck." *Ahata nad*, thus, is the sound that is produced by striking

—by a material sound source—while *anahata nad* is eternal sound: the "sound of the universe," *Nada Brahma*.

In one of the old books of Japanese Buddhism, *Shoji jisso-gí* (the title means something like "The True Sense of Human Singing"), we find the following passage:

> We are no longer able to hear the Buddha's voice. However, we can still hear voices that come close to his. When all things of this world that have a voice together raise their voices, retaining their individual character yet combining them in one large sound, then we are very, very close to the sound of the Buddha's voice.

When Zen monks in a monastery of the Shingon sect sing their *shomyo* ritual, one has the overwhelming feeling that they are following this instruction to the letter. They want to come close to the Buddha sound—and this Buddha sound is *Nada Brahma*. At his concert appearances or during lessons with his students, Pandit Pran Nath, the great master of Indian *kirana* singing style who now lives in New York, often says: "*Nada Brahma*. Sound is God. Show that in your singing. Meditate on it. Cleanse your karma by it. Sing so that people will understand that, even if you haven't told them before: Sound is God. *Nada Brahma*."

Allauddin Khan, one of the most outstanding musicians from Northern India, relates that his father practiced for twenty-two years "without interruption." He adds:

> Of course, that meant not only practicing music but also spiritual practice. It was like meditation, but it also was music. My father, Ustad Hafiz Ali Khan, was a deeply religious man. He taught me that music is not entertainment but that it represents a prayer. He was deeply convinced that through music you can reach "taseer," that indescribable quality which can touch the innermost soul of the listener. But, only if it is really played for God.

For centuries, the great musician families of India have been cultivating the "ceremony of binding the *ganda*," a string that symbolically binds together the disciple and his guru (quite often they are son and father). In the ceremony, the son has to pledge that he will never desecrate his art by using it for profane entertainment or even by passing it on to popular singers or dancing girls. Ultimately the *ganda* ties the disciple not to the guru but to Lord Brahma and to the Brahman, the cosmic principle.

Since playing Indian music implies a change in one's way of thinking, learning it is very time-consuming. Ustad Allauddin Khan (*Ustad* means "master" and is the approximate Muslim equivalent of the Hindu terms *pandit* or *guru*) tells how, for twelve years, he did nothing but learn *sargana, palta,* and *murchana* (vocalizing, scales, and études). He practiced between sixteen and twenty hours daily. "Sometimes during practice I tied my long hair with a string fastened to a ring on the ceiling. Then, when I would doze off, the string in my hair would tighten as soon as my head would nod, waking me up." Ravi Shankar took four years to practice his first ragas: "A student these days would grumble if he were to spend four weeks on them!" Ali Akbar Khan related that he had to practice fourteen to sixteen hours a day. As a child he used to like to run off and play, but his father would tie him up with a rope. Ravi Shankar reports of the training he received from Allauddin Khan: From 4:00 to 6:00 A.M., he had to practice basic scales. After that he bathed, did his morning prayers, and ate two boiled eggs and a piece of bread. At seven in the morning, he reported to the *ustad* and then had lessons until eleven. Shankar emphasizes that "total humility and surrender to the guru" were expected, "a complete shedding of the ego . . . The disciple is only the receiver." After that, he ate a meal, had a brief rest, and continued practicing alone, again for three to four hours. In the afternoon, the *ustad* would call for a second lesson, which again lasted at least three hours.

Shankar's descriptions of his life as a disciple are revealing: "The only entertainment I had was going for walks along the river or on the lovely hillside . . . Often Ali Akbar accompanied me."—"We would return to the house by dark and all have dinner about seven-thirty, then spend a few more hours practicing."—"During our lessons, we would lose all sense of time. Often we would cry because of the intense beauty of the music, and nobody would have dreamed of disturbing the magic."—". . . I would say that, from the first beginnings, at least twenty years of work and practice are necessary in order to reach maturity and perfection in our classical music."

More so than in other kinds of music, the student of Indian music grows up with a feeling of responsibility. Missed notes, imprecise rhythms, slurred embellishments, inattention, lacking concentration, a lack of *vinaya* (humility, respect, modesty, devotion) all serve to create confusion and, finally, chaos—not only in music but also in the world. A musical mistake is also a spiritual mistake. When Narada, probably the earliest great master of Indian music, whose history is lost in the haze of myth, was convinced that he had reached mastery after many years of work, Lord Vishnu led him to the dwelling of the gods. There—as Shankar relates the myth—he saw many men and women with broken limbs, all crying about their state. Vishnu approached them and asked them what was wrong. They answered that all of them were spirits of ragas and raginis . . . but a certain Narada, who could neither play music correctly nor understand it, had dislocated and broken their limbs with his singing. And they continued that they would never regain their unimpaired wholeness and health, if a truly great and accomplished musician would not come to sing their melodies correctly. When Narada heard that, he felt deeply ashamed and in all humility knelt down in front of Vishnu, asking him for forgiveness.

At this point, a brief look at the position of the musical cultures of Asia in the history of music is necessary—primarily the musical culture of India, but also of those in the Arabic world as well as those of Bali and Java, China and Vietnam, Korea and Japan. All of them are *classical* musics, and it is a sign of "colonialist" thinking (in the very sense of the word) when they are referred to as "folklore." One often hears such nonsense when Indian music is performed; someone will say that Hariprasad Chaurasia, for instance, the master of the "divine flute," plays "Indian folklore." In a way, that is the same as calling a Mozart divertimento "Salzburg folklore," or a Verdi opera "Milanese folklore," or a Gershwin song "American folklore." To call classical Indian music (or the old music of Persia or the great Bedouin music of Northern Africa) "folklore" is a sign of arrogance, making it sound as if classical music existed only in the European tradition, while all other traditions have folk music. (To be sure, there are popular music, light music, "top hits," and true folk music in India, too.)

Many of the great musical cultures outside of Europe and North America not only are of equal rank with Western music, but surpass it in certain fields. In terms of rhythm, for example, the music of Africa and that of India are far richer than almost anything brought forth in the West. Consider the *tala*s, the rhythmic series of Indian music. Even long *tala*s of fifteen or nineteen beats, structured in the most complex way, can be followed beat for beat not only by the musicians but also by many listeners in India. Western audiences, however, become unsure as soon as they are faced with rhythms more complex than simple three-quarter or four-four time, and Western musicians become uncertain about meters of more than five or seven beats. In the streets of towns in the Middle East, in India, Africa, or Indonesia one sees young boys drumming with their arms and legs on homemade percussion instruments (expertly built from buckets, tin cans, gasoline drums, steel drums, and cooking pots), keeping the most complex polyrhythms —seven or eight different overlaying rhythms—with absolute precision. To realize something like that with even approximate precision in the Western world, it would take half a dozen highly trained percussionists, each one of them singlemindedly sticking to his part —whereby, of course, the verve and vitality of the Asian performance would not nearly be reached.

The music of India is richer in tonality than the music of the West, because it uses microtones. Its tone repertoire is almost twice as large as that of our music. The ears of music lovers in India have not yet been spoiled by our "well-tempered" scale. To their ears, tones that have become "the same" to us in a long process of "auditory refinement" (D sharp and E flat, for instance, or F sharp and G flat), sound much more different than they do in the West even to most musicians.

Part of the Western concept of musical culture is history. In this respect also, many of the musical cultures outside the Western world are superior to ours. The great music of the Bedouins and of Western Arabia, for instance, had unfolded its entire wealth as early as the eleventh century C.E., at a point in time, in other words, when the European history of music had hardly begun. The history of classical Indian music can be traced back to the seventh century B.C.E., which means that today there is an uninterrupted musical tradition covering almost three millennia. It is high time that Western music lovers realize this. It might make them become more humble about their generation-old pretension of having a monopoly on musical culture and on "classical music" in particular.

The new musical-spiritual consciousness, to be sure, is seen not only in the fact that we now listen to music from Asia and that this music has become a success in the philharmonic halls of North America and Europe. It becomes even more obvious through the fact that countless Western musicians have begun to practice and play it. The first one to try to do so was a jazz musician, the great tenor and soprano saxophonist John Coltrane, who died in 1967. His influence can be seen even in rock and pop music and in fact in the consciousness of young people in general (even though many of them may never have heard the name John Coltrane). Coltrane's most famous piece, written in 1965, is entitled "A Love Supreme." Coltrane also wrote the lyrics, from which I quote the following excerpt:

> I will do all I can to be worthy of Thee O Lord.
> It all has to do with it.
> Thank you God.
> God is. He always was. He always will be.
> Words, sounds, speech, men, memory, thoughts,
>   fears and emotions—time—all related . . .

all made from one . . . all made in one.
Blessed be His name.
Thought waves—heat waves—all vibrations—
    all paths lead to God. Thank you God.
The fact that we do exist is acknowledgment
    of Thee O Lord.
God breathes through us so completely . . .
    so gently we hardly feel it . . . yet,
    it is our everything.
Thank you God.
May we never forget
that in the sunshine of our lives,
through the storm and after the rain—
it is all with God—
in all ways and forever.
All praise to God.
Thank you God. Amen.

Today it is difficult to appreciate the revolutionary meaning of such a text in a jazz piece. We have become accustomed to jazz musicians expressing such thoughts and writing texts of that kind. We have become familiar with it—through Coltrane. Before 1965, the lyrics of the jazz pieces we heard dealt with love, fidelity, and desire, and there was reason for gratitude when their grammar was halfway correct.

Coltrane, as American music critic Ralph Gleason put it, shifted the musical consciousness of the young people of the Western world from America to Asia. In the meantime, entire generations of young jazz and rock musicians in the United States, Europe, and even Australia, stemming from Coltrane, have come to know the music of Asia (above all, India) and that of the Arabic world, and many have come to master this music as well (or almost as well) as their own musical tradition.

The music being performed by these musicians from the East and the West differs from traditional European music by dint of the fact that it is "modal." That means, it is based not on continually changing chord structures like our occidental music, but on a "scale," a *mode*, or a single "chord." Which makes their music much more tranquil, much less "nervous" (if I may use this word in a neutral sense, simply in reference to the human nervous system) than our music, which is characterized by the fact that it is just that: referring to the nerves. Modal music has to do with a certain mental, spiritual attitude. Karl Berger, for many years the head of the Creative Music Studio, a well-known school for "world music" in Woodstock, New York, once said: "Modal playing is not simply 'playing modally.' You can't just go and use modal scales to improvise on instead of the conventional chord structures, and believe that that will produce meaningful music. If you don't *think* differently, all you'll get is études."

In 1976, at a Bicentennial symposium held in Washington, D.C., on America's cultural contribution to the world, I brought up the topic of modality in contemporary American music. Tenor player Nathan Davis (who teaches at the University of Pittsburgh) stood up and said: "Playing modally has to do with spirituality. What we really mean by saying spirituality is religiousness. Only we don't use that word, because we don't mean what the Christian world means by religiousness."

The way today's young musicians understand spirituality is exemplified by the John Coltrane lyrics quoted above. In the meantime, this kind of spirituality has long existed in many styles of Western music besides jazz—for instance, in rock music. One example is Santana, the group led by a San Francisco guitarist of Mexican descent. One of his most successful works is entitled *Caravanserai,* about which Santana has said that the "caravan journey" evoked by the music is a parable of a voyage of the soul into a new, unknown land. It is striking that such "journeys of the soul" have become more and more frequent in Western music since the late sixties. The jazz musician Wayne Shorter said about his "Odyssey of Iskra": "The piece is about a West African Odysseus by the name of Iskra. Perhaps you can relate this music to the journey of your own soul." And the jazz pianist McCoy Tyner entitled one of his pieces "Sahara" and quoted from the Arab historian Ibn Khaldun: "This desert is so long it can take a lifetime to go from one end to the other, and a childhood to cross at its narrowest point." It all makes sense: The desert, the caravan, the Odyssey are symbols for the voyage our generation has to make, a voyage into the world of a new consciousness. "Eternal Caravan of Reincarnation" is the title of the opening movement of Santana's *Caravanserai.*

There is a text by the great Sufi master Hazrat Inayat Khan that has been making the rounds among Western musicians since the end of the sixties. For years, its complete version existed only as a private printing of the London Sufi mission. In an abridged form, however, you can find it all over, in thousands of copies, quoted in articles and interviews. Occasionally, musicians will enclose a copy with a Christmas or birthday greeting. This text expresses the musical and spiritual consciousness of the young generation of musicians precisely and representatively. Here are some excerpts:

> What we call music in our everyday language is only a miniature from that music or harmony of the whole universe which is working behind everything, and which is the source and origin of nature. It is

because of this that the wise of all ages have considered music to be a sacred art. For in music the seer can see the picture of the whole universe. . . .

All the religions have taught us that the origin of the whole of creation is sound. No doubt, the way in which this word is used in our everyday language is a limitation of that sound which is suggested by the scriptures.

The music of the universe is the background of the small picture which we call music. Our sense of music, our attraction to music, shows that there is music in the depth of our being. Music is behind the working of the whole universe. Music is not only life's greatest object, but it is life itself.

What makes us feel drawn to music is that our whole being is music; our mind and our body, the nature in which we live, the nature which has made us, all that is beneath and around us, it is all music. . . .

We say that we enjoy nature. But what is it in nature that we enjoy? It is music. Something in us has been touched by the rhythmic movement, by the perfect harmony which is so seldom found in this artificial life of ours. . . .

When one looks at the cosmos, the movements of the stars and planets, the law of vibration and rhythm, all perfect and unchanging, it shows that the cosmic system is working by the law of music, the law of harmony; and whenever that harmony in the cosmic system is lacking in any way, then in proportion disaster comes to the world, and its influence is seen in the many destructive forces which are manifest there. The whole of astrological law and the science of magic and mysticism behind it, are based upon music. Therefore the whole life of the most illuminated souls who lived in this world, like the greatest prophets in India, has been music. From the miniature music, which we understand, they expanded the whole universe of music, and in that way they were able to inspire.

Every person is music, perpetual music, continually going on day and night; and your intuitive faculty can hear that music. That is the reason why one person is repellent and the other attracts you. It is the music he expresses; his whole atmosphere is charged with it.

There is a story of Omar, the well-known Khalif of Arabia. Someone who wanted to harm Omar was looking for him, and he heard that Omar did not live in palaces though he was a king, but that he spent most of his time with nature. This man was very glad to think that now he would have every opportunity to accomplish his object. And as he approached the place where Omar was sitting, the nearer he came the more his attitude changed; until in the end he dropped the dagger which was in his hand and said: "I cannot harm you. Tell me what is the power in you that keeps me from accomplishing the object which I came to accomplish?" And Omar answered: "My at-one-ment with God."

What did Omar mean by that at-one-ment with God? He meant being in tune with the Infinite, in harmony with the whole universe.

In other words, Omar was the receptacle of the music of the whole universe. . . .

The great charm that the personality of the holy ones has shown in all ages has been their responsiveness to the music of the whole being. That has been their secret. . . .

The difference between the material and the spiritual point of view is that the material point of view sees matter as the first thing, and considers that intelligence and beauty and everything else evolved from it. From the spiritual point of view we see the intelligence and beauty first; and from them comes all that exists. From the spiritual point of view we see that one considers last to be the same as first; and therefore in the essence of this whole being, as the basis of all that exists, there is music. One can see that in the essence of the seed of the rose there is the rose itself, its fragrance, form and beauty; and although in the end it may not be manifested, at the same time it is there.

The experience of harmony and at-one-ment one can make everywhere in the beauty of nature, in colour of flowers, in everything he sees and in everything he meets. In the hours of contemplation and solitude, and in the hours when he is in the midst of the world, the music is always there, he is always enjoying its harmony. And by breaking down those walls which surround him he experiences at-one-ment with the Absolute. This at-one-ment with the Absolute manifests as the music of the spheres.

The contemporary Western musician who first called attention to this text (at least, he was the first one for me, but I know that he was also the first for many others) is the trumpet player Don Cherry. His development has been exemplary for this entire generation of musicians, from jazz with its tie to the blues music of the black ghettos and to the gospel sounds of the Baptist congregations to ever greater musical and spiritual openness, in which all the cultures of the world come together like the pieces of a mosaic that is one great whole. Like thousands of other musicians the world over, Don Cherry lives today with a musical and spiritual tradition that makes it impossible for him to conceive of any one cultural stream or branch as more esoteric, more remote, more "exotic" than any other one. "Exotic for whom?" he once asked, "they for you, or you for them?"

Don Cherry's musical path is closely connected with my own. In the United States, he had only been playing in small groups—trios and quartets. For that reason, starting in the mid-sixties in concerts and recording sessions at several of the festivals I had founded (the New Jazz Meetings in Baden-Baden, the Berlin Jazz Festival, and my annual concerts at the Donaueschingen New Music Festival) I provided him with the opportunity to realize his ideas in a series of big-band works.

In Don Cherry's suite *Humus—The Life-Exploring Force,* written for the 1971 Donaueschingen Festival, one movement is entitled "Siddhartha," after Hermann Hesse's book of the same title. Here it is at last: another name has been used that inevitably must come up when we address the New Consciousness. John Coltrane and Hermann Hesse are surely not the founders of this consciousness, but young people throughout the Western world learned about it from them. This took place during the 1960s, the decade that has been called the most interesting of our century. It was a time that gave the "age of feature writing" (Hesse) a new way of looking at itself politically and socially, but it also paved the way for a new psychological and spiritual sensitivity. Today it seems that the latter effect is more permanent than the former. It was the decade at whose beginning (in 1961) John Coltrane had his first great success with "My Favorite Things," and during which Hermann Hesse, until then neglected by literary criticism as a philistine Swabian, advanced to the position of the most widely read German writer in both the United States and Japan.

In one of his "Fairy Tales," Hesse talks about an ancient sage who had "perceived the oneness of the world as a harmonious consonance of the heavenly spheres." As early as 1925, Hesse conjured the image of the "world music of the stars swinging freely." And about his *Glass Bead Game,* he wrote that in it "the cult of music and meditation intimately belong together." When Josef Knecht, the young hero of this novel, meditates, the world changes into tones, the sequence of notes turns into mathematical figures, into rhythmical ornaments. One might say that today's performers of minimal music (about whom I will have more to say later) have simply followed the instructions given by the player of the "Glass Bead Game," Josef Knecht, and thereby created their style of music—as, for instance, the composers Terry Riley, Philip Glas, Steve Reich, Peter Michael Hamel, and their followers all over the world.

With his musical realization of Hesse's poem "Organ Playing," one of the poetic precursors of the *Glass Bead Game,* Hamel has created a true work of genius. I know of no literary person, no literary scholar, who has grasped this text as precisely and as lovingly as this musician. Together with the members of his group Between, Hamel arranged the three levels of the text to three different planes of sound. To the first part of Hesse's text belongs the organ music of the old masters of the age of Johann Sebastian Bach, played on a church organ. The second part, played in a "fusion" manner on electronic keyboards, still on the same theme, deals with the "other sounds" and "other celebrations" of today's young people. The third part, finally, raises both tradition and modernity onto a "timeless" level. Hearing Hamel's music for

Hermann Hesse's "Organ Playing" means experiencing these three levels (which means, experiencing this text) more directly than would be possible through mere reading. Here are some excerpts from Hesse's poem (see also the discography at the end of this chapter):

Organ Playing

Sighing, droning through the vaulted room,
Organ playing. Pensive faithful raptly hear
This music, multi-voiced, in intertwining choirs,
Yearn, mourn, jubilate with angels,
    building dwellings for the spirit,
Gently rocked in blessed dreams,
Firmaments of sounding stars.
    . . . .

A miracle unequaled, is it not,
How note-sign covered leaves,
By interplay of organ pipes,
Transmute to star-spun cosmic choirs,
Which answer to the singly
Human powers of the player of the keys?
And listeners who, perceiving this,
Can glow and soar in sympathy,
Vibrate, resound and enter
With the music into a pulsing cosmos.
This was work, harvest
    of ten generations, with
A hundred humble masters toiling piously,
And thousands of disciples.
And as the musician at the organ plays,
Souls of revered and long departed
Masters listen midst the arches,
Held in close embrace by the
Structure that they had joined to build.
    . . . .

But perfection here below cannot endure.
Secretly as war in every peace,
    so decay in beauty dwells.
Organ playing echoes through the hall,
Euphonic sounds call out to
New guests: enter, rest and pray.
Yet, as old tone-poems rise again,
Like buildings or the spread of pipes,
Rich in piety and wisdom, joy,
Outside much has passed
To change both world and souls.
Other visitors, another youth have come

To whom half-familiar,
Antiquated, contorted seems
What before was holy and of treasured loveliness.
New drives sway their hearts,
Not to master torturously
Sternest rules of ancient music men,
Quicker challenges impress upon their tribe.
War at large and hunger raging.
Not for long do these new guests attend
The organ sound, its music true and deep,
Yet self-contained and safely
Clothed in sacral dignity.
Other sounds they wish and other celebrations,
Still sensing half-ashamed
The unwelcome admonition that demands so much
In those majestic, lavish organ choirs.
Life is short. And this is not a time
Patiently to spend on complicated games.
Inside the cathedral, of the many
Who once heard and shared that life,
Hardly any will remain.
One by one they leave, now stooped
And older, tired, smaller,
Chastizing the young as traitors,
Holding bitter silence,
Then to lie down with the fathers.

. . . .

No one knows if the old master
Still is playing, or if yonder fragile
Textures hovering in the room might
But ghostly echoes be of
Stubborn spirits from another day.
Now and then a passerby will pause
At the cathedral door to listen,
Nudge it quietly ajar, attend,
Transported to the distant silver stream of music,
Then to steal away with sound-touched heart.
Seek a friend to whisper word of that
Ethereal hour at the church in the
Scent of long-extinguished candles.
Even banished thus into the dark,
The sacred stream flows on,
Now and then its ripples rising from
The depths as sparkling tones.
He who hears them grasps the power
Of a secret, sees it fleeing,
Craves to hold it, burns with
Longing, for he has touched beauty.

The "Glass Bead Game," the "game of games," as Hesse put it, is unthinkable without the conviction that is the theme of our book: The world is sound. "During all ages, there was a close connection between the game and music; it was usually played according to musical or mathematical rules. . . . It meant an exquisite, symbolic form of search for perfection, a sublime alchemy, a process of getting close to a spirit which is one with itself, in spite of all images and variedness, that is, to God." *Nada Brahma*.

Herman Hesse called the "Glass Bead Game" a

> world language fed from all sciences and arts, which plays itself and heads toward perfection, toward pure being, toward completely fulfilled reality.
>
> All the insights, lofty ideas and works of art brought forth by mankind during its creative ages, all that for which subsequent periods of learned contemplation found the appropriate terms and of which they took intellectual possession, this entire, immense wealth of spiritual qualities is played by the player of the glass bead game the way an organ is played by the organist. And this organ is of a hardly conceivable perfection, its manuals and pedals sound out the whole spiritual cosmos, its registers are almost innumerable; theoretically the entire spiritual content of the world could be reproduced in playing this instrument.

Hermann Hesse dedicated his *Glass Bead Game* to the "Journeyers to the East," and millions of young people followed this dedication to the letter.

"Glass Bead Game" music, in an elevated sense, is created by the composers and performers of minimal music or, as it is sometimes called, Periodical Music, in which the streams of Western and Asian music flow together. One often has the impression that the same tone sequences are constantly being repeated, but during these repetitions barely noticeable changes take place. At the end of a piece, in minimal progressions, in a circular motion that (consciously or unconsciously) connects with the concept of infinity, something new and different is reached, another shore, another world. The musical phrases and movements of minimal music, its circling, correspond in a fascinating manner to the mantras of Asian tradition that in the course of meditation, in a way that is hardly noticeable to the meditating person, begin to develop, grow, and work according to their own laws.

The first composers of minimal music were three Americans: La Monte Young, Terry Riley, and Steve Reich. All three named jazz musicians as their crucial influences: the drummer Max Roach, the trumpeter Miles Davis, and, above all, John Coltrane. Terry Riley, who would much prefer his music to be called "maximal music" or, ironically, "Country 'n' Eastern," has said:

> In a sense my music is closely related to the techniques of classical Indian music, whose exponents are capable of developing endless sequences out of a single theme. . . . According to this concept, the composed portions remain unaltered, but the musician is quite free to spin them out within the limits of his imagination. . . .
>
> Music should be the expression of lofty, spiritual objectives: Philosophy, knowledge and truth—the most noble qualities of man. In order to give expression to these objectives, music must necessarily have tranquility and poise.

The most outstanding European exponent of this "new" new music is Peter Michael Hamel. In the introduction to his book *Through Music to the Self*, Hamel writes:

> It is the responsibility of spiritual music to learn from all musical traditions, to track down long-forgotten sources and to bring back into the limelight the original function of music—its links with the deepest in human experience—without, in the process, falling into naive eclecticism. At present there is a broad, strong urge to open up again those clogged wells of music which alone can reveal the way to a new type of musical experience encompassing man's being in its entirety. . . .
>
> Whether in avant-garde music, in jazz, or in pop music, we have been witnessing a trend towards a more spiritual, introverted musical language. The increasing public interest in spiritual music, both Western and non-European, . . . suggests that here, too, the future role of music will not be confined merely to one particular dimension of human existence.
>
> What we are concerned with are not so much new discoveries as the re-discovery of what has long been known to ancient cultures and nations and was only allowed to slip into oblivion due to the predominantly rationalistic development of the Western world. It is our task . . . to rediscover those links and to integrate them into the musical consciousness of the twentieth century.

Hamel also quotes the musicologist Gerhard Nestler:

> This new music requires "pure listening," that is, a listening free of all customary rational and emotional ingredients. This pure listening to the tone and to its dimensions as such harbors the strong stimulation

of this music. Music of instrumental colors is the most musical music since it is the music of the elementary existence of the tone.

Minimal music has meantime become *en vogue*; and like so many things that have become subject to marketing mechanisms, it has often acquired an unpleasant taste. Musicians, performers and conductors, began to "make" minimal music without having the slightest idea of the spiritual consciousness that this music carries. They simply play and conduct periodical music, knowing that it might bring them money or success. Music, however, has to do with consciousness. Great musicians are called "great" because they have scrutinized not only the music but also the thinking, the spiritual position and, often enough (when you think of Bach, for example), also the religious ness of the master whose music they play. Playing minimal music without spirituality means doing finger exercises, playing empty music.

Pandit Patekar, a master of classical Indian music, set forth some "absolutely essential rules of conduct":

1. Temporarily release yourself in thought from the usual way of thinking and concentrate on the higher, spiritual aspects of life. Music offers the best means for such concentration.
2. Place the universal in the forefront of your contemplation, and endeavor to lay aside or to forget the habit of looking at partial aspects only.
3. Immerse yourself in a mood of meditation and contemplation.
4. Establish a link with the supernatural aspects of reality.
5. Leave aside all inner preconceptions.
6. Try to think your way inside the artist. In other words, try to feel with him and to become one with both artist and theme.
7. Be still and spiritualized, both inwardly and outwardly.

The music we are talking about here—classical Indian music, the music of John Coltrane and of his musical heirs in jazz and rock, minimal music, and the best of the new meditation music—points toward an experience that in the Eastern tradition is referred to as "becoming one." To be sure, this music alone cannot bring about such "at-one-ment." No music can do that. Only years of meditation can do it. But this music paves the way—and this word *way* should be understood in its broader Chinese and Japanese meaning, as *tao* and *do*. It is a kind of music in which time is dissolved in a manner beyond words. Even though music has been defined as "art in time," this new music (which, as we know, is quite ancient, with ancestors also in the Western world—as for instance in Gregorian chant) is able to transcend time.

More than once I have talked about the illusory nature of our attitude to time. For modern man, this reveals itself above all in two instances: in the theory of relativity and—even more directly perceivable by the senses—in this "new, old" music. Time is, as Hermann Hesse once put it, the river that at its source, its middle, and its mouth simply is "the river." It is the river at whose banks Siddhartha meditated for years and found enlightenment. Rather than a brief excerpt, let's read the entire passage from Hermann Hesse's novel of the same name, because in it Hesse's wonderful mastery of language conveys the sense of time that concerns us here:

> Siddhartha stayed with the ferryman and learned how to look after the boat, and when there was nothing to do at the ferry, he worked in the rice field with Vasudeva, gathered wood, and picked fruit from the banana trees. He learned how to make oars, how to improve the boat and to make baskets. He was pleased with everything that he did and learned and the days and months passed quickly. . . .
>
> He once asked [the ferryman], "Have you also learned that secret from the river: that there is no such thing as time?" . . .
>
> "Yes, Siddhartha," he said, "Is this what you mean? That the river is everywhere at the same time, at the source and at the mouth, at the waterfall, at the ferry, at the current, in the ocean and in the mountains, everywhere, and that the present only exists for it, not the shadow of the past, nor the shadow of the future?"
>
> "That is it," said Siddhartha, "and when I learned that, I reviewed my life and it was also a river, and Siddhartha the boy, Siddhartha the mature man and Siddhartha the old man, were only separated by shadows, not through reality. Siddhartha's previous lives were also not in the past, and his death and his return to Brahma are not in the future. Nothing was, nothing will be, everything has reality and presence." . . .
>
> And once again when the river swelled during the rainy season and roared loudly, Siddhartha said: "Is it not true, my friend, that the river has very many voices? . . ."
>
> "It is so," nodded Vasudeva, "the voices of all living creatures are in its voice."
>
> "And do you know," continued Siddhartha, "what word it pronounces when one is successful in hearing all its ten thousand voices at the same time?"
>
> Vasudeva laughed joyously; he bent towards Siddhartha and whispered the holy OM in his ear. And this was just what Siddhartha had heard.

It is this river, the *nada* of OM, that is featured in one of the great Zen *mondo*s: "The master: 'Do you hear the rushing of the river?' —'Yes, master,' answers the disciple. The master: 'That is the way!'"

On this way is a repetition of what took place when *nadí* became *nada:* the amplification of the rushing of the river to the cosmic rushing of *Nada Brahma*.

The river—and the music that is our theme here—are NOW. They must not and cannot be taken apart, be separated, neither into past, present and future, nor—in terms of the river—into source, creek, river, stream, and mouth, nor—in terms of the music—into structural units, as is done, for example, when classical music is viewed as exposition, development, and reprise. This music "happens" in space as much as in time, the latter—from the standpoint of the music—only being a dimension of space anyway, just as it is from the standpoint of theoretical physics. It is a space in which one "is," in which one is NOW. It is striking how many contemporary musicians speak of spatial concepts, much more so than the musicians of classical and Romantic European music. The flute player Paul Horn described the sense of space he experienced when he made his famous recordings in the tomb of the Taj Mahal, that wonderful mausoleum near Agra in northern India, as follows: "The room came back to me like a thousand angel choirs. Actually, what I was doing was, I sat there deep down in the tomb and listened to the room. I answered it. I made music together with it. Much more than my flute, the room was the instrument on which I played."

In the *nada* of the *nadí*, in the rushing of the river, too, the sound has become space, a space like a temple, like a cathedral. You will enter this "temple of space" when you play and listen to music in that spiritual attitude that is of prime importance to the musicians I have quoted here.

In the meditation cultures of the world, music plays a special role, more than any other form of art. "And it came to pass, when the minstrel played, that the hand of the Lord came upon him [the prophet Elisha]" is written in 2 Kings 3:15. And even the sober world of Zen is full of references to music. The Japanese title of the 1783 koan collection of the monk and Zen master Genro (whom I have quoted several times in this book) is *Tetteki Tosui*. In his preface, Genro explains how an old Chinese hermit named Ryu was able to pierce clouds and crack large boulders with his flute playing, but even such flute playing produced only audible tones. Only when this flute was blown in the reverse direction would it tear apart the void with its inaudible sound. *Tetteki Tosui* means "the iron flute to be blown in the reverse direction"; and, since nobody can blow a flute in the reverse direction, the title is a metaphor of the absurdity of the world. The title itself is a koan. It is a symbol of an unplayable, inaudible music, a symbol of the sound that is meant in our Zen question:

> If you blot out sense and sound—
> what do you hear?

Zen has not only an iron flute to be blown in the reverse direction but also a "harp without strings"; and in reference to the famous koan that challenges the disciple to imagine what sound would be produced if he would clap with one hand, there is even a special Zen term for the inaudible voice of the one hand: *sekishu.*

Hsüeh-tou Ch'ung-hsien, a Chinese Zen master of the tenth century, once said: "Of course, an ancient melody can move you to tears. Zen music, though, goes beyond what you can hear and grasp. Therefore do not make music unless you have found the Great Tone of Lao-tzu . . ."—about which Lao-tzu wrote in his terse style: "Great tools take much time to be manufactured. . . . The Great Tone is the tone that goes beyond all usual imagination."

The Great Tone is the tone of being or, as the Indians put it, the tone of the self, of the *Atma.* The Great Tone is *Nada Brahma,* the tone from which God made the world, which continues to sound at the bottom of creation, and which sounds through everything. In Latin the term meaning "to sound through something" is *personare.* Thus, at the basis of the concept of the *person* (the concept of that which really makes a human being an unmistakable, singular *per-sonality*) stands a concept of sound: "through the tone." If nothing sounds through from the bottom of the being, a human being is human biologically, at best, but is not a *per-son,* because he does not live through the *son* (the tone, the sound). He does not live the sound which is the world.

When the Buddha returned to everyday reality after his enlightenment he first talked about a sound. Buddha called it the "drum of immortality." Here, too, it was Hermann Hesse who put this experience into words for our cultural realm. The "hero" of his short novel *Klein and Wagner,* who drowns in Lake Lugano, southern Switzerland (where Hesse lived), has the following experience at the moment of his death:

> Out of the song of the blessed and out of the endless cries of torment from the unblessed there rose over both universal streams a transparent sphere or dome of sound, a cathedral of music. In its midst sat God, a bright star, invisible from sheer brightness, the quintessence of

light, with the music of the universal choirs roaring around in eternal surges. . . . Now Klein heard his own voice. He was singing. With a new, mighty, high, reverberating voice he sang loudly, loudly and resoundingly sang God's praise. He sang as he floated along in the rushing stream in the midst of the millions of creatures. He had become a prophet and proclaimer. Loudly, his song resounded; the vault of music rose high; radiantly, God sat within it. The stream roared tremendously along.

MUSIC FOR LISTENING TO THE TENTH CHAPTER

The Genius of Pandit Ravi Shankar. With Chatur Lal, tabla.

Ravi Shankar and Ali Akbar Khan in Concert 1972. With Alla Rakha, tabla. Fantasy 24714 (2 LPs).

Ravi Shankar at Monterey 1967. With Alla Rakha, tabla. Bainbridge RSD 21.

Ustad Ali Akbar Shan. *Soul of the Sarod.* With Sri Swapan Chaudri, tabla. Oriental BGRP-1041.

Hariprasad Chaurasia. *Charm of the Bamboo Flute.* Oriental BGRP-1058.

Balachander. *The Virtuoso of Veena.* Music of South India. Denon CD-7275.

Shomyo:Buddhist Ritual. (See p. 50.)

Pandit Pran Nath: India's Master Vocalist. Shandar Records 83514.

John Coltrane. *A Love Supreme.* MCA/Impulse 5665.

Santana. *Caravanserai.* Columbia PC 31610.

Wayne Shorter. *Odyssey of Iskra.* Blue Note BST-84363.

McCoy Tyner. *Sahara.* Milestone 9039.

Don Cherry. *Humus—The Life Exploring Force.* Wergo 1010.

Hesse between Music. Selections from *Siddhartha, Klein and Wagner, The Glass Bead Game,* poetry, etc., including many passages quoted in this book. With music by Peter Michael Hamel and his group Between; read by Fred Haines. Produced by Joachim E. Berendt. Caedmon TC 1516.

Terry Riley. *In C.* CBS MS-7178.

———. *Descending Moonshine Dervishes.* Kuckuck 047.

Steve Reich. *Music for Eighteen Musicians.* ECM 1129.

———. *Music for Large Orchestra.* ECM 1168.

Philip Glass. *Glassworks.* CBS FM-37265.

Peter Michael Hamel. *Bardo.* Kuckuck 048.

———. *Colours of Time.* Kuckuck 046.

Paul Horn. *Inside the Taj Mahal.* Recorded live in the Taj Mahal. Kuckuck 062.

———. *Inside the Great Pyramid.* Recorded live in the Great Pyramid of Cheops and other pyramids. Kuckuck 060 (2 LPs).

11 ✍ The Myths Were Right: God Created the World from Sound

HAFIZ, THE GREAT Sufi poet of fourteenth-century Persia, told the following legend:

> God made a statue of clay in His own image, and asked the soul to enter into it; but the soul refused to be imprisoned, for its nature is to fly about freely and not to be limited and bound to any sort of capacity. The soul did not wish in the least to enter this prison. Then God asked the angels to play their music, and as the angels played the soul was moved to ecstasy, in order to make the music more clear to itself, it entered his body.

Hafiz is said to have added: "People say that the soul, on hearing that song, entered the body; but in reality the soul itself was the song." And Hazrat Inayat Khan comments:

> This is a beautiful legend, and much more so is its mystery. The interpretation of this legend explains to us two great laws. One is that freedom is the nature of the soul, and for the soul the whole tragedy of life is the absence of that freedom which belongs to its original nature; and the next mystery that this legend reveals to us is that the only reason why the soul has entered the body of clay or matter is to experience the music of life, and to make this music clear to itself.

173

In the beginning was the sound, the sound as *logos*. If you remember, God's command "Let there be . . ." at the beginning of the biblical story of creation was first tone and sound. For the Sufis, the mystics of Islam, this is the core of things: God created the world from sound.

Many of the world's cultures have passed down sagas and myths, legends and tales in which the world has its origin in sound, from the Aztecs to the Eskimos, from the Persians to the Indians and the Malayans. In fact, there is such a wealth of these myths that only a few can be mentioned here (in fact, others have been mentioned in earlier chapters).

In Egypt, the "singing sun" created the world with its "cry of light." In an ancient Egyptian scripture it is written that through "the tongue of the creator . . . all Gods and everything in existence were born. . . . Atum and everything divine manifest themselves in the thought of the heart and in the sound of the tongue." The symbol for "tongue" in Egyptian hieroglyphics can also mean "word"; it is the tongue that forms the sound that in turn carries the word. Thus the flowing transition from mantric sound to spoken word (which I spoke of in chapters 2 and 3) can still be detected in the early stages of the art of writing. In another Egyptian tradition, Thoth, the god of the word and of scripture, of dance and of music, creates the world by repeating his "laughing word" seven times.

Here is another version:

> Inaudible and motionless, says the mythology of the Aztecs of Mexico, was the creator. An iceberg! Silent as a stone. One day, however, he cast off the iceberg and broke his silence, as he was no longer able to resist his deepest wish to create the world and mankind. He sang: "This world shall be!" And the world came into being.

For almost all nations in the world, music and the divine are closely connected. Many ragas (the scales of Indian music) have a religious meaning; some of them refer directly to certain gods and their reincarnations. It is similar with the rhythms of most African cultures. The rituals of the West African Yoruba, for instance, have remained alive in Brazil in the widespread Macumba and Candomblé cults, their music forming the basis of the Brazilian samba and carnival rhythms. Even today, many Brazilian drummers and percussionists—even those working in television and recording studios—know which rhythm belongs to which "god." That's the way they put it: The rhythm "belongs" to a god. In the mid-sixties, when I was recording the Brazilian percussionists Rubens and Georghingho, suddenly they both began to call out the names of those deities who were being evoked by the particular rhythms they were drumming: First Xango, the great god of thunder and war, the Jupiter in the celestial spheres of the Yoruba; then Nana, the goddess of love, whose name was pronounced by Georghingho with particular tenderness; after that Ogum, the god of the jungles and forests; and finally Omulu, the god of the ill (whom Rubens called To-to). I was shocked by the intensity with which they did this. Everyone in the studio sensed that it was important to them. It had to happen right then and there. It was a ritual, albeit a miniature one, almost like the cipher of a Macumba rite, which they needed right now, at least as a cipher. After that, they swiftly proceeded with the recording work like the professionals they are, although in a much more relaxed manner.

In India, the Vedic creator-god Prajapati was himself hymn and song. "The rhythms," it is said, "are his limbs," the limbs, that is, of the god who created the world. "The first sacrificial offerings and the first gods were meters, and the seven archfathers of mankind were also rhythms." In the *Aitareya-Upanishad,* rhythms are compared to horses: As one travels with horses or oxen to reach a terrestrial goal, one needs rhythms and meters to reach heavenly goals. Of Brahma it is said: "He meditated a hundred thousand years, and the result of his meditation was the creation of sound and music."

Thus, the first act of creation was the creation of sound. Everything else came after and through it.

Plato, in his famous dialogue *Timaeus,* tells that the creator constructed the world-soul (which to Plato means the idea of the cosmos) according to musical intervals and proportions. And with his music, the divine singer Orpheus was able to cast formless matter into form (which for the Greeks meant: into structured beauty).

In Polynesia, on Samoa, Tahiti, Hawaii, there were originally —before all the other deities were added—three great gods. The three of them (another trinity!)—Tane, Tu, and Rongo (Lono on Hawaii) —created the world, and all three have to do with sound. Tane's symbol was the horn, Tu's the triton shell, and Rongo was the actual god of sound and tone who (consequently!) despised human sacrifice and was considered the mildest and best loved of the gods.

In the thinking of many cultures of the world, it was God (or several gods) who originally created music and somehow handed it down to humankind, usually by way of an especially gifted medium, for instance, through Orpheus in ancient Greece. For the African Ibuzo tribe in Nigeria, this medium was a singer called Orgadié. Having lost his way in the jungle, he heard the music of the spirits and gods of the trees there. They were making music on twigs and branches and stems, on blades of grass, on the tree leaves and vines. Hidden in the bush,

Orgadié listened, trying not to forget anything, and later brought it all back to his home village.

Following the account of an old Brahman priest, Swiss ethnologists Theo Meier and Ernst Schlager tell the following Balinese legend:

> Lord Shiva once sat on Mount Meru. . . . Out of the distance, he heard soft tones of a kind he had never heard before. He summoned Narada, the wise man, sending him to the Himalayan hermitages to find out where the tones were coming from. Narada went on his way and finally reached the hermitage of the sage Dereda. There the tones sounded stronger. He entered the hermitage. The hermit told him that the wondrous tones were, indeed, coming from his land. The hermitage was surrounded by a bamboo grove. Dereda had made holes in the bamboo canes to tie them together. Now, when the wind blew through the holes, the most diverse tones would be sounded. Dereda said he had been so delighted by this discovery that he had tied a bunch of bamboo canes with holes together and hung them up in a tree (creating a sound box like an aeolian harp), for no other reason than to produce a continual, pleasant sound.
>
> Narada returned to Lord Shiva to report to him what he had learned. Shiva decided that these bamboo harps were to form the basis of all music on Bali, because humans had thereby received the ability to pay their reverence to the gods and to please them in a new way. Whereas music had been in a state of chaos before, Lord Shiva provided it with an orderly system.

A particularly moving legend about the way sound, music, and dance bring order and harmony to the chaos resulting from the creation of the world comes from Japan. It relates how Amaterasu, the sun goddess, sought recluse in a cave. There was no sunlight, everything was dark and desolate. Then Izanagi, the creator-god, took six giant bows and tied them together, creating the first harp. On it he played wonderful melodies. Lured by them, the charming nymph Ame no Uzume appeared. Enraptured by the harp music, she began to dance—and finally to sing. Amaterasu, the sun goddess, wanted to better hear the music that reached her ear from far away. For this reason she glanced outside her cave—and in the same moment the world was showered with light. The sun came out to be seen and felt, flowers and plants and trees began to grow. Fish and birds, animals and humans entered the light-filled earth. The gods, however, decided to cultivate music and dance so that the sun goddess would never return to her cave again, because they knew: It was the sun who had produced life, but without the harp music of the six great bows and without the singing of the nymph Ame no Uzume, the sun goddess Amaterasu would never have taken up her place on her heavenly throne. She would have stayed in her cave for all eternity. So it was sound, music, and dance, with which the world began.

Since God created the world from sound, and since sound and music were given to humankind by the god(s), you will find that in most cultures it is music whose sounds disclose God's will and the deepest secrets of creation to man. In China, there is the story of the great Taoist Huan Yi, who was not only an enlightened sage but also a gifted flute player. A Taoist dignitary had heard that Huan Yi would come to that particular area on his travels. The dignitary sent an envoy to Huan Yi, asking him to pay him a visit and share his wisdom with him. Then Huan Yi "descended from his coach, seated himself on a chair, and played the flute three times. Thereupon he entered the coach again and drove off." The two did not exchange a single word, but legend has it that the dignitary was an initiate from that time on.

There is also a Zen version of this story. When Kakua, one of the early pioneers of Buddhism in Japan, returned from a voyage to China, the emperor asked him to tell him about all the wisdom he had brought back from China. Kakua took out his shakuhachi (bamboo flute), played a melody, took a polite bow, and walked off. The emperor, however, was enlightened in that moment.

There are certain ceremonial rites in Islam that do not permit any kind of music. Hazrat Inayat Khan tells of a wonderful experience from the lifetime of the saintly Khwaja of Ajmer. To visit this saint, Khwaja Abdul Qadir Jilani, a great master who was also an advanced soul, came to him from Baghdad. Now the saint was very strict in his religious observance and would not have any music. His guest, of course, wanting to respect this rule, had to sacrifice his daily musical practice. He did continue his daily meditation routine, however. But when he started to meditate, the music began to sound by itself, and everybody listened. It continued this way for some days. Qadir Jilani did not touch his instrument, but whenever he started to meditate, the music began. Hazrat Inayat Khan comments: "Music is meditation and meditation is music. The enlightenment which we can find in meditation we can experience in music, too."

There is another, similar story, also told by Hazrat Inayat Khan, about the Mogul emperor Akbar and Tansen, a famous musician at his court:

> The Emperor asked him, "Tell me, O great musician, who was your teacher?" He replied, "Your Majesty, my teacher is a very great musician, but more than that. I cannot call him 'musician,' I must call him 'music'!" The Emperor asked, "Can I hear him sing?" Tansen answered, "Perhaps, I may try. But you cannot think of calling him

here to the court." The Emperor said, "Can I go to where he is?" The musician said, "His pride may revolt even there, thinking that he is to sing before a king." Akbar said, "Shall I go as your servant?" Tansen answered, "Yes, there is hope then." So both of them went up into the Himalayas, into the high mountains, where the sage had his temple of music in a cave, living with nature, in tune with Infinite. When they arrived the musician was on horseback and Akbar walking. The sage saw that the Emperor had humbled himself to come to hear his music, and he was willing to sing for him. And when he felt in the mood for singing, he sang. And his singing was great; it was a psychic phenomenon and nothing else. It seemed as if all the trees and plants of the forest were vibrating; it was a song of the universe. The deep impression made upon Akbar and Tansen was more than they could stand; they went into a state of trance, of rest, of peace. And while they were in that state, the Master left the cave. When they opened their eyes he was not there. The Emperor said, "O, what a strange phenomenon! But where has the master gone?" Tansen said, "You will never see him in this cave again, for once a man has got a taste of this, he will pursue it, even if it costs him his life. It is greater than anything in life."

When they were home again, the Emperor asked the musician one day, "Tell me what raga, what mode did your master sing?" Tansen told him the name of the raga, and sang it for him, but the Emperor was not content, saying, "Yes, it is the same music, but it is not the same spirit. Why is this?" The musician replied, "The reason is this, that while I sing before you, the Emperor of this country, my Master sings before God; that is the difference."

"Master of the tone" was the name given to a wise old man whom Alexandra David-Neel encountered in a remote monastery somewhere in the Himalayas near the Sino-Tibetan border. In a temple of the monastery, the old master (whose real name was Bönpo) played the *chang*, the ancient Tibetan cymbal whose edges are bent upward. All of a sudden, "an unearthly sound, similar to a confused screaming, shook the hall and pierced my brain." The peasants and the escorts of the European voyagers cried out in horror—and there was not one among them who was not totally sure he had seen a fiery snake: "The snake came out of the *chang* when the Lama struck it," one of them said, and the others agreed with that. Afterwards, the Lama told the voyagers:

I am the master of the tone. With the tone, I can kill living things and revive dead things. . . . All creatures, all things, even the seemingly lifeless ones, give off tones. Each being, each thing produces a special, characteristic tone which, however, changes as the states of the being or thing by which it is produced change. Why? Beings and things are conglomerations of smallest particles, the so-called *rdul phra;* they dance, and with their movements they produce tones.

This is what the teachings say: In the beginning was the wind. With its whirl, it created the *gjatams,* the primordial forms and the prime base of the world. This wind sounded; thus it was the sound which formed matter. The sounding of these first *gjatams* brought forth further forms which, by virtue of their sounds, in turn created new shapes. That is by no means a tale from days long passed, it is still that way. The sound brings forth all forms and all beings. The sound is that through which we live.

To our Western mind, legends and myths hail from ancient times, but the only reason they do so is because we have banished them there. In reality, they are *now.* They have come into existence because people need them. The rationalist believes he can do without myths. He doesn't want to be made uncertain of his "belief" that the rational mind is omnipotent. But perhaps this, too, is part of the change of consciousness we are witnessing: Contemporary man has a need again for myths and mythical things. One indication of this is the worldwide success of such authors as J. R. R. Tolkien, the enthusiasm with which young people devour his books. And, of course, there is a mythical core in the better Western and fantasy films and comic strips. Some of them are pure myth.

In Tolkien's *Silmarillion,* sound plays a decisive role in crucial passages. In the very first pages of the book, the world begins with a "song." When the patriarch Ilúvatar assigns to the Ainur—the elves and forefathers of mankind—the "fair regions" of "the Void" as their place of residence, he says:

> "Behold your music! . . . Of the theme that I have declared to you, I will now that ye make in harmony together a Great Music. And since I have kindled you the Flame Imperishable, ye shall show forth your powers in adorning this theme, each with his own thoughts and devices, if he will. But I will sit and hearken, and be glad that through you great beauty has been wakened into song."
>
> Then the voices of the Ainur, like unto harps and lutes, and pipes and trumpets, and viols and organs, and like unto countless choirs singing with words, began to fashion the theme of Ilúvatar to a great music; and a sound arose of endless interchanging melodies woven in harmony that passed beyond hearing into the depths and into the heights, and the places of the dwelling of Ilúvatar were filled to overflowing, and the music and the echo of the music went out into the Void, and it was not void. Never since have the Ainur made any music like this music, though it has been said that a greater still shall be made before Ilúvatar after the end of days. Then the themes of Ilúvatar

shall be played aright, and take Being in the moment of their utterance, for all shall then understand fully his intent in their part, and each shall know the comprehension of each, and Ilúvatar shall give to their thoughts the secret fire, being well pleased.

In Tolkien's world, evil also manifests itself musically at first; in fact, in the end it is musical dissonance that causes the dissonance in creation:

> But now Ilúvatar sat and hearkened, and for a great while it seemed good to him, for in the music there were no flaws. But as the theme progressed, it came into the heart of Melkor to interweave matters of his own imagining that were not in accord with the theme of Ilúvatar; for he sought therein to increase the power and glory of the part assigned to himself. . . .
>
> Some of these thoughts he now wove into his music, and straightway discord arose about him, and many that sang nigh him grew despondent, and their thought was disturbed and their music faltered; but some began to attune their music to his rather than to the thought which they had at first. Then the discord of Melkor spread ever wider, and the melodies which had been heard before foundered in a sea of turbulent sound. But Ilúvatar sat and hearkened until it seemed that about his throne there was a raging storm, as of dark waters that made war upon another in an endless wrath that would not be assuaged.

Another great author of modern myths is Michael Ende. His *Momo* relates the beautiful story of a "glittering pendulum" that brings forth ever new buds and blossoms and flowers, more and more beautiful with each swing of the pendulum. The actual force, however, that drives the "glittering pendulum" and the "shaft of light" beaming down from the dome of the heavenly vault, is a sound:

> At first it reminded her of wind whistling in distant treetops, but the sound swelled until it resembled the roar of a waterfall or the thunder of waves breaking on a rocky shore.
>
> More and more clearly, Momo perceived that this mighty sound consisted of innumerable notes whose constant changes of pitch were forever weaving different harmonies. It was music, yet it was also something else. All at once, she recognized it was the faraway music she had sometimes faintly heard while listening to the silence of a starry night.
>
> But now, as the sound became ever clearer and more glorious, she sensed that it was the resonant shaft of light that summoned each bud from the dark depths of the lake and fashioned it into a flower of unique and inimitable beauty.
>
> The longer she listened the more clearly she could make out

individual voices—not human voices, but notes such as might have been given forth by gold and silver and every other precious metal in existence. And then, beyond them, as it were, voices of quite another kind made themselves heard, infinitely remote yet indescribably powerful. As they gained strength, Momo began to distinguish words uttered in a language she had never heard before but could nonetheless understand. The sun and moon and planets and stars were telling her their own, true names, and their names signified what they did and how they all combined to make each hour-lily flower and fade in turn.

Since God created the world from sound, all music is directed back to God and the gods. That is why all music, first and foremost, is praise of God. This idea can also be found in the music concepts of almost all cultures of the world.

Ancient Indian mythology says that "the carriage of the sun had a shaft consisting only of songs of praise." In the *Rig-veda* of ancient India, the primordial rhythm and the primal sounds are fused into a "rustling song of praise" that "encouraged creation to grow and prosper."

The most beautiful expression of this thought, however, has been created by those singers who stand at the outset of Christian and Jewish poetry (and music!): the psalmists. Thousands of years ago, in the four final hymns of the Psalms (from Psalm 147 to 150), they created the following verses, which have inspired musicians and composers (from Johann Sebastian Bach to Duke Ellington) time and again in the course of centuries to musical settings filled with thanks and praise:

> Sing unto the Lord a new song. . . .
> Let them praise his name in the dance: let them sing praises unto him with the timbrel and harp.
>
> (Psalm 149)

> Praise ye the Lord.
> Praise God in his sanctuary: praise him in the firmament of his power.
> Praise him for his mighty acts: praise him according to his excellent greatness.
> Praise him with the sound of the trumpet: praise him with the psaltery and harp.
> Praise him with the timbrel and dance: praise him with stringed instruments and organs.
> Praise him upon the loud cymbals: praise him upon the high sounding cymbals.
> Let everything that hath breath praise the Lord. Praise ye the Lord.
>
> (Psalm 150)

Music for Listening to the Eleventh Chapter

Folklore e Bossa Nova do Brasil. Includes the piece "Macumba" by the Brazilian percussionists Rubens and Georghingho. Produced by Joachim E. Berendt. MPS/Polydor Intern. 00821 8561.

Johann Sebastian Bach. *Motets: "Singet dem Herrn ein Neues Lied."* Angel S-36804.

Duke Ellington. "Praise God" from the *Second Sacred Concert.* With the Ellington Big Band and Alice Babs, soprano. Prestige 24045 (2 LPs).

PART TWO

PART TWO

1 🐚 Zen and Modern Japan

I.

A FRIEND OF MINE travels to Japan in order to meditate at a Zen monastery. After visiting a number of wrong addresses, he is finally directed to a temple near the Sea of Japan at a point west of Tokyo. The abbot there, the Zen master, is supposed to speak English, and it is said that they accept foreigners. When he arrives at the monastery, the only person he finds is a man working in the garden, transporting manure in a wheel barrow . . . My friend asks him if it is possible to see the master. The gardener ushers him to the portico, where he is made to wait. For more than an hour. Then another monk appears and invites him inside, and finally he stands before the Zen master, who is sitting on an elevated platform. It is—the gardener who was carting the manure.

The Japanese word *zen* comes from the Chinese *ch'an*, which in turn comes from India, from the Sanskrit word *dhyana*, meaning "teaching, lore" and "meditation."

Modern linguists (the wiser ones among them) have pointed out how mysteriously "right" our language is in that concepts, perceived as incompatible opposites by Western rational man, have grown from the same linguistic root. Word pairs with such contrary meanings as *hell* and *holy*, *must* and *muse*, *cold* and the Italian *calda* (which means "warm"), *whole* and *hole*, *logos* (the word and the spirit that were "in the beginning") and *lie*, *divine* (from French *dieu*, which comes from

Sanskrit *deva,* "god") and *devil,* all go back to the same "primal words" and "primal roots." What appears to us as "duality" is, in reality, "nonduality." Duality is *maya,* mere appearance; it is void and nothing.

The Japanese words *ku* ("void, hollowness") and *mu* ("nothing") are key words in Zen. Meditators continually repeat "Mu! Mu! Mu!" either silently or out loud, even screaming it (toward the end of a long meditation), for hours, days, even weeks in order to become empty, empty of all the trivia with which we stuff ourselves, to make room for the only fullness that counts, the fullness of being that is the fullness of nothing (whichisthefullnessofbeingwhichisthefullnessofnothingwhich isthefullnessofbeingwhichis . . .).

"The fullness of being that is the fullness of nothing" seems an absurdity to the rational, Western mind. That is just the point: Part of Zen is absurdity, and part of absurdity is laughing about it. "What is the basic principle of Zen?" a pupil once asked the Zen master Joshu. The answer: "The cypress tree in the courtyard." Or, "The Goddess Kannon (the goddess of mercy, who is especially well loved by the Japanese) has a thousand hands, each hand has an eye, which is the true eye? Answer me quickly!" A famous Zen exercise is this: Go into the mountains early in the morning and roar with laughter at the rock face in front of you. (You might try that sometime! You will continue laughing inside all day long, and all of your problems will become laughable.)

The *Bhagavadgita,* one of the great books of Indian wisdom from a time long before Zen came to Japan, speaks of laughter as the "source of meditation": One is supposed to meditate on the roaring laughter of Lord Vishnu, imagining that it keeps on roaring in one's own abdomen.

II.

North of Tokyo, we are led into a large factory hall, where 3,032 female workers (the exact number is part of it; in the Western world, you would probably say "more than three thousand"), working with magnifying glasses, are placing minute electronic parts on printed circuits in matchbox-sized casings. At the end of each hour, there is a five-minute break. The 3,032 women in their white smocks get up and do breathing exercises, following instructions from the intercom: inhaling when a high tone is sounded, exhaling when a deep tone comes. Subsequently they all bow and, speaking in chorus, wish their company business success; then they sit down again, place their magnifying glasses over their eyes, and continue working.

Zen may have to do with modern-day Japan as little as the teachings of Christ have to do with present-day America or Europe. When touring Japan, in the hotels where you stay, in the companies you visit, among the people you meet, you will hardly find anyone who truly understands Zen; and yet, as Eshin Nishimura, professor of Zen sciences at Hanazono University in Kyoto, has remarked, "there has probably never been a time where Zen was as widespread as it is today." The high-ranking executive who, each morning on the way to his office, makes a stop at a Zen monastery to meditate there for an hour, is nothing unusual. He meditates in *zazen*, "sitting", for twenty-five minutes; then for ten minutes while walking, in so-called *kinhin*, slowly putting one foot in front of the other; then twenty-five minutes more in a sitting posture. Afterward he drives to his office, and all day he is filled with the kind of concentration and precision, quick-wittedness and speed which are so strikingly characteristic of the Japanese business world. The executive is convinced that all these characteristics come from meditation. A friend told me: "You have no idea how many people do that. Surely some of the best."

A famous haiku, written by Basho, the eighteenth-century master of the Japanese miniature poem, is the following:

> When I look carefully
> I see the *nazuna* blooming
> By the hedge!

The nazuna is a very small flower. It is easily overlooked, for it grows hidden in hedges and ditches, underneath bushes and rocks. It blossoms for a few days only. One really has to look for it to find it. Basho wants to say: The laborious search for the nazuna blossom, the keen attention is worth the effort, because the nazuna flower is very beautiful.

Basho's haiku is totally Zen. But it is also totally modern-day Japan. A Japanese university professor with whom I discussed the living conditions in Tokyo, the largest, loudest, wildest, most turbulent, most confusing, most frantic city of the world, said: "The twelve million people living in those narrow streets, in those tiny, rickety houses with papier-mâché walls, love the small things: a single flower—often not even that, simply a dry twig, perhaps a leaf—or a nicely grained rock, an ink drawing consisting of a few lines only, or even just a single character of traditional Chinese writing in an otherwise empty room. . . . The flower stands for spring, the twig for the forest, the rock for the ocean or the mountains, the Chinese character for the wisdom of the world. . . . These people are able to survive in their city only because the small things symbolize to them what in their everyday lives is so unreachably far removed from them."

Tokyo—I don't know whether people in America or Europe can imagine what that means: almost forty thousand people per square mile, the largest mass of human beings in the world; four square feet is the average living space per person, which means that most people have much less.

Hardly anyone living in this "largest slum of the world" (as the Japanese newspaper *Asahi* once put it) knows anything about Zen. But the twig in an empty, unfurnished room—that *is* Zen, the beauty of emptiness and hollowness, of *ku* and *mu*.

III.

If Christianity means what is written in the Sermon on the Mount, then only very few Westerners are Christians. What this Western world thinks and feels and does, however, is unthinkable, incomprehensible without two thousand years of Christianity. In fact, philosophers and sociologists have emphasized that even Marxism is nothing other than a Christian "counterworld" unthinkable without the Christian ideals and principles that are ever present in the concept of Marxism, much more so than they are in capitalism.

In this sense (only much more so) Japan is unthinkable without Zen. D. T. Suzuki, the great Japanese philosopher of Buddhism, once said: "Whether the Japanese realize it or not, Zen is present everywhere. If you know Zen, you will find its traces all over Japan." In his book *Zen: Weg zur Erleuchtung ("Zen—Path to Enlightenment")*, Father Hugo Makibi Enomiya-Lassalle writes: "There was and still is hardly a Japanese who is not influenced by Zen in his innermost feelings." He talks about the famous Japanese *do*s, the "ways": the "way of tea" as displayed in the Japanese tea ceremony; the "way of the bow," the *kyu-do* of the archers; the "way of writing" *(sho-do*, the ancient Japanese art of calligraphy); the "way of the flowers" *(ka-do)*; the "way of wrestling" *(ju-do)*; or the "way of fencing" *(ken-do)*: "There is *one* spirit in all these paths, and that is the spirit of Zen."

The *do*s of Zen are paths into everyday life. That's what the ancient Chinese and Japanese sages created them for. Take a ride out into one of the classical Japanese landscapes—to Matsushima, for instance, a half day's trip north of Tokyo: a sea of islands, hundreds of rocky isles in shimmering colors; on each—or almost each—of them just one or two pines bent by wind and weather, the archetype of a Japanese landscape. Thousands of tourists travel there, also Americans and Europeans; yet there is a difference in the way the Japanese people look at it: totally immersed, even devoutly. Sometimes you will see someone bowing, and you have the sense that in their thoughts they all bow down. To the islands. To the gnarled pines. And in springtime to the *sakura*s, the cherry blossoms . . . In writing this, I am committing one of those typically Western faults of imprecision. It is not enough to say simply *"sakura."* Any Japanese knows that there are four *sakura* periods, each one with its own name. Any Japanese, including the modern big-city dweller, associates precise concepts with each of the four cherry-blossom states: Whether the blossom has four or eight petals, what hue it has, whether the petals are blown away by the wind or pushed off by new shoots, which form they have, and—this is also important—what all of that symbolizes. Entire books have been written on cherry blossoms.

In the evening, after returning to Tokyo, the Western guest will tell his Japanese friends about his trip to the country to see the *sakura;* and they will ask about the number, the form and hue of the petals, the way the petals drop, and the names of the strains of cherry tree. All of these are topics for long conversations. If his answers are as imprecise as they usually are from Westerners, the Japanese think: Maybe he didn't go to the country after all and he is telling us about it only to make us feel good. They simply cannot imagine that someone who *really* saw something has not perceived and remembered it all precisely.

What has actually made Japanese industry so successful? Is it not, here too, the love for detail? The precision? The attentiveness? The care for each single, minute element? The "finickiness" that goes into realizing in a minute space the most complex constructions and circuitry: the Japanese are masters thereof. It is no accident that electronic "chips"—integrated circuits capable of commanding one hundred thousand (and soon many more!) electronic functions on a slice of material smaller than half a square inch, although not invented in Japan, have been implemented and developed there much faster and more widely than anywhere else—and all that with an enthusiasm as if it were something arch-Japanese (as was also the case with the transistor, the printed circuit, the quartz watch, and so on—in fact, with everything requiring that technical processes be condensed into very small spaces).

In all cultures, it is the women who preserve tradition. At no time in Japan is the Western observer more surprised to realize that preciseness and love for detail are part of the great heritage of that country, as when a Japanese woman dons a kimono, especially a precious one worn only on festive occasions. On the surface, there is not much to it: the actual kimono (which is only the outer garment) and the obi (the belt). When I counted, I found thirty-eight parts belonging to a kimono, including sashes, ribbons, strings and cords, stockings and socks. An inexpensive one will cost you upward of two thousand dollars, and it takes two to three hours (often longer) to put it on correctly. Again and again in the process, it will happen that the woman will deem it necessary, absolutely imperative, to begin again at a certain point. She will then take off five, six, seven parts of the outfit, because (supposedly) she has made a "mistake" somewhere, with one of her undergarments that nobody will ever see; with one of the many ribbons or strings that, were it left out, would not be missed by anyone, not even by the woman herself; or when draping a fold that will be covered by half a dozen further folds. Often, when she is finished—after hours not of dabbling around but of intense activity—she still may not be able to go to the party or to the reception for which she has put on the kimono, because she is so exhausted now that she needs to rest, at least for an hour. It is a hard day's work to don a kimono. When she wears it, however, smiling and laughing, talking and chirping and giggling the whole evening, all trouble is forgotten. Any other woman, no matter in what country (if it were possible anywhere else to get a woman to undergo such a process) would be jaded all night long after such torture.

Once I was co-producer of a television program with a Japanese television company. After we had worked out the entire show with the typical Japanese delight in detail in a series of day-long conferences, the director asked me to attend one further meeting. The entire staff was invited. The topic was: How was the program to be opened by a Japanese MC in Japanese and by me in German? Obviously, the question would have been answered in the Western world in a matter of ten or fifteen minutes. In Japan, the discussion of this small problem lasted seven hours. After three hours I was tired, after five hours I became highly irritable, after seven hours I was totally exhausted. There was not one detail that was not mentioned, discussed, and flogged to death. And everyone in the staff took part in it, more than a dozen persons, each with extreme care and in full detail. Many of them made small graphs and sketches, as almost everything in Japan is perceived graphically.

On the following day, Mr. Domei (Domei-san, as the director was called) asked me to come to another meeting, again labeled as "final" but "absolutely necessary." I attended reluctantly, and I made him feel that. There really was nothing left to talk about. After an hour I said I would have to leave. Now he became annoyed in that traditional Japanese way of self-control which radiates annoyance and anger so much more effectively than the ranting and raving that is usual in the West. He gave me the impression I had left the staff at the most important moment of our whole collaboration. During the following days I sensed that I had hurt his feelings. But it took years of working in Japan with Japanese to understand why. I had violated the form. Part of this form is the ancient consciousness, which has remained alive and active for most modern Japanese, that the details are crucial. This consciousness has to do with the order of things, and this, in turn, with "style," with the "correct" way of living. That was the reason why Domei-san had reacted the way he did. He had sensed a danger to this order. It is possible, however, that he himself was not even aware of that, since he is a modern television director used to thinking in Western categories.

IV.

No nation does so much photographing as the Japanese do. Wherever they are, they carry their cameras with them and shoot, shoot, shoot . . . The average Japanese consumption of photographic film is four times greater than that in the Western world. What in heaven's name do they do with all these pictures? I discussed this question in a circle of Japanese friends. The Westerner that I am says: Industry has manipulated the individual. And I point out the gigantic advertising efforts of the Japanese photo and film industry. But my friends are correct when they counter: Manipulation by industry and the flood of advertising exist in America and Europe, too. After an extensive discussion back and forth we arrive at the following: Photography preserves the moment, that one unrepeatable, uncomparable moment which otherwise would now—now!—be forgotten, lost forever . . . The clicking of millions of Japanese cameras in the hands of Japanese people all over the world seems to be constantly saying: Now! Now! Now!

The "now" is just as important for Zen as the nothing and the void, the *mu* and the *ku*. It is practical Zen wisdom to do everything as if it were the only time, with utter concentration on doing it at this very moment and without thinking of future or past. And it is a deep Zen conviction that eternity is "now!"—not, as Christianity says, something beyond the foreseeable future and beyond death, something one might enter into at some undefined point in time. You enter eternity at each and every moment, with each and every "Now!" Hence the "now" counts and the idea of an endless period of time hardly exists. The past has passed, even only by seconds, and the future does not yet exist. It might exist tomorrow. Or in a few minutes. But not "now." Whoever is not living in the "now" lives nowhere.

In the garden of the famous Kokedera moss temple in Kyoto (but also in other Zen gardens all over Japan), small creeks are regulated by bamboo lever pumps that periodically fill with water, tip over, and run out. Each time they tip, they generate a hollow, wooden bamboo sound to be heard all over the Zen garden and the entire temple area; this tone has been sounding for centuries, varied only by the creek's changing water-level. "Do you know what the bamboo says when it goes 'click'?" asked the monk who was guiding us through the garden. Then he answered his own question: "Now! Now! Now!" It is almost unnecessary to add that a Christian perceives this bamboo tone quite differently, as a reminder that time keeps running, that we keep getting older, that we all must die, and perhaps as a reminder of the hereafter. But not of the "Now!"

Occasionally one reads reports in Japanese newspapers about lovers who have died together, at the moment when their love was at its highest fulfillment. These lovers will gaze at a landscape all night long—a waterfall, a rock in the sea, or the full moon—but not for the sake of saying: Now I could die! That would suit Western romanticism, but the attitude of the Japanese is quite the opposite: They do not talk about it. They just do it. They die. As one way to preserve the "now." There is something commonplace in the way they do it: "It's nothing worth talking about." Along with this goes the effort to cause as little trouble as possible for everybody else. If they leave anything written at all, it will most likely be a note of apology for certain unavoidable problems they are causing like the blood that has to be cleaned up or the bodies that have to be removed.

The Japanese consciousness of the "now" is shown impressively in Nagisa Oshima's famous movie *Ai no korida* (which means something like "The Struggle of Love," a much more fitting title than *In the Realm of the Senses,* the international title given to this film). The "Struggle of Love," the "Now!" of this struggle and of this love culminates in the final scene of the movie, when death comes at the moment of orgasm, a death that preserves the most extreme form of "Now!" human beings can experience: the victory of "now" over time. Love is always "now." That's why it has to be experienced over and over again.

V.

Connected with the century-old training to do a thing in its entirety, to do it now, with extreme concentration on this "now," are precision, devotion, endurance, exactness, a stoic composure, and a love for detail—all characteristics of millions of people (who know little or nothing of Zen) working in Japanese industry, which owes its power, its superiority, and its stability to these characteristics.

For centuries, the Zen masters have taught their pupils exactly that: Do one thing. Only this one thing. Again and again. Do it completely. In each moment. Do not think of anything else—neither anything which was before nor anything still to come. Think of the Now!

How different this attitude to life is from our Western attitude, where one is constantly under pressure to do different things at the same time (in fact, where one is considered all the "better" the more things one is able "to take care of" simultaneously)! In everything we do is an awareness of history, of past and future, and of something further, of a "further meaning" of the matter of concern . . .

For this reason, because the only thing that matters is the "Now!" and "doing one thing only," meditation is the central concern of Zen. That is what meditation insists upon, on being totally "there," being "clear, open, cloudless," as a chant by the Chinese Zen patriarch Seng-ts'an puts it.

The concentration on the "Now," doing one thing fully, becoming empty so that fullness may appear—all these things make one active. There is no doubt in my mind that this is the actual reason for the immense, fascinating, antlike activity of the Japanese people.

"The body of one single truthful man exhausts the ten directions of the universe," says the Zen master Dogen. To which Kakichi Kadowaki, a contemporary Japanese Jesuit, adds: "This means that body and spirit, when they are permeated by absolute nothingness, are overflowing with activity." Then he tells the story of a young Catholic nun who had meditated in Zen fashion for eight days, eight to nine hours each day, and then, by a wide margin, won a series of sports competitions, which she had not been particularly interested in before. Said the nun: "Since I had learned Zen, I was able to forget myself and to participate actively in the different competitions without inhibitions." And Kadowaki comments.

> The nun had grown up in the usual lifestyle of a Catholic convent. . . . But before taking part in the meditation course, she had displayed

none of this exuberant vitality. Hers was more the unobtrusive, solid life you find among the sisters of a Christian convent, and you hardly had the impression that she was living with all her energy and heart.

What Kadowaki describes here is the path to success in the many Japanese sports connected with Zen: archery, judo, karate, aikido, and the various martial arts—and it is striking that these are all disciplines wherein one has to become "entirely one" with the target or the opponent, putting oneself in the position of the target or the opponent, identifying oneself with them.

VI.

Let me tell you about a special meeting with a Japanese woman on my first trip to Japan in the early 1960s, when I was still unaware of all these things. It was in the Nikko temple region, north of Tokyo. We were tourists, mostly Japanese, a few Westerners. At the temple entrance, we drew fortune sticks from a vessel. There were a few Japanese characters on each stick, and the monk who was holding the vessel interpreted them for us. From the group surrounding the monk with his fortune sticks, it was the turn of a young woman standing directly in front of me. The monk told her what her stick meant. She laughed. Then it was my turn to draw a stick. The monk talked to me in Japanese, and she translated for me. It had to do with women and love. As it seemed, her fortune stick had to do with men and love. Both of us had to laugh, and that's the way we met.

We talked, went for a walk, drank tea, went for another walk, talked some more, listened to music at a hi-fi sales stand, went to dinner and afterward to a movie—all things young people in the Western world would also do. After the movie, however, she took the initiative—and then things took a different turn:

All night long (let me be more precise, because it sounds unbelievable: from eleven that night, when the movie was over, until five or five-thirty in the morning, when the sun was rising) we sat by Lake Chuzenji near Nikko, watching the full moon and in its light a rock island with a cedar on it, the classical Japanese "moon-watching party." She and I each sat on a rock, five feet apart from each other. Not once did we touch.

I am still not sure why I went along with that. Perhaps I thought it would be interesting to have a totally Japanese experience. We hardly talked at all; for seven hours, all we did was gaze at the full moon, the lake, the rock, and the cedar.

When morning came I understood: It was a test. Perhaps I understood it better than the Japanese woman herself, who was only following a convention without giving it a lot of thought. From that point on, she was my girlfriend. Of course it was a Zen test, although she had no idea of Zen. A test that was far more difficult, more productive, more precise, and more fulfilling than the endless talk with which Western men try to come on to women.

Naturally this night was torture for me, the man from Europe. But the longer we sat there, the more it became clear to me that something else existed next to the strain of the situation: I felt—I began to sense it even after one or two hours, and the feeling grew all night long—how the moon was filling me, how I—there are no other words for it—"became one" with it. Even days after this experience, I had a different body feeling, lighter, more transparent, clearer, more vibrant, filled with light . . .

VII.

I can understand it if a reader should say: The things you describe in this chapter as the effects of Zen are only remnants, many of which show signs of degeneration and decay. That may be so, but if even *de*ficiency is so *ef*ficient, is still capable of permeating life and lifestyle in all their manifestations so strongly and powerfully—how powerful the heritage of Zen must be even today!

The thought that this heritage is being swept aside by Japan's "turn to the West" presents itself, but it does not hold true upon closer inspection. The opposite is true. In the same way as the idea that Japan is losing its own tradition in the wake of modern high technology is itself a Western one. Japan is not only one of the most "modern" countries of the world but at the same time also one of the most "conservative" nations, in the true and original sense of the word "conservative." Again and again, one can find support for the impression that both "modernity" and "conservativism" grow under each other's influence in a dialectical process for which there is no comparison in the Western world.

Experts in Japanese art and culture have emphasized that new discoveries in literature, painting, sculpture, architecture, music, science, and so forth have never displaced tradition, but rather have supplemented and enriched it. Almost nowhere has the new taken the place of the old (as has often been the case in the development of Western art). Almost always the effect of a new development is one of opening up and widening.

In their many cultural encounters with China and Korea in the course of hundreds of years, whatever the Japanese adopted from these nations sooner or later led to finding typically Japanese solutions. The more Japanese art seemed to become "Chinese," the more intensely it demonstrated typically "Japanese" traits only a few years later. It was as if the foreign influences mainly served to strengthen the Japanese elements. The saturation with Chinese education and Confucianist ethics in the poetry of the Nara period (during the eighth century), for instance, only two generations later (at the Kyoto court), led to the crystallization of a highly developed aestheticism that differed fundamentally from anything comparable in China. In painting and sculpture, the Nara and early Heian periods were characterized by a truly overwhelming Chinese influence, but during the later phases of the Heian period (around the year 940) the pendulum began to swing in the opposite direction. When the Kamakura period began (around 1185), Japanese artists had absorbed the Chinese influences so totally that the latter were barely perceivable as cultural stimuli, while the art reappeared as "purely Japanese." Architecture also provides us with examples. Twice in its history (during the seventh to eighth centuries and again during the thirteenth century), Japanese architecture experienced a "Chinese wave," each time with the same result: Immediately afterward, the Japanese character came through all the more clearly. And we have not yet said anything about the uniquely Japanese element of refinement, which did not come in the wake of the adaptation of foreign stimuli but rather became effective parallel with it (as has been seen again since the Japanese have begun to adopt modern Western technology).

Chinese art has a tendency to transport a "message," a moral, a maxim, an instruction to take to heart. Japanese art, however, wants to transport nothing but itself. There is a strange absence of "message" almost everywhere in Japanese art. A famous example is the tea ceremony, the *chanoyu*. Almost everything belonging to it came from China; yet the ceremony, as it developed during the fifteenth century under the patronage of Yoshimara, is so Japanese that its Chinese origins today have only academic relevance. The point of the ceremony is—the ceremony. Again we find the Zen ideal that a thing be done for its own sake—only this *one* thing, but that completely. This leaves no room for messages. (I am aware of the fact that this ideal also originated in China, but there it was covered up by the Confucianist ideal to constantly aim for something.)

When Japan opened itself up to the Portuguese and the Dutch during the sixteenth century it showed all signs of enthusiasm and an apparently unlimited will to adapt. Only a few years later, however, isolationism began and with it an even stronger accent on "Japanese" elements. It makes no difference whether this process took place consciously or unconsciously. Quite the opposite, the fact that it took place more unconsciously during some phases of Japanese history and more consciously during others, makes it appear that much more elementary. It is important to understand that there is no parallel to this kind of reaction in the Western world. If you take a look at the European history of art and culture, for instance, you can assume that at a certain point in time and in a particular location, say, Gothic style took the place of Romanesque, or Baroque that of Renaissance. If you use similar concepts when looking at the Japanese development, however, you commit the sin of oversimplification. In their comprehensive work on Japanese art and culture, the French cultural historians Danielle and Vadime Elisseeff draw the following conclusion: "Perhaps one has to look for one of the sources of the extraordinary wealth of Japanese art in the fact that one style was never abandoned exclusively in favor of introducing something new. Innovations served to enrich, not to replace."

It is not very plausible to assume that this type of cultural reaction, having been repeated over such a long period of time—from the sixth to the nineteenth century—should suddenly be relinquished in our century. Of course, the phenomenon, which can legitimately be called the Japanese trait *par excellence,* remains alive in the encounter of Japan with the Western world and (which makes us return to the outset of this deliberation) in the meeting of Zen and Western technology. Here too, you find the Japanese dialectic of mutual enrichment.

The fact, by the way, that in Japanese art an earlier period is not so much suppressed by as supplemented by the succeeding period has an ethical (if not to say: moral) basis that is directly connected with Zen (and also with Confucianism). This basis can be found in *giri.* Once more Danielle and Vadime Elisseeff: *"Giri* expresses grateful respect, a feeling of enrichment as well as of obligation, also the essence of the ties linking the pupil to his master. . . . Because of *giri,* the pupil may never ignore the capabilities of his master as that would mean committing an impropriety."

Giri has led to an "astounding continuity" in Japanese art. *Giri* is still alive in modern-day Japan, even in the way factory workers feel respectfully affiliated with their foreman, office workers with their department head, or artists with their teacher. *Giri* is the reason why all these fields (and countless others) clearly remain Japanese even though they may seem "westernized" in the eyes of the superficial observer. The model for the *giri*-relationship is the association between the *roshi,* the Zen master, and his pupil.

VIII.

You may have been asking: How come we keep hearing that the Japanese are adverse to anything religious? I can tell you fairly exactly where that comes from, because I witnessed the creation of this misconception several times—the last time in 1975 when visiting with a group of Protestant church people from the United States who were on tour in Japan. Again and again they asked their Japanese hosts with embarrassing directness: "Do you believe in God?" Almost always they received evasive answers—or a straightforward "No," both given with the typical Japanese smile. None of the visitors was aware that the question whether one believes in God can actually be posed only from the viewpoint of three world-religions (Christianity, Judaism, Islam) because of its fixation on a so-called "personal God." If you ask the wrong question you will get a wrong answer. That is what the smile means: I'm sorry, but your question doesn't mean anything to me.

Elias Canetti's statement, which forms one of the epigraphs at the beginning of this book, has been made reality in no other country more intensely than in Japan. Nowhere else have so many people what can be called their "own religion."

From guitarist John McLaughlin I learned a wonderful statement by Vivekananda: "God comes to Earth to found a religion and everything is very beautiful, but the Devil comes right behind him and organizes it." Apart from a few so-called "new religions," there is no "organized religion," no "church" in Japan. Many Western visitors to Japan who miss religion in that country confuse religion with institutionalized churches, something they also do in their own countries, thus further damaging their own Christian religion. (It seems to me that this is one of the greatest miracles of Jesus Christ: that even the remnants left of Him, after two thousand years of misuse by the appointed representatives of the various Christian churches, are able to help so many people and to still bring some grace to the whole world).

To ask whether someone believes in God has something indiscreet and nagging about it, something that violates the private sphere. It is almost as if one were asking: Who did you sleep with last night? A society that takes as much care in protecting privacy and the personal sphere as the Japanese do is sensitive in this field.

It is also true that the Japanese are a nation "living in this world." Nothing said so far contradicts that statement, not even the countless "new religions" professed by millions of Japanese, who are "simultaneously" Buddhists or Shintoists or both. They get married in a Shinto ritual, their burial is Buddhist, and in between they may belong to one or two "new religions." According to Western thinking, if you have religion, it should be one religion. The Japanese idea is rather the opposite: the more religions, the better! We have to understand that the word "religiousness," as it is used in the Western world, is much too heavily influenced by Christian concepts and hence is not the appropriate term for other parts of the world. For that reason, it is being replaced more and more by the concept of "spirituality." Zen is certainly no religion, but Zen is "spiritual."

IX.

In his book *The Three Pillars of Zen,* Philip Kapleau tells a story in which anyone who has frequent contact with Japanese will recognize today's Japan:

> One day a man of the people said to Zen Master Ikkyu [1394–1481], "Master, will you please write for me some maxims of the highest wisdom?"
> Ikkyu immediately took his brush and wrote the word "Attention."
> "Is that all?" asked the man. "Will you not add something more?"
> Ikkyu then wrote twice running: "Attention. Attention."
> "Well," remarked the man rather irritably, "I really don't see much depth or subtlety in what you have just written."
> Then Ikkyu wrote the same word three times running: "Attention. Attention. Attention." Half-angered, the man demanded: "What does that word 'Attention' mean anyway?"
> And Ikkyu answered gently: "Attention means attention."

2 🐚   India and Jazz

I want the windows and doors of my house to be wide open. I want the
cultures of all lands to blow freely about my house, but I refuse to be
blown off my feet by any of them.

—Mahatma Gandhi

1. Indian Music and Its Relationship to Jazz

THE FRENCH ETHNOMUSICOLOGIST Alain Daniélou, one of
the West's top experts in the field of Indian music, once said:

> Two basic traits are characteristic of music in India. For one thing,
> in all its various forms its basic concept is vocal; thus even pure
> instrumental music always shows that the human voice, its tone color
> and its breathing technique, served as a model. For another thing,
> Indian music is modal music in the true sense; it knows no change of
> keys, that is, it sticks to one steady, unvarying ground tone. . . . A
> crucial role is played by embellishments, tone colors, and, above all, by
> intervals that do not exist in Western well-tempered music. A music
> created from this vantage point . . . can find its musical expression
> only in improvisation.

Daniélou is not a jazz specialist; yet his statement shows immediately
(and perhaps more convincingly than it would if he were a jazz expert)
how many similarities exist between jazz and Indian music. Jazz, too, is
vocally conceived, even in its instrumental forms. Nor does jazz limit
itself to the tone reservoir of Western tempered tuning. Jazz musicians
—singers and instrumentalists alike (except, of course, piano players,
who have no choice)—have never limited themselves to the well-
tempered scale. Theoretically, the Indian octave consists of sixty-six

shrutis (microtones); in musical praxis there are twenty-two tones per octave, almost twice the number in the Western octave! You can find approximately that number of tones in the singing of the great old blues men like Blind Lemon Jefferson or Leadbelly or their countless successors all the way down to modern black soul and funk, or in the free-jazz improvisations of players like Albert Ayler, Joseph Jarman, Roscoe Mitchell, and dozens of others all over the world. Of course, their music is "modal," too.

The existence of so-called *blue notes* most clearly demonstrates the inadequacy of European tempered tuning for jazz. The idea that there are only two blue notes in jazz, the third and the seventh (the classic blues notes of traditional jazz), should once and for all be discarded. Since the emergence of bebop in the forties, the fifth step, the so-called *flatted fifth*, can also be considered a blue note; and since the advent of free jazz, practically every note in the scale can be played "flatted," can be felt and played "blue." Jazz and fusion guitarist Larry Coryell was completely right when he said, "I hear a lot of blues in Indian music."

The first jazz musician to emphasize the parallels between jazz and Indian music, not only in his music but also in theory, was the trumpeter and band leader Don Ellis, who died in 1978. Between 1965 and 1976, he contributed a number of articles to the (unfortunately now defunct) outstanding American magazine *Jazz*. Ellis was particularly fascinated by the wealth of rhythmical possibilities in Indian music. He wrote:

> Jazz musicians like to think of themselves as masters of rhythm (and in comparison to European music they are in the forefront), but I would like to demonstrate how crude and primitive the conventional jazz musician's grasp of rhythm is in comparison with Indian music. . . . The best and most advanced jazz drummer that ever lived is a mere novice compared to a good tabla player from India. . . . The same thing applies not only to players of rhythm instruments but also to players of melody instruments.

One has to add, however, that jazz musicians have been so receptive to Indian music because of their strong interest in rhythm. They have sensed that they could learn from it. Don Ellis again:

> Any jazz musician who desires to really acquire a grasp of rhythm should, if at all possible, study Indian music. . . . If a number of jazz musicians would do so, this could pave the way for one of the most important advances jazz could make. It would broaden the whole rhythmic vocabulary of jazz.

Ellis said this in 1965, and in the meantime precisely that has happened. Drummer Milford Graves, for instance, said that studying Indian music and tabla "opened me up, gave me ideas . . . , another direction to look into." Similar experiences have been reported by dozens of modern jazz drummers, from Andrew Cyrille and Paul Motian in the United States to Pierre Favre and Edvard Vesala in Europe.

It also was Don Ellis who pointed out that Indian music is played with a different—non-Western—concept of time. In India a single piece of music can last many hours, even an entire night. Since the early sixties, under Coltrane's influence, jazz pieces have become increasingly longer. Of course, the duration of a piece is only a superficial indication of a different time concept. In *The Jazz Book* I showed (in more detail than space allows here) that a non-Western time feeling plays a decisive role in jazz, and that the phenomenon of swing arises from the fact that jazz is played with two different concepts of time, one Western and one non-Western. That is the actual reason why all technical-academic analyses of swing are unsatisfactory and, indeed, are considered inadequate by musicians as soon as they are applied to practical music-making. Here, too, the spiritual aspect is more important than the technical one—which is another reason why so many jazz musicians are fascinated by Indian music: they recognize in it a time concept they can relate to, one that is richer and markedly more intricate than that of Western music.

It is necessary at this point to say a few words about the mysteries of Indian music. Its *tala*s, its rhythmic sequences—incomprehensible for Western listeners—can be as long as 108 beats; yet the Indian ear is constantly aware of where the *sam* falls (jazz musicians would call it the "one") as easily as if it were simple 4/4 or 6/8 time. However far apart the players may have moved in their elaborations of the most intricate rhythmical subdivisions, on the *sam* they have to come back together again. When they do so, the audience will often break out in loud cheers, thereby venting the enormous tension that has built up in the constant, anxious question: Are they going to make it? Are they going to meet? *Tala:* the word combines the two syllables *ta* (from *tandava*, Shiva's cosmic dance) and *la* (from *Lasya*, the name of one of Shiva's [dance] partners), implying a cosmic as well as an erotic musical union, one standing for the other.

The ragas, too, can be dealt with here only in a cursory manner. They are not keys in the Western sense (in India the keys are called *tāt*), although ragas combine all those things that in Western music break down into theme, key, tuning, phrasing, form, and even composition. The ancient Sanskrit sages gave the following definition: *Ranjayati iti ragah* ("That which colors the spirit is a raga"). Many musicians have emotional qualms about identifying themselves as composers of ragas, because actually a raga is not a work of composition. A raga is "discovered as a zoologist may discover a new animal species or as a geographer may discover a new island" (Ravi Shankar). In other words, a raga—each raga—exists from the beginning; it is a musical archetype.

In theory the number of ragas is unlimited. In South India alone, there are 5,831 ragas known by their individual titles. Even an average musician is expected to have mastered at least seventy to eighty ragas. This word "mastering," as I mentioned earlier, implies years of practicing—a study that goes far beyond the comparable studies of scales and études in Western music. Each interval, each individual tone, is packed to the brim with content, expressivity, and individuality: The octave is a peacock (with fanned tail), the major second a bull, the third a sheep, the fourth a crane, the fifth a cuckoo, the sixth a horse (for some also a frog), the seventh an elephant. Others connect the seven main tones (in India SA, RI, GA, MA, PA, DHA, NI) with the human being: SA, the tonic, is the soul, followed in sequence by the head (the directive through the second!), arms (third), chest (fourth), neck (fifth), hip (sixth), and feet (seventh).

In the face of the wealth of parallels and relationships between these two musical worlds, it is surprising that jazz musicians did not become interested in Indian music much earlier, because all these features interest them: widening the range of rhythmical possibilities, enlarging and "stretching" the tempered scale, gaining the freedom to have more tones at their disposal than is possible in tempered tuning, as well as improvisation, modality, vocal conception of instrumental music, and the strong accent on the personal sound . . . Parallels can be found even in details: The principle of *call* and *response*—of crucial importance in the development of black music from Africa all the way down to the "conversations" between the various sections of a big band—exists in the music of India, too. There it is called *javab savad*. Of course, both cultures are also familiar with the concept of the musical *battle* (a "sportive" competition that is actually foreign to the European mind) or the *chase*, when the musicians "run" after each other, initially changing turns after eight bars each, then changing in shorter and shorter turns, tossing phrases of four bars, two bars, one bar at each other, and in the end only single notes. *Larant* (which means "battle" or "struggle") is the name given to this technique in India. In playing together with the tabla player Alla Rakha, Ravi Shankar developed it to perfection as did the tenor players Gene Ammons and Wardell Gray in jazz. Nor is it surprising to find that the singers of both cultures also have their common ground: They both love what in jazz is called *scat* or *bop vocals,* in Indian music *tarana;* both terms refer to the seemingly senseless casting out of syllables just for the fun of it.

Thus a broad base underlies the energy and open-mindedness with which many jazz musicians turned to Indian music once it had entered their consciousness. This also makes it clear why jazz musicians were the first Westerners to develop a sensibility for Indian music. In the early 1970s, Ravi Shankar said:

> What I find today that is different from five or ten years ago is that . . . in the past it was the jazz musicians and the jazz buffs. They took to Indian music like a fish does to water. It was very natural to them. . . . The second group of people I found was the folk group. And then came this young group of people, rock 'n' roll and pop music. Classical audiences, I have always felt, take a little more time in the sense that they are more regimented.

II. A Brief History of the Encounter of Jazz with Indian Music

Jazz had hardly come into existence when there were already echoes of Indian music, sentimental ditties of the commercial pseudo-jazz of the twenties and thirties in pieces like "The Snake Charmer" or "My Sweet Indian Princess" or "Moonlight on the Ganges" and, as early as 1922—with a first "oriental" (more Chinese than Indian) tint—in Philip Braham's "Limehouse Blues," which was (and still is!) a favorite of many New Orleans and Dixieland bands. I mention this only for the record. Viewed with the insights provided by black writers like Aimé Césaire and Léopold S. Senghor, this was a kind of primitive "cultural colonialism," lacking in depth and respect.

One generation later, the first serious attempts to use elements of Indian music in jazz were made by the saxophonist, flutist, and oboist Yusef Lateef (who became known through his work with Cannonball Adderley's group), on his 1957 record *Before Dawn* (Verve). Lateef employs a wide range of exotic instruments from Arabia, Africa, India, and other Asian countries, among them the shenai (an Indian oboe) and the argol (an Arabic reed flute). Lateef comes from Detroit, and since 1949 has been involved in the Black Muslim movement, which was especially active in that city. (Ever since the forties, quite a few jazz musicians have been Black Muslims, and as such many were active in the civil rights movement of the 1960s.) As a consequence of his Muslim beliefs, Lateef has dealt with "exotic" kinds of music again and again in the course of his career, as, for instance, in his 1964 composition "India" (Impulse). As early as the fifties, he told music critic Nat Hentoff that what he had in mind was to give his music an "East Indian–African flavor"—an illuminating term, for it links India with Africa from the very outset.

The next person to connect jazz with Indian music was not a musician, but a producer: Dick Bock, head of World Pacific, a California-based record company, one of the most important companies for the popular West Coast jazz of the fifties. In 1957 Bock, who had seemed contented with the relatively tame Californian jazz up to that time, was the first American record producer to collaborate with Ravi Shankar. It acted as something like a signal, since World Pacific was a successful label for jazz buffs and musicians. Many of them sensed immediately that this was going to have an effect on them. What is more, they realized this earlier and more instinctively than other musical audiences.

In the years that followed, Bock released records of many of the great masters of classical Indian music, among them the sarod player Ali Akbar Khan, the South Indian vina player Balachander, the tabla drummer Chatur Lal, and the vocalist Subbulakshmi. It was obvious from the beginning that Dick Bock was expressing, from a genuine inner impulse, his love for Indian culture and spirituality. In 1961, he produced the first recorded meeting of a jazz musician, the California alto and flute player Bud Shank, with an Indian musician, the sitar player Ravi Shankar (who was not yet very well known at that time). Shank and Shankar improvised on a theme from Shankar's score for the highly acclaimed Indian film *Pather Panchali*. The flutist Paul Horn, who has meanwhile become a key figure in "meditation music," also made a few early recording sessions with Ravi Shankar for Bock's World Pacific label.

In the ensuing years, Bock initiated recordings of the virtuoso jazz drummer Buddy Rich with the Indian tabla player Alla Rakha, thus producing the first representative encounter of the rhythmical conceptions of both cultures. Paul Horn was part of this work, too, and two of the pieces on that album were directed by Ravi Shankar. Alla Rakha, by the way, is the father and teacher of tabla player Zakir Hussain, who became the most sought-after percussionist for "Jazz-cum-India" productions in the seventies. Since he had lived in the United States from the age of six, Hussain incorporated both Indian music and jazz from the beginning. (Later he became the drummer of the two most important groups emerging from this fusion: Shakti, led by John McLaughlin, and Ali Akbar Khan and John Handy's group Rainbow. I will have more to say about these two groups later.)

The setting for most of this early activity was California. The fifties were the grand era of the beat poets—Kerouac, Corso, Ferlinghetti,

Snyder, McLure . . . Allen Ginsberg was successful with his "Howl," *the* poem of an entire era, dedicating it to Kerouac as the "new Buddha of American prose." The spiritual center for them all was San Francisco, and they were paving the way for the developments of the sixties—for social consciousness, the civil rights and protest movement, the rise of hippie culture, and, above all, for the awakening of a new spirituality. India, Buddhism, Hinduism, Zen, and Hermann Hesse played an increasingly important, though still undefined role in this process. It was as if these pioneer writers were "invoking" Asia without knowing much about it. By constantly referring to Asia, they called it to the attention of an entire generation that would begin to deal with it, that much more intensely, only a few years later. In 1958, British-born Alan Watts, a writer and university lecturer in San Francisco, published his article "Beat-Zen, Square-Zen, Zen," which was widely acclaimed on the beatnik and jazz scene. For the first time, the jazz terms *beat* and *square* were connected with the concept "Zen"; and again, this was something like a signal.

One of the meeting places for beat poets and jazz musicians was the San Francisco–based jazz and poetry movement. Clearly under the influence of the beat poets, Dick Katz, a cellist and anthropologist living in California, entitled an album *Zen;* of course, this record was released on Dick Bock's World Pacific label.

The artists whose names I have mentioned so far all simply paved the way for what was going to come. It was John Coltrane who really built the bridge between jazz and India—a bridge that initially was based more on Indian spirituality than on Indian music—and who made all of us, far beyond the jazz realm, aware of this bridge. As early as 1955, a critic writing for the American magazine *down beat* had heard something "oriental" in Coltrane's music. In 1965, Coltrane told composer Dave Amram that he found the improvisation principle of Indian ragas "ideal" for jazz. In 1960, Coltrane had his first extensive success with "My Favorite Things" (Atlantic, later versions on Impulse). The piece is based on a simple waltz from a musical, but it was played on the soprano sax in a manner that reminded critics at the time of the nasal, "preaching" tone of the Indian shenais or the Arabic zoukras, both oriental reed instruments. It was followed by "India" in 1961, "A Love Supreme" in 1964, "Om" and "Meditations" in 1965 (all on Impulse). Said drummer Billy Hart: "John was deeply religious, he always had a religious attitude." The musicians influenced by Coltrane were impressed at least as strongly by his religiousness as by his musical technique, his modality and sound, as demonstrated by a comment made by Billy Harper, tenor player from Texas: "The main thing I got from

John Coltrane was that his spirituality came through in the music."
Many other jazz musicians have made similar statements.

In 1961, before most of the above-named records were made,
Coltrane said: "I've really got to work and study more approaches to
writing. I've already been looking into those approaches to music, as in
India, in which particular sounds and scales are intended to produce
specific emotional meanings."

According to the late San Francisco critic Ralph Gleason, Coltrane
shifted the musical consciousness of young people from the United
States, where it had been centered until then, to Asia. This shift in
awareness extends far beyond jazz, not only into rock and pop music,
but also into the way people think and live. The fact that today
thousands of rock and pop groups all over the world play modally, is
inconceivable without Coltrane. It is obvious that such a universal
influence cannot be limited to music. Had it not always also been
spiritual, it would never have become so meaningful for so many people
who have only a marginal interest in music in general and in Indian
music in particular.

All of a sudden, in the sixties, many jazz musicians both famous and
unknown were working with Indian music, obviously most of them
influenced by Coltrane, but others also as a result of their own inner
shift in consciousness. In any case, it is rather impossible in most
instances to discern "personal experience" from "Coltrane's influence." The fact that both aspects are so strongly interwoven is yet
another indication of how elementary this process was (and still is).
The musicians (and young people in general) found their way to
"Trane," as he was called, because they had already been searching
—many of them for years. Coltrane helped them in their search. He
was the "medium."

It is imperative at this point to realize that the discovery of Indian
music by jazz musicians is only one aspect (albeit an important one) of a
much more comprehensive process, namely the discovery of the great
non-Western musical cultures. The pioneer of this development, Yusef
Lateef, illustrated that point early on, as he included in his work not
only Indian music but also sounds, motifs, phrases from American
Indians, China, Japan and—since he was a Muslim—above all from
Arabia. Arabic music stood, and still stands, at the focal point of
Lateef's interest in non-Western musical cultures.

In the second half of the sixties, after Coltrane's death in 1967, Don
Cherry became the most universal jazz musician—or, to put it differently, the jazz musician with the strongest and most comprehensive
awareness of world music. In 1964, Cherry moved to Europe, residing
primarily in Sweden. His first major world-music works were created

in Germany. The very first one was based not on Indian but on Balinese music. I had spent quite some time on Bali and brought Don a number of recordings from there, which inspired him to compose his piece "Eternal Rhythm" (MPS-Metronome), a work commissioned by the Berlin Jazz Festival in 1968. The composition was based on a number of experimental recordings made at the New Jazz Meeting Baden-Baden in 1967. In his next major orchestral works, Cherry, who was following Tantric Buddhism at the time, turned to Indian music: in 1970 he composed the "Whole Earth Catalogue," again a piece presented at the New Jazz Meeting Baden-Baden, and in 1971 "Humus —The Life-Exploring Force" (Wergo-Spectrum) at the Contemporary Music Festival in Donaueschingen. Before each rehearsal and each performance, Cherry went into deep meditation on Tibetan mantras. Since then (as we mentioned), he has worked with musical elements form China and Japan, the American Indians, Arabia and Africa, Lapland and Tibet. He studied Indian vocal technique with the great master of Indian singing, Pandit Pran Nath. What became increasingly evident (not only for Cherry but for the entire movement) was the fact that the interest in what was called "world music" centered around India.

The stream kept getting wider and wider. Around the turn of the decade from the sixties to the seventies, even skeptics, if they had their ears open, realized that this new music was not a passing fad but a permanent opening of musical and spiritual consciousness. The styles (the musical "fashions," so to speak) kept changing. Rock-jazz, so-called *fusion music*, took the place of the free jazz of the sixties—or, more precisely, it attracted the main attention of jazz audiences, but free jazz stayed alive and kept developing. The interest in Indian music, however, remained; in fact, it kept growing. Many successful fusion players at some point or another became interested in Indian music, in Indian or generally Asian spirituality: Herbie Hancock, Joe Zawinul, Chick Corea, Bennie Maupin, Wayne Shorter, and others. For years, many of them (the circle of people around Herbie Hancock, for instance) sang and meditated on their Nichiren Buddhist mantras and chants each time before they went on stage and again immediately after each performance. In fact, it got to the point where a musician not doing so found himself more or less isolated. Trumpeter Freddie Hubbard, for instance, said he felt out of place when he was on tour with Herbie Hancock's group VSOP in the late seventies. The Asian hymns that were chanted several times a day literally "persecuted" him, for, he said, "my roots still are what we have had for generations: the black gospel tradition of the Southern Baptists."

For many musicians the spiritual aspect was more important than the musical one. Even those who dealt with Indian music in very few pieces only (in Herbie Hancock's case, I know of no such piece) still felt a commitment to the spiritual tradition of Asia. I will return to this point.

A further development was exemplified by the work and personality of John McLaughlin. There are three pertinent stages in his career: In 1971/72, this British-born guitarist, who had become known through his work with Miles Davis, formed his Mahavishnu Orchestra, to play what was (and still is) the most compact, complex, and artistically demanding music to be brought forth by fusion music. The titles of the compositions already indicate their spiritual orientation: "The Dance of Maya," "Awakening," "Sapphire Bullets of Pure Love," "One World," "A Lotus on Irish Streams," and (the title of a solo LP released earlier) "My Goal's Beyond" (all on CBS). In 1976, McLaughlin presented his new group, Shakti (also recording on CBS), in which he was the only Western musician. The three other players—all Indian —included the outstanding violinist L. Shankar and the previously mentioned tabla player Zakir Hussain. In 1978, under pressure from his record company, McLaughlin disbanded Shakti and formed another electric fusion group, One Truth Band (CBS); but he retained his Indian violinist L. Shankar for this new group (thus also retaining elements of Indian music). Since the beginning of the eighties, McLaughlin has appeared mainly in solo performances or in various fusion groups consisting mainly of Europeans, including his French wife, Katja Labèque, a well-known classical pianist. His contacts to Indian music, however, have remained intact. What is true about all stages of McLaughlin's development, and what is expressed in the names of his three major groups, is expressed here in his own words: "India is part of my home on this planet. India is a part of me, not only psychically but also physically." And in a different context: "I am the tool. God is the master musician."

The many musicians who have been influenced by John McLaughlin have included famous players like Larry Coryell and Carlos Santana as well as unknown ones, and usually it was not only a musical but also a spiritual influence. Together with Santana, McLaughlin recorded "Love, Devotion, Surrender" (CBS). Sri Chinmoy, McLaughlin's guru at the time, said the following about the final movement of that work:

> Unfortunately, in the West surrender is misunderstood. We feel that if we surrender to someone, he will then lord it over us. We will have no individuality or personality. From the ordinary point of view, the human point of view, this is true. But from the spiritual point of view,

it is absolutely wrong. When the finite enters in the Infinite, it becomes the Infinite all at once. When a tiny drop enters into the ocean, we cannot trace the drop. It becomes the mighty ocean.

Coltrane, Cherry, and McLaughlin were only the key figures in opening jazz to Indian music. The most frequent voyager to Asia among the jazz musicians of the sixties was the American clarinetist Tony Scott, who comes from a southern Italian family and now resides in Rome. Starting as early as 1961, Scott lived in various East Asian and Southeast Asian countries for a total of almost ten years. Anyone traveling through Asia during those years, as I did, could almost depend on running into Tony somewhere in the region, on Java, Bali, in Singapore or Hong Kong, in Vietnam, Taiwan, or Japan. Everything that others began doing around that time, Scott had already done a few months or years earlier, particularly so in Indonesia. In 1967, I was invited to Djakarta to be on the jury of a contest for the best Indonesian jazz musicians. When I asked the members of the prizewinning quintet of this first Indonesian Jazz Competition where they had learned to play such outstanding jazz, they answered in unison: "Tony Scott. He was our teacher." From Djakarta, I called Scott (who was in New York at the time) to tell him how good his former students had become. That same year, I was able to reunite the teacher and his students at the Berlin Jazz Days, as well as on a recording entitled *Tony Scott and the Indonesian All Stars* (MPS-Polygram). Scott's most successful Asian record *(Music for Zen Meditation;* Verve), which has been highly influential since its release in the sixties, was recorded in Japan with Shinichi Yuize, the "grand old man" of the koto (the "harp" of traditional Japanese music) and teacher of entire generations of koto musicians, and the equally outstanding shakuhachi flutist Hozan Ya-mamoto. This record was later followed by the much less satisfying *Yoga Meditation and Other Joys* (Verve).

As early as the mid-sixties, the late trumpeter and composer Don Ellis and the Indian musician and university professor Harihar Rao had founded in Los Angeles the Hindustani Jazz Sextet, a group that incorporated Indian music more thoroughly than any other group had done before. Some years later, Ellis turned away from avant-garde experiments and formed a big band, which—stimulated by the *tala*s, the rhythmical series of Indian music—played meters more compli-cated than anything previously known in jazz (and in Western music in general). For example: 17/8 or $3\frac{2}{3}/4$ or 19/4, the latter subdivided into 3–3–2–2–2–1–2–2–2 (on Pacific and CBS). Said Ellis: "The longest meter I have attempted so far is a piece in 85." And: "When my band has to play a piece in simple 4/4 time, it's best to explain it to them as 7/4 minus 3, otherwise it's too easy for them."

Surprisingly enough, even musicians who do not use technical elements of Indian music refer to India. The tenor saxophonist Pharoah Sanders, for instance, whom Coltrane considered his true successor, claims that he acquired his breathing and falsetto technique through his study of Indian yoga; the same is claimed by Sonny Rollins (for many jazz buffs the greatest tenor player of modern jazz next to Coltrane). Again, although nothing Indian is to be heard in his music, Rollins is deeply involved in Indian spirituality; he meditates and employs Indian breathing methods. The violinist Michael White is another jazz musician who incorporates yoga breathing and concentration methods on records such as *Pneuma* (Impulse). The bassist Gary Peacock studied Zen and meditated in Japan for years.

Another noteworthy encounter between jazz and Indian music occurred in San Francisco when the alto player John Handy, known for his work with Charles Mingus, got together with the famous Indian sarod player Ali Akbar Khan, the two fusing jazz and Indian music in improvisations of great compactness and beauty. *Karuna Supreme* (1975) and *Rainbow* (1980) were the resulting records (which I produced for MPS-Polygram). *Karuna* in Indian philosophy of religion refers to the "highest divine love and compassion"—precisely what Coltrane had wanted to express with the title of his album *A Love Supreme* (Impulse).

On *Karuna Supreme* there is a piece entitled "The Soul of the Atma," which John Handy and Ali Akbar Khan call a "dialogue between Lilah and Manju" (referring to the well-known lovers of Sufi tradition). Lilah symbolizes the East, Manju the West. Lilah "is" Ali Akbar Khan, Manju "is" John Handy. "In the end," explained Ali Akbar Khan, "Lilah and Manju have a child. They have created something new, something they share. And they sing the joy and melody of life." *Atma* (or *atman*) in Indian philosophy is the innermost, most sacred self of a person. It corresponds to the highest concept of what in the West is referred to as "soul."

On *Rainbow*, Handy and Khan are joined by L. Subramaniam, a scion of a great family of violinists from South India (L. Shankar, who played with John McLaughlin, is his brother). Thus this record features three musical cultures "in concert": North Indian–Hindustani music (represented by Ali Akbar Khan), South Indian–Carnatic music (represented by L. Subramaniam), and jazz (in the person of John Handy). (I will come back to the two musical cultures of India at a later point.)

Of similar importance are the previously mentioned recordings made in 1968 by Paul Horn in the tomb of the Taj Mahal and released under the title *Inside* (Epic). Similar to Don Cherry's descriptions of his practices around this same time are Paul Horn's words: "Before each piece I sat in deep meditation."

The alto saxophonist Charlie Mariano lived in Asia for a number of years, in Malaysia, Japan, and India. In a tiny, squalid village in South India, without electricity and the other "blessings" of modern civilization, he studied the nagasvaram with his guru and returned to him regularly for a number of years to deepen his knowledge. The nagasvaram is an oboelike instrument of Carnatic (South Indian) music, which Mariano used for years in his concert appearances and recording sessions for especially expressive Indian solos (as on *October,* Contemp Records). He said: "You know, I have observed that your jazz gets better when you have mastered Indian music. Not only in my Indian pieces, but also in others which have nothing to do with India. You simply go deeper. You say more. And what you play has more meaning."

How far the jazz-India fusion had progressed was demonstrated exemplarily in the late seventies by the music and the personality of Indian drummer-percussionist Trilok Gurtu (who settled in West Germany back then, but also plays in the United States, with the group Oregon, for instance). Gurtu can be referred to as the first Indian musician of international fame to be both intimately connected with the musical (and spiritual) tradition of his homeland—he is an outstanding tabla percussionist—and an excellent jazz musician, a swinging drummer in the best sense of the jazz tradition.

Of course, there is also the corresponding phenomenon from the American side, exemplified especially impressively by the late percussionist Collin Walcott, who was a congenial player of the tabla and sitar—and an intense Buddhist. There is an inner logic in the fact that Gurtu became Walcott's successor in the group Oregon when Walcott died in a traffic accident in East Germany in 1984.

To be sure, there are many who are only superficially involved in Asian music, to whom deep spirituality is something foreign, who understand this whole process as nothing more than a "fad," and who want to jump on that bandwagon, if only for commercial reasons (which usually end in disappointment). It seems inevitable that any development of this kind also has those aspects that are degenerations of the original idea. One characteristic example is the album *Jazz Raga* (Impulse), recorded by the late Hungarian-born guitarist Gabor Szabo in 1966.

Any musician who considers the opening of his music to the great exotic musical cultures—especially that of India—as a "fad" will do no

more than combine styles and thus remain on the surface of things. Karl
Berger, whose Creative Music Studio in Woodstock was so important
in creating the New Consciousness (regrettably, the studio no longer
exists, but it was highly active all during the seventies), once said the
following:

> I see from the people who come here—Nana from Brazil, Trilok
> Gurtu from India, Ismet Siral from Turkey, Ayib Dieng from
> Senegal—that playing together is not difficult. The idea is not so
> much to combine styles but to look at the elements common to all the
> different forms of music, the idea of harmonics and rhythm that have
> been treated by different cultures in different ways, and learn from
> each other, and then come up with personal ways of playing.
> Personalize the music more, not less, rather than identify with styles
> that may not be your own. You learn to see the basic human elements
> that carry all the different musics and build the music from there. This
> may sound theoretical and philosophical, but what we do is very
> practical. We've had some bands like that here and they've sounded
> like real units. . . . Theoretically I've always known that music was
> some sort of universal language, but now we're beginning to see the
> practice of it.

III. The Encounter between Jazz and India in Europe

Everything that happened through Coltrane and because of him would
have been impossible if it did not—as it still does—meet a need of the
times and the people. Hence the emergence of the beat poets in the
fifties. Hence the rediscovery of Hermann Hesse in the sixties,
especially *Siddhartha* and *Journey to the East*. (Don Cherry once said:
"For many people, Hermann Hesse was the first person who taught
them about the eternal cycle of energy.") Hence the great impact of
Asian religiousness particularly on young people, even though they may
not be interested in music. Hence a similar development in Europe,
which had its beginning independently of the one in the United
States.

   In 1952, a young composer, John Mayer, arrived in London from
Calcutta to study at the Royal Academy of Music. Mayer literally dove
into the combination of Western and Indian music. The first person to
understand Mayer's goals and to support him in this endeavor was a
Hungarian-born composer, Matyas Seiber. In the late twenties, Seiber
had founded the first German jazz school in Frankfurt. Later, the Nazis
forced him to emigrate to London. Mayer's efforts initially centered

around Western concert music. His symphonic composition *Raga Jaya Javanti* had its premiere in 1957 with the London Philharmonic Orchestra, conducted by Sir Adrian Boult. Subsequently it was performed in the United States, India, Israel, and Australia. Mayer, however, soon realized the limitations inherent in European concert music. He sensed that the academically trained orchestra musicians and conductors did not understand that the approach to Indian music entailed a different way not only of playing but also of thinking. With this in mind and following Seiber's advice, Mayer began to look for a jazz musician who would be a congenial partner for his ideas. In the early sixties, he had found his man: the Jamaica-born alto saxophonist Joe Harriott (who was to die in 1972). The fruit of this collaboration was the *Indo-Jazz-Suites*, released (on EMI) in various versions in 1966/67.

The attempt to take one further step was made by the encounters of jazz and Indian music that I produced for the 1967 Donaueschingen Contemporary Music Festival and for the Berlin Jazz Days of the same year, under the thematic title "Jazz Meets India" (record versions contained in the double LP *Jazz Meets the World*, MPS-Polygram). Here a jazz trio, that of the Swiss pianist Irene Schweizer, was confronted with an Indian trio, that of the sitar player Devan Motihar. In the tension field between these two trios, two jazz soloists, the German trumpeter Manfred Schoof and the French saxophonist Barney Wilen, blew their improvisations. A critic called it an "exchange of sensitivities, of differentiated rhythmical impulses, a chamber symposium of ancient Eastern and modern Western music."

Immediately thereafter, in 1968/69, similar experiments were made in other European cities. The results were particularly interesting in Vienna, where again European musicians played with colleagues from India, mostly in the format developed for the Donaueschingen festival (a jazz group confronting an Indian ensemble, with improvisations in the energy field between them by one or two wind instruments).

In continental Europe, the interest in Indian music was initially generated by German musicians. In 1964, the trombonist Albert Mangelsdorff, returning from a tour of Asia sponsored by the Goethe Institute, recorded his version of Ravi Shankar's "Pather Panchali," which he entitled "Three Jazz Moods on a Theme by Ravi Shankar Based on a Bengali Folk Song" (on the album *Now Jazz Ramwong*, L + R Records). It was the same theme that Bud Shank had recorded with Ravi Shankar for World Pacific in 1961. At the time, Mangelsdorff was not familiar with the Bud Shank version, which makes it all the more remarkable how much more intensely and deeply integrated and emotional the music is on this record, produced only three years after Shank's collaboration with Shankar. The process had progressed.

As of the mid-sixties, various groups of Indian musicians had found an audience in London, not only among the jazz enthusiasts and jazz musicians but also among the young British pop movement. Ravi Shankar and Devan Motihar, for example, introduced the Beatles (especially George Harrison) to music from India. There followed the "big sitar explosion," as Shankar put it. Guitarists all over the world bought sitars as their second (or third or fourth) instruments—and occasionally provided a painful reminder of the original meaning of the word *sitar: seh tar* in Persian means "three strings"; even though most sitars today have seven strings and twice as many sympathetic strings, many of these "pop sitarists" sounded as if they were able to play on three strings only. In 1966, George Harrison went to Bombay (a pilgrimage, from his point of view) to study Indian music with Ravi Shankar. When he arrived, he was besieged and harrassed so much by screaming Indian teenagers that for weeks he was unable to get down to work. Finally he had to escape with his teacher to Kashmir and Benares. A few years later, the sitar player Devan Motihar collaborated with Herbie Hancock on the music to Michelangelo Antonioni's movie *Blow-Up*.

In 1966, Ravi Shankar and Yehudi Menuhin played their first duo in England, at the Bath Festival. (The two had first met in Paris in 1934 when they were children: Shankar was fourteen when young Yehudi took lessons from Ravi's brother Uday Shankar, whose influence today as a dancer is even greater in India than that of Ravi Shankar in the field of music.) In 1967, Menuhin and Shankar gave their historic concert for the United Nations in New York. Together they made their *East Meets West* records (EMI), which were immensely successful with concert music audiences.

The ensuing years saw a series of concerts with Indian musicians in Europe as well as in the United States, which found appreciation primarily with non-jazz audiences. The most famous one was the 1971 Concert for Bangladesh at New York's Madison Square Garden, featuring many of the top pop musicians of the day (Eric Clapton, Bob Dylan, Billy Preston, Leon Russell, Ringo Starr) as well as the two best-known contemporary musicians from India, Ravi Shankar and Ali Akbar Khan. More than any other event, this concert (recorded by Apple Records) created an awareness of Indian music among the rock generation.

IV. Social Motivation

Around the turn of the century, jazz had come into existence in the encounter of the musical feeling of Black Africa with the musical techniques of Europe. In the course of jazz history, the European element of this encounter took up more and more space. For jazz musicians, the definition of European music became wider and wider. The ragtime pianists of the turn of the century, when they talked about "European music," meant nineteenth-century piano compositions. New Orleans musicians meant French opera music, Spanish circus music, and brass bands. Bix Beiderbecke and his Chicago-style colleagues of the twenties discovered the music of Claude Debussy. Some of the great swing style arrangers studied the art of orchestration from symphonic music of the late Romantic period. By the time the development had produced cool jazz (which was influenced by Bach and counterpoint), jazz musicians had put to use almost everything in European music from Baroque to Stockhausen. Free jazz went into the few remaining fields.

The role of European music as an "opponent"—at least as the exclusive "opponent"—had thus been exhausted. While jazz musicians were confronted with this musical exhaustion, they also gained a new consciousness of their African roots and began to understand that limiting themselves to European music as the only "counterpoint" to these roots meant exactly what spokesmen of the newly developed nonwhite Third World consciousness called "remnants of colonialist thinking." To accept this limit was to kowtow to the claim of supremacy that had always been part of the European tradition. This fact was recognized   not only by musicians (and their vociferous spokesman of the mid-sixties, the poet and novelist LeRoi Jones, later known as Amiri Baraka) but by many black people of all classes. Thus in 1967, students and teachers of a predominantly black high school in New York boycotted concerts that featured classical European music. They did not do so because they were not interested in European concert music. Quite the contrary: musical activity at this school was higher than average. They took action because the students felt it to be wrong that they were offered concerts only of European music, but not of music from Africa, India, Arabia, or Japan: "This limitation is arbitrary. It may be justified by European history, but not by our own."

Thus, the musical discovery of the Third World was paralleled by its discovery as a social and political reality. Musicians began to realize that their true musical and political partners were not the conservatory-trained composers of European music but far more their "brothers" in the underdeveloped countries of the Third World. In this way, the discovery of world music by the jazz musicians is one of the few functioning aspects of what today is referred to as "cultural Third-World solidarity."

V. TWO CULTURES:
HINDUSTANI AND CARNATIC MUSIC

We have been dealing with Indian music as if it were one single musical culture. In reality there are two: the North Indian type, called Hindustani music, and the South Indian type, Carnatic music. The music from South India is the older of the two, it is pure Hindu music. In North Indian music, the influence exerted by the Muslim cultures—from the Arab world and from Persia—is important. South Indian music is purer, less flexible; some consider it to be "atrophied," but that makes it "clearer" and less the product of a cultural mix. When the Muslims took over the North Indian government and administration, many of the most devoted and religious Brahmans fled to the south, where they carefully preserved their traditions; in doing so they infused their music with a certain amount of rigidity.

Composition plays a larger role in South Indian than in North Indian music. Improvisation, on the other hand, is more important in northern India. Up to ninety percent of Hindustani music may be improvised. South Indian music, in turn, has a greater wealth of rhythms. The people in southern India are "black." (Indeed, there are ethnological theories claiming a relationship between the original Dravidic population of South India and the black populations of Africa. Originally, *all* people in India were Dravidians before the dark-skinned tribes were pushed southward by the fair-skinned Aryans coming from the North). In terms of rhythmic intensity and complexity, the music of South India is closer to black rhythms (in the African sense) than is Hindustani music; in fact, many musicians feel that Carnatic rhythms are "hot" in a jazz sense. Carnatic music, on the other hand, does not have the freedom and the "soul" of black music from Africa. North Indian music, though, allows for a freer, more individual and "jazzlike" expression, which is more or less taboo in Carnatic music with its many rules and codes.

In spite of all that, however, the Carnatic music of southern India is closer to the common people than the art of the North. Since the Muslim moguls and princes attracted the best Hindu artists to their courts, North Indian music became more and more an art of the educated upper classes. More so than in North India, where music and dance developed in different directions, Carnatic music still shows its proximity to dance, to the great classical dance styles of *kathakali*, a kind of "dance drama" telling stories and myths, and to the oldest Indian style of dancing, the *bharatanatyam*.

The most important part of *all* of Indian music, however—and that which shows the difference between the two cultures most clearly, even though this difference is almost impossible to put into words—is made up of the embellishments, the musical ornaments and "ameliorations," the tone shading, the nuances and inflections. Compare this to jazz, where the point also is not *what* is played but *how* it is played. The musician plays "around" the notes, he almost never hits a tone directly. In Indian music, sound and phrasing are as important as they are in jazz and much more important than they are in European music. Ravi Shankar has gone so far as to say: "The embellishments are just as essential to our music as harmony and counterpoint are to Western music."

There is the trill of *kampita*, the turns of *ahata*, the accentuation of *tiripa*, the swinging of *andola* and *andolita*, the glissando of *meend*, the sobbing of *gamaka*, the "butterfly" effect of the violinists—and all these specialities, which are so crucial to the Indian feeling of music, are totally different in North India and South India. Like everything in Indian music, such differences have to do with language. In the North they have stronger ties to Sanskrit and the "Arian" languages; in the South they are tied more to the various South Indian and Dravidian languages. Generally speaking, Indian music in North and South is first and foremost the sound of language, the musical echo of words, vocal music, even when it is instrumental. "In the beginning"—the word always comes from Brahma, the creator of word and sound. Musicians from North and from South India, Hindus as well as Muslims, know that the source of power is the word of Brahma, *Nada Brahma*. (It is with gratitude that I take this opportunity to note that it was a North Indian Muslim, a musician from what today is Bangladesh, who first pointed out to me the importance of the Hindu concept of *Nada Brahma* for all of Indian music and spirituality: the great sarod player Ali Akbar Khan.)

VI. SPIRITUAL MOTIVATION

The sociopolitical aspect of "anticolonialism" also has spiritual implications (as I will show not only in this part of the chapter but also in the following part, which talks about Muslims and Hindus). The musical and spiritual elements, however, are so intertwined that the main structural problem of this essay—how to separate the two—remains unsolved: it is unsolvable. The "act of love" between music and spirituality is eternal; it has no end, at least not in the music we are dealing with. Three terms are important in this statement, not only *music* and *spirituality*, but also *love*. Love does not simply "happen"; it has to be acted out, it has to be "done." In music, it is "done" when a musician plays.

In reference to music, spirituality *is* Nada Brahma. Remember what tenor saxophonist Nathan Davis said: "What we really mean by saying spirituality is religiousness." Davis and others have emphasized that one of the main reasons why the word *spirituality* has gained acceptance so quickly is that young people no longer like to speak of "religiousness" with its associations to Christianity as the established churches like to view it.

James Baldwin wrote that anyone who really wants to become a moral, humane being must first of all "free himself from the taboos, the misdeeds and the hypocrisy of the Christian Church. . . . The concept of God is valid and useful only if it can make us greater, freer and more capable of love." Millions of black Americans, "after two hundred years of searching devoutly, ardently and in vain," no longer believe that the Christian God can give that to them. That's why, according to Baldwin, the time has come to "get rid of Him." Blacks have always been the most devout Christians in America. During the forties, however, young blacks especially in Harlem and on the South Side of Chicago turned from Christianity to Islam. They did not just give up their Christian faith, the way millions of whites have done in similar situations; rather, they needed, and immediately embraced, another faith: Islam. This group of blacks has grown immensely in the years since then—particularly among jazz musicians, who have always belonged to the forefront of the black community. Hundreds of jazz musicians became Muslims, and occasionally they even took Arabian names: the drummer Art Blakey, for instance, became Abdullah Ibn Buhaina for his Muslim brothers, and the saxophonist Ed Gregory became Sahib Shihab; other well-known performers include Yusef Lateef, Ahmad Jamal, Idrees Sulieman, and Ahmed Abdul Malik.

The religious commitment to Islam was followed by a musical one. Musicians like Yusef Lateef, Ornette Coleman, John Coltrane, Randy Weston, Herbie Mann, Art Blakey, Roland Kirk, Sahib Shihab, and Don Cherry expressed their fascination with Arabia in compositions and improvisations. In fact, as jazz opened up to Third World music, the initial impression was that Arabian music was the main focal point and not Indian music. Furthermore, it can be demonstrated that, from a technical point of view, the parallels between jazz and Arabian music are at least as strong as those between jazz and Indian music. Even so, the fact that interest in Indian music grew steadily while the fascination with Arabian music diminished somewhat can only be partially accounted for by the greater complexity of Indian music. This phenomenon becomes more understandable only when the spirituality of Indian music is taken into account. When the protest movement of the sixties had reached its peak (1966 in Berkeley, 1967 in Berlin, and 1968 in Paris), more and more musicians and young people all over the world developed a new feeling of fraternity, of spiritual unity, an awareness of universal oneness.

This, however, meant an awareness of Indian spirituality. No doubt many of the same elements can also be found in Islam—for instance, in the wonderfully rich tradition of Sufism. But as time passed, more and more people began to be aware of and be shocked by the growing fanaticism, aggressiveness, militancy, and intolerance in Islam. Militancy, aggressiveness, and intolerance had been the reasons why they had turned away from Christianity. There was no reason to accept these patterns anywhere else.

VII. On Muslims and Hindus

It will be useful for us to consider the fascinating symbiosis of Muslim and Hindu culture that has developed—above all in North India—in the course of the centuries. It represents one of the most admirable and fruitful "acculturations" in the history of mankind, involving not only music but all forms of art. Think of the Taj Mahal, that eminent edifice that is neither Muslim nor Hindu but "Muslim-Hindu." Even though North Indian music is referred to as "Hindustani" music, in reality it is the result of a mixture of Mogul (Muslim) and Indian (Hindu) cultures. Ravi Shankar's music, for example—the embodiment of what Westerners associate with the concept of "Indian music"—in reality is *khyal* music, which means it is Muslim as much as Hindu. (In this sense, it is comparable to the *saeta* of Andalusian flamenco, a similarly fascinating acculturation, again with Muslim participation, although, in the case of

Spain, the encounter is with European-Christian music.) Ravi Shankar's teacher, his musical and also spiritual guru, was a Muslim, the eminent Ustad Allauddin Khan (Shankar: "An inner flame seemed to glow in him"). Allauddin Khan is the father of Ali Akbar Khan, which means that today's two most famous Indian musicians, both Bengali, lived and received their training under the same roof: one, Ravi Shankar, as a Hindu, and the other, Akbar Khan, as a Muslim; and both in a Muslim family in the Bengali Hindu village of Maihar, where the wise *ustad*, the Muslim guru, was admired as "holy man" by the Hindus even more than by his Muslim brothers (who mostly saw "only" the great musician in him). Before the spread of the racial and religious fanaticism that so troubles India today, it was a general rule that Muslims also respected and honored the holy Hindu Brahmans in their village or city, just as Hindus paid their respect to the wise and holy Muslim sages. The integration of Muslims and Hindus in North India (and also in a few areas in South India) could not find a better demonstration than this phenomenon.

Surprisingly many outstanding Indian musicians are not Hindus but Muslims, as, for instance, Ustad Bismillah Khan, the most eminent shenai player; or Sheikh Chinna Maulana Sahib, the great master of the nagasvaram, who, by the way, comes from the much more Hindu-oriented South (his favorite places to play are Hindu temples; there is no music in Islamic mosques anyway); or Ustad Vilayat Khan, whom many people consider to be a better sitar player than Ravi Shankar. The most "authentic" of all Indian vocal styles, the so-called *dhrupad dhamar* (which was cultivated hundreds of years before Islam came to India and was the forerunner of such later styles as *khyal* and *thumri*), today is sung almost exclusively by the Dagar Brothers, the Muslim family of the Dagars. All these great Muslim musicians possess a special kind of emotional power; the Hindus call it *bhav*, a term that in many respects is comparable to what jazz people call "soul." *Bhav* is inconceivable without the sound of Brahma, without *Nada Brahma*. *Bhav* is Hindu, but experts are of the opinion that today more Muslim musicians play with *bhav* than Hindus.

Experts have always assumed that many of the eminent Indian musician families—who play an important role as they pass on their playing styles, their technique, and their tradition from one generation to the next—were Islamic, because for centuries, from the sixteenth to the nineteenth century, the Mogul rulers summoned the best artist of India to Delhi or, more generally, to their capitals and palaces. These rulers had conquered India, but India also conquered them, with its vast wealth of art and spirit. This becomes particularly clear in the case of the greatest of its rulers, the emperor Akbar (1556–1605), under whose sponsorship the Hindu *dhrupad* vocal style reached its highest fruition. Four hundred years later, the great Allauddin Khan, Ali Akbar Khan's father, after having to sleep in the streets of Hindu cities or in the stables of Hindu villages for years, found his first worthy residence at the court of a Muslim prince, the Nawab of Rampur. The Nawab had attracted five hundred (!) artists to his court during the second half of the nineteenth century, for he had made it a point to have the outstanding players of each instrument (vina, sitar, rabab, surbahar, sarangi, shenai, tabla, etc.) in his palace.

Ever since the Arabs invaded India in the eleventh century, there were struggles and bloody confrontations between Muslims and Hindus. These confrontations continued even after the historic victory of the Islamic side in 1192. Yet once the Mogul empire was established, the tendency ran toward tolerance and acceptance on both sides. During the Mogul empire itself (1526–1748), no Hindu artist or musician was forced to convert to Islam. The generosity and kindness of the Mogul emperors, kings, and princes was sufficient reason, especially for the educated and the well-to-do, to convert to Islam in droves. Some of these rulers, as a gesture to their subjects which everyone understood, had three or four (favorite) wives: a Muslim, a Hindu, a European, and once even a black woman from Africa; and they left no room for doubt that they loved all of them with equal intensity. In 1580, Akbar officially renounced Islam and founded a new religion uniting the best elements of Islam, Hinduism, Jainism, Buddhism, and Christianity. There were Jesuits among his religious advisors. Even though this religion regrettably did not gain widespread acceptance, most of Akbar's successors realized that the symbol he had thus set forth was a lasting commitment to tolerance and religious freedom.

The Muslim cultures in southern Spain and on Sicily, with their outstanding historical achievements, would also have been unimaginable without a high degree of religious openness (for which there was no parallel in medieval Christianity). Thus, the intolerance and aggressiveness displayed today by so many Islamic countries are not a basic trait of the Muslim faith. I would prefer to look at them as distortions or degenerative stages (which, to be sure, can with a certain amount of legitimacy be related to Muhammad, the founder of Islam, who was undoubtedly a fanatic). In any case, the enmity between Muslims and Hindus in India is a carefully cultivated product of British colonialism (as is the enmity between Catholics and Protestants in Ireland, and as are enmities in so many parts of the world where the British once ruled). All the more absurd is the fact that Indian and Pakistani politicians, whose public image is vociferously anticolonialist, so carefully nurture this aspect of the British legacy.

Musically, however, the integration of Muslim and Hindu culture still is very much alive. When I began to work with Ali Akbar Khan in the early seventies, the possibility that "Khan Sahib" could be a Muslim did not even cross my mind. He was constantly talking about Hindu Gods and Hindu traditions. The same is true of the other Muslim artists in India. They sing and play about Hindu deities, Rama, Krishna, Shiva, Brahma, but almost never about Islamic things. Even in Pakistan, a Muslim country of the first order where it is against the law to sing about Hindu deities on the radio, Muslim vocalists with their century-old traditions still like to sing about Shiva, Krishna, and Rama—in secrecy if necessary.

The question arises whether jazz enthusiasts perhaps are better equipped to understand this situation than most other people. There is hardly a better parallel to the Indian integration of the Hindu and Muslim cultures than the integration of the black and white cultures in the United States, whose culturally most convincing result is jazz. In both countries, primarily in the southern United States and in North India, there is the same painful and indissoluble mixture of love and hate, of insoluble relatedness and yet not being able to live together. In both cases, it is a "marriage" without end, whose power of love and procreation is still effective and fertile, in love as much as in hatred. Deep down in the people's hearts, the unconscious realization of not being able to live *without* each other is stronger than the conscious conviction of not being able to live *with* each other, even though the latter may be expressed in words and deeds. The knowledge and feeling that they are in the same boat forever needs no expression; it is a given.

VIII. Nada Brahma

Back to music. One common denominator for both cultures, Hindu and Muslim (as for the various fusions and subcultures formed under Islamic influence, all the way to Tunisia and to Andalusian flamenco music), is modality. As I mentioned earlier, it was Miles Davis and John Coltrane who made the jazz world conscious of modality, or, to put it more precisely, revived that consciousness: because modality is inherent in jazz from the beginning. All of archaic blues, the rich store of black folk-music, is modal, not only in America but (earlier) in Africa. Generally speaking, all musical cultures of all periods and eras of mankind have been modal—with the exception of European "art" music from the Renaissance onward. That is why the composer Peter Michael Hamel was right when he said: "The root of modality common to all non-European *and* European cultures is the first step toward a world music, toward a common language, *without* anyone losing their identity."

Historically, the awareness of modality in jazz was gradually suppressed, beginning with New Orleans and even more so with the advent of the Chicago style of the twenties. In the second half of the fifties, Miles Davis and John Coltrane brought modality back into the limelight with their pioneer recordings. It has never been clearly established which of the two was first, Davis or Coltrane. Perhaps it is fair to say that initially the more powerful impulse came from Davis, if for no other reason than that he was a successful, highly acclaimed bandleader at the time while Coltrane was still working as a sideman. In the sixties, on the other hand, when the tendency to play modally became important all over the world, Coltrane was more at center stage than Davis, until the turn of the decades from the sixties to the seventies, when Davis started the trend toward fusion music with his records *In a Silent Way* and *Bitches Brew* (both CBS). This means that in the decade when modal playing conquered jazz and rock, Coltrane's influence was stronger than Davis's. Why was this so? There is no more convincing answer than that Davis's turn to modality was purely a matter of musical technique, while Coltrane shifted directions both musically *and* spiritually. Coltrane's spirituality gave the necessary "push" to modality that he and Davis had rediscovered, a push that was felt all over the world.

Coltrane's musical development was driven forward, motivated, supplemented, enlarged, and enriched by its interaction with his spirituality. Trane himself supported this view in countless statements, such as this one from 1957: "I have experienced, by the grace of God, a spiritual awakening which was to lead me to a richer, fuller, more productive life." Or in 1962: "I think the main thing a musician would like to do is give a picture to the listener of the many wonderful things he knows of and senses in the universe. That's what music is to me—it's just another way of saying, this is a big beautiful universe we live in, that has been given to us." Or finally in 1965: "My goal in meditating through music remains the same."

All this could have been said in remarkably similar words by Indian musicians, Hindu or Muslim. There is not one among them who does not understand music first and foremost as something spiritual, which means: religious! They all have grown up with *Nada Brahma*, with an awareness of the Brahma sound that is reflected in their music. For this reason, each tone they generate comes from Brahma, from God. Ali Akbar Khan put it into the following words: "You can't play it if God hasn't given it to you." (And Coltrane, without being consciously aware of the context: "Words, sounds, speech, men, memory, thoughts, fears . . . all made from One. . . .")

There is no doubt in my mind that of the three components that led to the development I have been describing—the musical, the socio-political, and the spiritual—the spiritual element is the most important one.

It is no coincidence that John McLaughlin, when asked for the beginning of his musical interest in India, first speaks of spiritual things and then of musical matters: "I opened myself to Indian music, because I felt a tie with Indian culture."

One thing has to be realized: What is actually manifested in the meeting of Indian music and jazz—and in general of India and the Western world—is a turning away from Christian, Western rationalism and aggressiveness, toward a holistic worldview; a worldview no longer characterized by such Western dualisms as good/bad, beautiful/ugly, divine/demonic, right/wrong, moral/amoral, etc., but by the age-old wisdom of the great religions and philosophies of Asia: "All is one." The fact that this is the actual, basic motivation behind the "Jazz Meets India" movement can be corroborated by the statements of dozens of musicians, including those quoted in this book. Here, once more, is Don Cherry: "Don't look to the outside. You will see too many different things. Look inside. You will see truth. The one."

For many jazz musicians and for the new species of "world musician" in general, Indian music is a memory of what music should actually be and what it was in the beginning. It is a memory of the "archetype" of music, which is deeply rooted in them and which, at some point in their early years, led them to the decision to become musicians.

C. G. Jung has shown that such archetypes are alive in our dreams. That is precisely so: this music is alive in dreams. It is an echo of the primordial music, an echo of the Brahma sound. Once you awake from that dream you find yourself so much harder at work to realize the vision which made you dream. It is a vision of becoming one, of union, of love—a vision of *Nada Brahma*.

MUSIC FOR LISTENING TO THIS CHAPTER

Many of the records listed here can be found in specialty record stores only. Moreover, many of them, particularly the older and historic ones, are no longer in print or readily available. Even so, real music buffs have their ways of getting hold of even these hard-to-find items.

The records here are listed following the structure of the chapter, beginning with some of the most important timeless recordings of classical Indian music. Still others are listed at the end of chapter 10.

Ustad Allauddin Khan. EMI ECLP 2757.↓

Ustad Vilayat Khan (sitar). His Master's Voice ALP 1946.

Chatur Lal (tabla). *The Drums of India.* World Pacific WP 1403.

Ravi Shankar, Ali Akbar Khan, Balachander. *The Anthology of Indian Music.* Vol. 1. World Pacific WDS-26 200 (3 LPs).

Vilayat Khan (sitar), Bismillah Khan (shenai). *Duets from India.* Capitol ST 10483.

Dagar Brothers. His Master's Voice EMI EALP 1291.

Ram Narayan. *Sarangi: The Voice of One Hundred Colors.* Explorer H 72 030.

Pandit Pran Nath. (See p. 172.)

Yusef Lateef. *Jazz 'Round the World.* Includes "India." Impulse AS 56.

Yusef Lateef. *Blues for the Orient.* Prestige 24035 (2 LPs).

Ravi Shankar, with Bud Shank and others. *Improvisations and Theme from Pather Panchali."* World Pacific WP-1416.

Paul Horn in India. The Blue Note Reissue Series Bn-La-529-H2 (2 LPs).

Rich a la Rakha. With Buddy Rich, Alla Rakha, Paul Horn, and others. World Pacific WPS-21 453.

Dick Katz. *Zen.* With Chico Hamilton and Paul Horn. Pacific Jazz PJ-1231.

John Coltrane. *The Art of John Coltrane: The Atlantic Years.* Includes the first version of "My Favorite Things." Atlantic ATL SD 313 (2 LPs).

———. *Selflessness.* Features "My Favorite Things." MCA 29026.

———. *A Love Supreme.* (see p. 172.)

———. *Om.* MCA 290224.

———. *The Other Village Vanguard Tapes.* Includes "India." MCA 4137 (2 LPs).

Music of Bali. Request 10101.

Bali: Gamelang and Ketjak. Nonesuch 72028.

Don Cherry. *Eternal Rhythm.* MPS-Polygram 68.225.

———. *Humus.* (See p. 172.)

The Carnatic Music Ensemble. Oriental BGRP-1046.

L. Subramaniam. *Virtuoso Violin of South India.* Lyricon 7390.

South Indian Classical Carnatic Music. With Balachander. Oriental BGRP 1021/21 (2 LPs).

John McLaughlin. *My Goal's Beyond.* Elektra Musician EI-60031.

———. *John McLaughlin Mahavishnu Orchestra.* Columbia PC-36394.

———. *Shakti.* With Zakir Hussain and L. Shankar. Columbia PC-34162.

———. and Carlos Santana. *Love—Devotion—Surrender.* Columbia PC-32034.

L. Shankar. *Who's to Know.* With Zakir Hussain. ECM 1195.

The Don Ellis Orchestra Live in $3\frac{2}{3}/4$ Time. Pacific Jazz PJ 10 123.

Pharaoh Sanders. *The Creator Has a Masterplan.* Karma MCA 29 057.

John Handy and Ali Akbar Khan. *Karuna Supreme.* MPS-Polygram.

Ali Akbar Khan, John Handy, L. Subramaniam. *Rainbow.* MPS-Polygram 0068.268.

Paul Horn. *Inside.* (See p. 172.)

Charlie Mariano. *October*. Inner City 1023.

———. *Charlie Mariano with Carnataka College of Percussion*. ECM/PSI 1256.

Tony Scott. *Music for Zen Meditation*. With Shinichi Yuize (koto) and Hozan Yamamoto (shakuhachi). Verve V6-8634.

John Mayer. *Indian-Jazz Suite*. With Joe Harriott. Columbia/Great Britain SCX 6025.

The Joe Harriott Double Quintet under the direction of John Mayer. *Indo-Jazz Suite*. Atlantic SD 1465.

Jazz Meets the World. Includes "Noon in Tunisia" (Bedouins), "Folklore e Bossa Nova do Brasil," "Jazz Meets India," Don Cherry's "Eternal Rhythm," "Japan Meets Jazz," Tony Scott and the Indonesian All Stars, etc. MPS-Polygram 29-22520-8 (2 LPs).

Albert Mangelsdorff. *Now Jazz Ramwong*. Includes "Three Moods on a Theme by Ravi Shankar." L + R Records 41.007.

The Concert for Bangla Desh. With Ravi Shankar, Alla Rakhar, George Harrison, Billy Preston, Leon Russell, Bob Dylan, Ali Akbar Khan, and others. Apple Records STCX 3385 (3 LPs).

Collin Walcott. *Cloud Dance*. ECM/War. ECM 1-1062.

———. *Grazing Dreams*. ECM ECM/PSI 1096.

Don Cherry. *Codona*. With Nana Vasconcelos and Collin Walcott. ECM/War. ECM 1-1132.

———. *Codona 2*. ECM/War. ECM 1-1172.

———. *Codona 3*. ECM/War. 23 785-1.

3 🐚   Postscript on Science

THE TOPIC OF this final chapter is the role of the sciences, the question of methodology, in *"Nada Brahma."* This question is not really part of the book, but I have constantly made reference, both positive and negative, to scientific findings, and I am sure that the alert reader will have become aware of the ambivalence of my position. This ambivalence needs to be clarified.

Let me first state the prerequisite: I admire the breadth of vision and the subtlety of thought of many of the scientists quoted in this book. I realize that we need the sciences. We cannot live without science. Nor do we want to fall back into a prescientific state.

Now let me be specific: In a book wittily entitled *Smog im Hirn* ("Smog in the Brain") the physicist and mathematician Claudio Hoffmann deals with the "necessary dissolution of the *predominant* sciences." Hoffmann shows that science does not serve to further communication but rather domination. In physics, the number of all publications written since the beginning of humankind has doubled every thirteen to fifteen years; of these, ten times as many studies have to do with the destruction of life as with research aimed at the preservation of life: "The death drive, once presented to people by a scientist as a theoretical concept, is now imposed on people by scientists as an actual destructive force."

228

Even a man of such conservative stature as the nuclear physicist Carl Friedrich von Weizsäcker has posed the question whether what scientists "are doing to the world is perhaps objectively criminal."

Since analysis is more important to the predominant sciences than synthesis, scientists tend to encapsule themselves, to think narrowly and rigidly rather than widely and flexibly. Thus—even at a time when logic and cybernetics point to the often higher efficacy of non-Aristotelian systems of logic and of analogous (instead of logical) thinking, as well as to the existence of nonlinear patterns of causality—most scientists still cling stubbornly to Aristotelian logic and to linear causal chains. As a result of this rigidity, scientists accept findings that are a product of their own methodology within a few years or even months after they are published, but pass over all those findings that represent a danger to their traditional methods, even half a century after these findings are made.

The main handicap of predominant science is the fact that it takes one reality for all of reality. Science is like a creature that inhabits the realm where land and sea meet but perceives only the land, or only the sea. Such a creature could not survive. "Nobody has ever had access to objective reality through science" (neuro-scientist Robert B. Livingston). "We do not deal with truth in science. We deal with approximate descriptions" (Fritjof Capra).

The failure of the conventional methodology of science is especially apparent in the field of medicine. In the last 150 years, there has hardly been a single pioneering figure in medicine who has not been denounced as "unscientific" by tenured university professors—from Ignaz Philipp Semmelweis (who introduced asepsis) to Robert Koch (who founded modern bacteriology, against the almost total opposition of his colleagues) and Werner Forssmann (who invented the cardiac catheter in 1929, tried it out on himself, and was discriminated against as a "quack" as late as the fifties), all the way to Louis Pillemer (who discovered properdine, a substance of crucial importance to the human immune system, and who, after being ostracized by his colleagues for years, committed suicide in his laboratory in 1954; only a few months later, scientists all over the world began to accept his findings).

In medicine, positive concepts like "helping" and "healing" are perverted into negative ideas like "fighting" and "going to war" against diseases or "destroying" and "exterminating" their causes. It's an absurd situation: Medicine, the science most directly concerned with highly differentiated living organisms, still looks at its "object," man, as if he were a "machine" or a chemical plant. The science of physics, on the other hand, whose findings in the early years of the modern era led to the invention and development of machines, is giving up its mechanistic thinking more and more and now looks at the world as a web of dynamic relationships. Conventional medicine simply does not seem to be able to understand that it is still orientated toward a physical worldview that, in its basic conception, is outdated. There have always been close ties between physics and medicine. Yet conventional medicine has not even begun to draw consequences from the obvious fact that a holistic physics implies a holistic medicine.

The positivistic thinking of predominant science has had a disastrous effect on research in evolution. More than a century ago, in 1859, the founder of the theory of evolution, Charles Darwin, formulated this warning: "The concept that the eye, with all its unique devices for accommodation, adaptation, and for correcting spherical and chromatic aberrations, might be the result of 'natural selection' is, as I freely admit, highly absurd." Robert Kaspar cites a simple example:

> Assume that the eye of a vertebrate comes into existence, which—in a simplified view—consists of five substructures: cornea, lens, iris, vitreous body, and retina. Each individual substructure is supposed to be a result of mutation; present evolutionary theory assumes that substructures develop independently of each other.
>
> We know that mutation takes place at about each ten-thousandth (10^4) reproductive step and that maximally one out of every hundred (10^2) mutations is a success. Thus, it takes an average of one million (10^6) mutations to "improve" a given structure. That figure applies to only one characteristic. In order to "improve" two characteristics, it would take one trillion $(10^6 \times 10^6 = 10^{12})$ mutations, etc. If we make the generous assumption that only one (positive) mutation is necessary for each substructure of the eye, evolution would have needed $10^6 \times 10^6 \times 10^6 \times 10^6 \times 10^6 = 10^{30}$ tries to produce all five structures. That would be possible only if, ever since the beginning of the universe (about 10^{17} seconds ago), 10^{13} mutations per second had taken place in the eye.
>
> One must consider the fact that this absurdity is nothing other than a conclusion drawn from evolutionary theory as it is explained in our textbooks.

D. T. Suzuki has proposed that we progress at last from the conventional scientific to a "metascientific" attitude. He writes:

> The scientific method in the study of reality is to view an object from the so-called objective point of view. For instance, suppose a flower here on the table is the object of scientific study. Scientists will subject it to all kinds of analyses, botanical, chemical, physical, etc., and tell us

all that they have found out about the flower from their respective angles of study, and say that the study of the flower is exhausted and that there is nothing more to state about it unless something new is discovered accidentally in the course of other studies.

The chief characteristic, therefore, which distinguishes the scientific approach to reality is to describe an object, to talk *about* it, to go *around* it. . . . But the question still remains: "Has the complete object been really caught in the net?" I would say, "Decidedly not!" Because the object we think we have caught is nothing but the sum of abstractions and not the object itself. . . .

. . . The scientific way kills, murders the object and by dissecting the corpse and putting the parts together again tries to reproduce the original living body, which is really a deed of impossibility.

Science and taboo-type reactions actually should be mutually exclusive, because science should be characterized by openness. In reality, however, the various contemporary sciences are closed systems, whose representatives watch over them Argus-eyed so that virtually nothing can invade them that is not rooted in their own thought and memory processes. The bias of conventional medicine, for instance, is so great that the mere fact that a therapy or medicine has been developed by a school of thought other than the predominant one is sufficient reason to reject it. An unbiased examination of the therapy or medicine in question is usually considered to be superfluous in such cases.

Carl Friedrich von Weizsäcker has pointed out that it is "part and parcel of the methodological foundations of science" that "one does not ask certain fundamental questions." In order to exclude such fundamental questions, science has no choice but to employ taboo reactions similar to those of "primitive" societies. Again and again in the critical writings of contemporary philosophers of science, you can find one observation: What a totem is to an African tribe—that is precisely what a "proven theory" is for certain groups of scientists. These scientists dance around it as if it were the golden calf. Both the African tribe and the scientific community have manipulated their living and working conditions in such a way that they constantly "prove" that the totem or the theory are "correct." In reality, the theory is no more "correct" than the totem and, essentially, is in no way different from it. Both have exactly the desired "effects," and thus confirm themselves just as their creators want them to.

A prime example is the role played by coincidence in the worldview of certain evolutionary positivists. We are aware by now of what speaks against coincidence. I cited Darwin's example of the eye, which cannot possibly be the result of mutations as would be implied by the theory of evolution. A further example is the enzyme cytochrome c, a chain molecule consisting of 104 amino acids, without which living organisms could not have developed. With reference to Einstein's famous statement, "I will never believe that God is playing a game of dice with the world," the scientist Hoimar von Ditfurth, a positivist, has indicated that the entire universe consists of hardly more than half the number of atoms necessary as "possible throws of the dice" for coincidence to produce cytochrome c "accidentally." Even assuming that ever since the beginning of the universe "the dice had been thrown" once per second, the resulting 10^{17} "throws of the dice" would not be near enough to "coincidentally" produce a chain molecule for which there are 10^{130} possibilities. The majority of scientists, however, still cling to their "god of coincidence," with a blinker mentality that shows all the signs of a mental block.

It has long become obvious that "coincidence" is a much greater fetish than (as the positivists believe) the "good Lord" is for those who believe in God. A fetish like the totem that the medicine man in Africa uses to make certain things "understandable" for his people. All of conventional scientific thinking is full of totems and fetishes like that. The name of the fetish may be "coincidence" or "rationality," "cause" or "effect," "time" or "matter," "experiment" or "plausibility" (What's plausible to whom?); it may be "evolution," "mutation," or just a formula or any term that scientists toss into the debate as if the mere term could already work "magic"—just like the bundle of straw that works magic in the African village or the gods and ghosts of the medicine man.

The most fetishlike of these terms is the word *science* itself. I have experienced dozens of times how a physician, for example, will claim that something is "not scientific" and, having pronounced that judgment—as if it worked some sort of magic—believes himself to have made a pertinent statement about the matter at hand. I think it is helpful in this context to refer once more to Carl Friedrich von Weizsäcker, who has remarked that scientists are "not sufficiently self-critical," that they are "not fully aware of their responsibility." Finally, an eminent biologist and the founder of modern systemic ecology, Jakob von Uexküll: "Today the word 'science' is used to maintain a ridiculous fetishism."

Science could, in fact, remain the way it is (at least it could be useful), were it not so consistently marked by moral failure. It is the scientists who keep the arms race going and who have accelerated it to a degree that now threatens the existence of the world. It is the scientists who are always ready to do whatever is feasible, however detrimental it may be to the health of others. It is the scientists—medical doctors in this case—who (according to official statistics) are three times more likely to do breast removal surgery if it means additional income for them, than they are if the surgery is paid for as part of a flat overall rate for therapy. Every day, biogeneticists and bio-engineers are committing crimes against life, although the best of them have warned us often enough about the inevitable consequences of what is being done in these fields the world over.

No doubt we owe our standard of living to the scientific work that has helped us to survive epidemics and other threats or crises. We should be thankful for that work, but that does not mean overlooking the fact that the hypertrophy (nothing else is meant here!) of the rationalistic, mechanistic way of thinking, the one-sidedness and arrogance of this thinking, has itself become a threat to our survival.

Paul Feyerabend writes:

> There will always be people who prefer being scientists to being masters of their fate and who gladly submit to the meanest kind of (intellectual and institutional) slavery provided they are paid well and provided also there are some people around who examine their work and sing their praise. Greece developed and progressed because it could rely on the services of unwilling slaves. We shall develop and progress with the help of numerous willing slaves in universities and laboratories who provide us with pills, gas, electricity, atom bombs, frozen dinners and, occasionally, with a few interesting fairy-tales. We shall treat these slaves well, we shall even listen to them, for they have occasionally some interesting stories to tell, but we shall not permit them to impose their ideology on our children in the guise of "progressive" theories of education. We shall not permit them to teach the fancies of science as if they were the only factual statements in existence. . . .

This, Feyerabend continues, "may be our only chance to overcome the hectic barbarism of our scientific-technical age and to achieve a humanity that we are capable of but have never fully realized."

Let's stay with moral categories for a moment. We have become increasingly aware that the cynicism and egotism of society not only are reflected in the way scientists work, but are virtually programmed by the "findings" of science. In bioengineering and in conventional medicine, for instance (but also in other sciences), cynicism is almost part of the job description. Erich Jantsch, an eminent American astrophysicist and advisor to the Organization for Economic Cooperation and Development (OECD), was repelled by the enthusiasm of leading scientists in Berkeley in discussing a discovery by the well-known British anthropologist Colin Turnbull. Turnbull had found a small tribe in a remote mountain village in Uganda whose members had reacted to their involuntary resettlement ("in a situation of hunger and despair") with the reduction of all human relations "to the crudest level of egotism." Mothers were denying their children the warmth of the fire, old people were abandoned as too great a burden for others, murder and robbery were daily incidents. Turnbull and other scientists from various fields celebrated the misdeeds of the tribe as the "absolute reduction of man to his 'objective' survival functions," which they saw in turn as the true goal of human development. Here perversion had become a model. Jantsch concluded his report as follows:

> The scum turned into the avant-garde of evolution—if it works that way, it's reason enough to be proud of one's misdeeds. . . . The parallels between science, robbery and murder remained uncontradicted. . . . Instead of horror, I saw glowing eyes. . . . I realized that reductionism in the academic world is not simply a kind of abstract mental shrinking but a phenomenon that threatens all of society.

Where I have employed the term "predominant science," I have used the word *predominant* in a double sense: as the science most widely accepted at a certain moment in time and as the science that dominates us, more powerfully than politicians or even dictators can do. However, there is such a thing as an "attendant" science. It is this science I mean when I quote people like Einstein, Heisenberg, Weizsäcker, Bohr, Jantsch, and all the others I have mentioned in this book. They possess an open-mindedness that implies freedom from rule and that is the opposite of the "ruling science." The truly outstanding ones among the scientists see that phenomenon as "objectively criminal" and "lacking any sense of responsibility" (Weizsäcker), as an "imperialistic attack on nature" and a "step backward" (Erwin Chargaff, the discoverer and decipherer of the genetic code).

The critics of science I have quoted (particularly those who have contributed brilliantly in the academic realm) are speaking not only of the scientists who have invented atom and hydrogen and neutron bombs, who practice gene manipulation and produce nerve gas, who keep the arms race going, and who are ready, whenever they are called upon by the nuclear and chemical industry, to testify to politicians and judges that whatever is happening is guaranteed to have no potential dangers.

They are speaking not only of the murders for which science is responsible, but also its thinking, which suppresses, manipulates, restricts, robs, impoverishes, reduces, makes cynical and egotistical, which excludes what is essential. They mean, as the great German poet Gottfried Benn put it, "the thoughtless and irresponsible depersonalization of the world." Along with Winston Churchill they fear that "it might be that the stone age is returning on the glowing wings of science."

Sources·Literature·Notes

Introduction

Part One

Chapter 1

Mystik, ed. Hans Dieter Zimmermann (Frankfurt am Main: Insel Verlag, 1981).

17 *Upanishads:* part of the Vedas, the holy scriptures even though they were unified as a text collection only much later. The Sanskrit word (from *upa-ni-sad*) translates literally as "sitting down with it," meaning "Sit down with this scripture and meditate on it."

Chapter 2

19f. *Zen masters: Aussprüche und Verse der Zen-Meister,* compiled by Peter Weber-Schäfer (Frankfurt am Main: Insel Verlag, 1978).

If you blot out sense and sound—: Else Madelon Hooykaas and Bert Schierbeek, *Zazen* (Weilheim: Otto Wilhelm Barth Verlag, 1972).

20 *Were I to know the answer:* There is, in fact, a collection of answers to Zen koans. It is interesting for the study of Zen, but the meditating person learns from it as little as a student learns by copying someone else's homework. The title: Yoel Hoffmann, *The Sound of the One Hand* (New York: Basic Books, 1975). I will refer to this work frequently, especially to its introduction, written by Ben-Ami Scharfstein.

tao: In the *Tao te ching,* Lao-tzu writes of the *tao:* "It stands alone and does not change. . . . It is capable of being the mother of the world./ I do not know its name. / So I style it 'the way.' . . . /Man models himself on earth,/ Earth on heaven,/ Heaven on the way,/ and the way on that which is naturally so" (Trans. D.C. Lau). For the Chinese word *tao,* whose original meaning was "the (royal) way," the most diverse translations have been proposed—for instance, "God," "reason," "sense," "word," and "logos."

Hakuin: See note to p. 20 *(The Sound of the One Hand).*

21 *Richard de Martino:* Richard Martino, Erich Fromm, D. T. Suzuki, *Zen Buddhism and Psychoanalysis* (New York: Harper and Brothers, 1960).

27 *Angarika Govinda: Creative Meditation and Multidimensional Consciousness* (Wheaton, Ill.: Theosophical Publishing House, 1976). All subsequent Govinda quotes are from this work.

29 *Sivananda Sarasvati:* in the Sufi journal *Sifat* 8:2 (Summer 1978; Oberwil, Switzerland).

30 *"Hail to the jewel in the lotus!": The Tibetan Book of the Dead; or, The After-Death Experiences on the Bardo Plane,* comp. and ed. by W. Y. Evans-Wentz, with a psychological commentary by C. G. Jung (London: Oxford University Press, 1960).

31ff. *MU:* See part 2, chapter 1, "Zen and Modern Japan," pp. 185ff.

Joshu, the court lady Kasuga: See note to p. 20 *(The Sound of the One Hand).*

32   *"How old is Amida Buddha?":* See note to p. 20 *(The Sound of the One Hand).*

33f.   *Hazrat Inayat Khan:* "The Power of the Word," in *The Sufi Message of Hazrat Inayat Khan,* vol. 2 (Geneva: International Headquarters of the Sufi Movement, 1962).

34f.   *Vilayat Inayat Khan:* (Geneva: International Headquarters of the Sufi Movement, 1959).

            Tantric sexual practices: See Arthur Avalon, *Tantra: A Translation from the Sanskrit* (London, 1913) and Ashley Thirleby, *Tantra: The Key to Sexual Power and Pleasure* (New York: n.p., 1978).

36   *Nichiren Shoshu Buddhism: World Tribune: A Journal of Nichiren Shoshu Buddhism in America* (Santa Monica, Calif., 10 November 1980; 17 March 1980; 11 February 1980).

37   *Faust:* (New York: Grollier Press, 1968).

38   *The Tibetan Book of the Dead:* See note to p. 30.

            Hazrat Inayat Khan: Music (Geneva: International Headquarters of the Sufi Movement, 1959).

            The Way of a Pilgrim. Trans. Helen Bacovcin (Garden City, New York: Doubleday/Image, 1978).

41   *Vilayat Inayat Khan:* See note to p. 34f.

            John Blofeld: Mantras: Sacred Words of Power (London: George Allen and Unwin, 1977).

42f.   *Suzuki:* See note to p. 21 (De Martino).

44   *Erich Fromm:* See note to p. 21 (De Martino).

            Aristotelitis: according to Bhagwan Shree Rajneesh, in *The Search* (Poona, India: Rajneesh Foundation, 1977).

            Carl Friedrich von Weizsäcker: Die Einheit der Natur (Munich: Hanser Verlag, 1971).

            Hakuin: See remark to p. 20 ("The Sound of the One Hand").

46f.   *thinking behind the Japanese language:* according to Ryogí Okochi, "Sprache ohne Subjekt. Europäische und japanische Denkstrukturen im Vergleich," unpublished manuscript.

48   *Frederic Vester: Neuland des Denkens* (Stuttgart: Deutsche Verlags-Anstalt, 1980).

50   *"Quantum mechanics are . . .":* See note to p. 104f. (Capra).

            Chapter 3

51   *fluid transition between mantric sound and the spoken word:* See chapter 11, p. 174. (Egyptian legends and hieroglyphs).

            Wassily Kandinsky: "Über das Geistige in der Kunst," in *Rationalität und Mystik,* ed. Hans Dieter Zimmermann (Frankfurt am Main: Insel Verlag, 1981).

            Jean Gebser: Ursprung und Gegenwart (Munich: Deutscher

Taschenbuch-Verlag, 1973). Translated into English as *The Ever-Present Origin* (Athens, Ohio: Ohio University Press, 1985).

Main source for this chapter: Arnold Wadler, *Der Turm von Babel* (Wiesbaden: Fourier Verlag, 1981).

52f.   *leg and regh:* The paleolinguist Richard Fester (whose work I was unfamiliar with when writing this chapter) has shown that both roots go back to the primal female root *kall*. Needless to say, the fact that *light, loud, right, rex, beginning,* and *lie* all derive from a primal female root is of great import. See Fester's *Urwörter der Menschheit: Eine Archäologie der Sprache* (Munich: Kosel, 1981). The train of thought only touched upon here is carried out in detail in my subsequent book, *The Third Ear;* see note to p. 8.

53   *Sukie Colegrave: The Spirit of the Valley: Androgyny and Chinese Thought* (London: Virago, 1979).

Chapter 4

57   *Kippenhahn:* personal communication, 1982.

58   *pulsars:* See Isaac Asimov, *The Collapsing Universe: The Story of Black Holes* (New York: Walker, 1977).

Jeff Lichtman and Robert M. Sickels: "Amateur Radio Astronomer's Notebook," privately published, copyright © 1977. See also p. 75.

Isaac Asimov: See note to p. 57.

Tunguska region: See Asimov, *op. cit.*

59   *Johannes Kepler, Gesammelte Werke* (Munich: Beck, 1938).

59f.   *Faust:* See note to p. 37.

60–63f.   *overtone scale, interval proportions, Hans Kayser:* This discussion of harmonics is based on the works of Hans Kayser, the founder of the science of harmonics, as well as the work of Rudolf Haase. However, I have not cited here the countless "theorems," "axioms," and computations that accompany the works of these experts (or the wealth of detailed tables and graphs included in their studies). The following works were my primary sources: Hans Kayser, *Akróasis* (Basel: Benno Schwabe Verlag, 1946), translated into English as *Akróasis: The Theory of World Harmonies* (Boston: Plowshare Press, 1970; this edition is cited on pp. 63–64); *Vom Klang der Welt* (Zurich and Leipzig: Max Niehans Verlag, 1937; *Grundriss eines Systems der harmonikalen Wertformen* (Zurich and Leipzig: Niehans, 1938); *Abhandlungen zur Ektypik harmonikaler Wertformen* (Zurich and Leipzig: Niehans, 1938). Rudolf Haase founded the Hans Kayser Institute in Vienna, where he carried on Kayser's work congenially. Literature: Rudolf and Ursula Haase, *Literatur zur harmonikalen Grundlagenforschung,* 5 vols. (Vienna: Verlag Elisabeth Lafite, 1969–1983); Rudolf Haase, *Die harmonikalen Wurzeln der*

Musik (Vienna: Lafite, 1969); *Der messbare Einklang: Gründzüge einer empirischen Weltharmonik* (Stuttgart: Ernst Klett Verlag, 1976); *Leitfaden einer harmonikalen Erkenntnislehre* (Munich: Ora, 1970).

62   *Lambdoma:* Hans Kayser, *Lehrbuch der Harmonik* (Zurich: n.p., 1950); Rudolf Haase, "Das pythagoreische Lambdoma" and "Lambdoma, I Ging und Genetischer Code," both in *Grenzgebiete der Wissenschaft* (Innsbruck: Resch Verlag, n.d.).

65   *Thomas Michael Schmidt: Musik und Kosmos als Schöpfungswunder* (Frankfurt am Main: privately published, 1970).

quotations (from Blaesius, Plotinus, Keyserling): quoted in Thomas Michael Schmidt, *op. cit.;* see note to p. 65.

Willie Ruff: American Scientist (May/June 1970).

"Song of the planets": for more information about this topic, see my book *The Third Ear* (note, p. 8).

68f.   *Wilfried Krüger: Das Universum singt* (Trier: Editions trèves, 1983).

Jean E. Charon: L'Esprit, cet inconnu (Paris: n.p., 1977).

70   *Periodic System of Elements:* Examples of octave relationships are formed by the series of rare gases helium (2)—neon (10)—argon (18)—then a double octave step to krypton (36); or by the series lithium (3)—sodium (11)—potassium (19); or the series boron (5)—aluminium (13), etc.

71   *Planck's constant:* It is defined by physicists as an energy locatable in space, multiplied by its duration delimitable in time: $h = (6.626176 \pm .00036) \times 10^{-34}$ J $\times$ s.

Planck inspired by overtone scale: according to Haase: *Der messbare Einklang;* see note to p. 60–63f.

72   *black hole:* according to Charon; see notes to pp. 68f. (Charon) and 58 (Asimov).

electron: Its inconceivably small size is described with a radius of 2 $\times 10^{-13}$ cm.

73   *elementary particles that do not disintegrate:* Only protons, neutrons, electrons, neutrinos, and photons are stable particles. Their lifetime is close to that of the universe, except in cases of "accidents"—for instance, when they collide at very high energy levels. Then they disintegrate into unstable particles, often existing only for fractions of a second.

74   *Oscar Ichazo:* quoted in Anand Margo, *Tantra* (Schwebda: Sannyas Verlag, 1982).

Solié: quoted in J. Charon; see note to p. 68f. (Charon).

75   *Sounds of DNA, Earth magnetism, solar winds:* for more information, see note to p. 65 ("song of the planets").

Chapter 5

77   *drums and croakers, spot snappers, etc.:* according to information furnished by Dr. Johannes Kinzer of the Institute for Oceanography, University of Kiel.

        Cetacea: according to findings of the Pacific Studies Section, Canterbury Museum, Christchurch, New Zealand.

78   *whales:* Joan McIntyre: *Mind in the Waters* (Sausalito, Calif.: Project Jonah, 1974).

        David Cahen, Gordon Kirkbright: Bernhard Dixon, "Listening to Life," *Omni* magazine (1980).

        Peter Tompkins and Christopher Bird: The Secret Life of Plants (New York: Harper and Row, 1973).

80f.   *The golden section and the laws of harmonics:* See also the remarks on "deviations," p. 86ff.

81   *"Harmonologia Musica"* and *T. M. Schmidt:* quoted in Thomas Michael Schmidt; see note to p. 65.

82   *Agrippa von Nettesheim, Kepler:* quoted in Thomas Michael Schmidt; see note to p. 65.

        chromaticism in ancient China: The eminent musicologist and expert on Asian musical cultures Alain Daniélou has also pointed out the amazing concurrences among musical cultures of the world.

82f.   *sexuality, thirds, sixths:* In my book *The Third Ear,* I devote an entire chapter to the mysterious connection between sexuality and music; see note to p. 8.

85   *"as a hidden, encoded music notation":* Marius Schneider, "Singende Steine," and Dieter Rudloff, "Romanische Kreuzgänge und Singende Steine," in *Die Kommenden,* March 1982 (Basel/Kassel 1955).

86   *Hans Kayser:* See note to pp. 60–63f.

88   *"corrective hearing":* Rudolf Haase, *"Der messbare Einklang;* see note to pp. 60–63f.

89f.   *George Leonard: The Silent Pulse* (New York: E. P. Dutton, 1978).

Chapter 6

92f.   *Imagine we were observing . . . :* Lyall Watson, *Supernature* (Garden City, N.Y.: Anchor Press, 1973).

94   *Sir Arthur Eddington:* quoted in Schmitz; see note to p. 106 (Jeans).

94f.   *P. D. Ouspensky: Tertium Organum* (London: Routledge and Kegan Paul, 1921).

96   *processes of the microworld also appear in macrophysics:* An example for this "printing through" in the border region between macro- and microphysics, often cited by scientists, is the

"spooking" in the microchip-laden electronic system aboard modern jetliners, for example the short-range Boeing 737-200. Insiders speak of "phantom phenomena" and of "motrons" and "gremlins." The (supposedly benevolent) electronic system —a Lufthansa pilot told the German news magazine *Der Spiegel*—"may determine correct data, but computations result from them that you must not follow, because they may be misleading." As early as 1980, 232 German jet pilots, among them 221 Lufthansa captains, had observed such "phantom phenomena." To be sure, a single chip with its 64,000 memory units would produce only one "phantom" in 117 years, but a bank containing a thousand chips would produce one every six weeks. Since modern jetliners are equipped with well over a thousand chips, there is hardly a flight without "gremlins." The crash of a Lufthansa jet near Nairobi, Kenya, and that of an Air New Zealand DC-10 on an ice-covered mountain in the Antarctic are attributed to them. A leading Federal Aviations Authority executive commented: "The chances of reliably testing such circuitry are near zero." Pilots themselves are quoted as saying: "Most of us push aside and suppress the idea of such phantom phenomena" *(Der Spiegel*, August 1983).

Ilya Prigogine was awarded . . . : according to Hoimar von Ditfurth, *Wir sind nicht nur von dieser Welt* (Hamburg: Hoffmann and Campe, 1981).

Heisenberg has shown . . . : quoted in George Leonard; see note to p. 89f.

97   *Dogen:* quoted in D. T. Suzuki; see the following note.

D. T. Suzuki: Mysticism: Christian and Buddhist (New York: Harper and Brothers, 1957).

Einstein: quoted in D. T. Suzuki; see the preceding note.

Saichi: quoted in D. T. Suzuki; *op. cit.*

Buddhism and Christian mysticism: quoted from Erich Fromm, *To Have or to Be?* (New York: Harper and Row, 1976).

98   *Meister Eckehart: Predigten und Traktate,* ed. Josef Quint (Munich: 1955).

Franz Kafka: "Betrachtungen über Sünde, Leid, Hoffnung und den wahren Weg," in *Rationalität und Mystik,* ed. Zimmermann (Frankfurt am Main: Insel Verlag, 1981).

Gorbach: See note to p. 9 (Genro). In his book *Mysticism: Christian and Buddhist* (see note to p. 97) D. T. Suzuki compares the teachings of the medieval German mystic Meister Eckehart with Buddhism, finding surprising concurrences (which, however, make the differences between them all the more illuminating).

99   *fighters in the French Revolution 1789:* The incident has been mentioned by various authors, as for example by Walter Benjamin, *Gesammelte Schriften,* vol. 1 (Frankfurt am Main: Suhrkamp Verlag, 1974).

100   *muezzin:* in Muslim countries, a crier in a minaret who calls the people to prayer, generally five times a day.

          net of time: The Swiss jazz composer Mathias Rüegg has called my attention to the fact that it certainly is not without irony (or a deeper meaning) that Switzerland, the country where "rule by the church" most quickly and thoroughly turned into "rule by capital," was for generations the most proliferous producer of clocks and watches.

101   *Penelope Shuttle and Peter Redgrove: The Wise Wound* (London: Victor Gallancz, 1978).

102f.   *"The Silent Pulse"* by George Leonard: See note to p. 89f.

103   *size of the Empire State Building:* according to George Leonard; see note to p. 89f.

          a human being, compressed . . . : See note to p. 58.

          Isaac Asimov: See note to p. 58.

104f.   *Fritjof Capra: The Tao of Physics* (New York: Bantam Books, 1977).

105   *Niels Bohr:* quoted in Capra; see preceding note.

          shikisokuseku: See *The Sound of the One Hand,* note to p. 20.

106   *Niels Bohr's family coat of arms:* according to Capra; see note to p. 104f.

          Sir James Hopwood Jeans: quoted in Emil Heinz Schmitz, *Das Zeiträtsel—Die erweiterte Gegenwart der Psyche* (Geneva: Ariston Verlag, 1979).

          "spatially separate events . . . independent of each other": quoted in George Leonard; see note to p. 89f.

107   *Ch'an-sha Ching-ts'en:* quoted in *The Sound of the One Hand;* see note to p. 20.

110   *Wolfgang Büchel:* quoted in Emil Heinz Schmitz; see note to p. 106 (Hopwood Jeans).

111   *"If you blot out sense and sound—":* See note to p. 19f.

Chapter 7

113   *György Ligeti:* liner notes to a Ligeti album (Deutsche Grammophon DGG 137 003).

114   *Richard Norton:* "Musik als tonale Geste," in *Die Zeichen: Neue Aspekte der musikalischen Ästhetik II,* ed. Hans Werner Henze (Frankfurt am Main: Fischer Taschenbuch, 1981).

          Dane Rudhyar: The Magic of Tone (Boulder: Shambhala, 1982).

116   *Wilfried Krüger:* See note to p. 68f. (Krüger).

116f.   *George Leonard:* See note to p. 89f.

117   *William Condon:* quoted in George Leonard; see note to p. 89f.

Paul Byers: quoted in George Leonard; see note to p. 89f.

118   *Brian L. Partridge:* quoted in *Der Spiegel,* July 1982.

119   *Gunther Hildebrandt:* quoted in Rudolf Haase, *Der messbare Einklang;* see note to pp. 60–63f.

123   *In opposition to harmonization:* These thoughts (like those in the second part of chapter 4, p. 71ff.) are based on the insights of Jean E. Charon; see note to p. 68f. (Charon).

124   *electrons . . . smaller in size than we can imagine:* see note to p. 72.

125   *black hole . . . seen as an "embryo" of a new universe:* according to Asimov; see note to p. 58.

Chapter 8

128   *group sound:* It is interesting that, parallel to the discovery of the "group sound" in rock music, "group sound" has been playing an increasing role in "classical" music since the late seventies, in the consorts working to reproduce the authentic, original sounds of early music, for instance. This is a trend that does not contradict the state of affairs discussed here, but rather supplements and corroborates it as corresponding to our times. Certain composers of modern concert music are now becoming "sound-conscious" in their works to a degree heretofore known only in jazz. Wolfgang Rihm, a German composer born in 1952 who has become one of the most outstanding contemporary composers, said in an interview: "I have a utopia—that I can touch the sound, that, while composing, I almost become the sound itself. . . ." This statement corresponds almost exactly to the sound-consciousness of most jazz and rock musicians.

129   *Arnold Wadler:* See note to p. 51.

130   *Rudolf Steiner: Das Wesen des Musikalischen* (Dornach, Switzerland: Steiner Verlag, 1981).

Perry Robinson: in an interview for Südwestfunk Broadcasting at the New Jazz Meeting Baden-Baden, November 1978.

131   *not only chest, stomach and belly will be vibrating:* Special emphasis is laid upon the effect of saying or singing OM on the pineal and the pituitary glands, which in turn pass the vibrations on to the interior glandular system (and thus to the entire organism), giving order and a better functioning to the entire system.

133   *"When you blot out sense and sound—":* See note to p. 19f.

133f.   *Silvia Ostertag: Eins-Werden mit sich selbst* (Munich: Kosel Verlag, 1981).

Chapter 9

135   *Temple in the Ear:* This chapter is the "springboard" to my next book, *The Third Ear* (see note to p. 8). Almost all the topics

touched on in this chapter are discussed there in detail and with a wealth of different sources: for example, the differences between eye and ear, the independence of the ear from the dimensional nature of the world, the aggressiveness of the eye, the feminity of the ear, the problems caused by radio and TV, and so on.

137   *Jacques Lusseyran: Et la lumière fut* (Paris: 1963); translated into English as *And There Was Light* (Boston: Little, Brown, 1963). The Lusseyran quotations gain all the more weight if you realize that they are based on personal experience. The author, born in France, lost his eyesight at the age of seven. Even so, he took an active part in the French Resistance movement during World War II and was incarcerated in a German concentration camp. Later he was a university professor in the United States.

  our ear informs us more correctly about reality: But the ears can also be misused—for the purpose of subjugation, which, translated literally from the Greek of the New Testament, means "under-hearing." The apostle Paul uses this expression, but interestingly enough not in his letters. For Paul, the sexually inhibited zealot, 84 percent of whose adhortations are directed to slaves (only 16% to the masters, and then in noticeably more polite language, hardly ever demanding, and certainly never expecting "fear and trembling" as he does from the slaves), the words *obedience* and *heed (hypakouein, hypotasesthai, hypakoe, hypotage)* are favorite terms. In his letters, they appear 49 (!) times, while in all four Gospels together the word *obey* appears only 8 times. Moreover, Paul hardly ever uses the word *ear!* "He was not interested in hearing but in heeding" (according to Anton Mayer; *Der zensierte Jesus*, n.p.: Walter-Verlag, 1983).

138   *"They do it just like that on TV!":* This statement was made by a twelve-year-old boy who had hanged a thirteen-year-old friend. *(Badische Neueste Nachrichten,* Karlsruhe, 15 January, 1983).

  Botho Strauss: Paare, Passanten (Munich and Vienna: Hanser Verlag, 1981).

140   *Stefan Zweig: Die Monotonisierung der Welt* (Frankfurt am Main: Bibliothek Suhrkamp, 1976).

141   *Bhagwan Shree Rajneesh:* See note to p. 44 (Bhagwan).

142   *Robert May: Sex and Fantasy: Patterns of Male and Female Development* (n.p.: Wideview Books, 1981).

  Anneliese Korner: "Sex Differences in Newborn with Special Reference to Differences in the Organization of Oral Behavior," in *Journal of Child Psychology and Psychiatry* 14 (1973). On the same topic: Jerome Kagan and Michael Lewis, "Studies of Attention in the Human Infant," *Merrill-Palmer Quarterly* 11 (1965).

144   *Lusseyran:* See note to p. 137.

145f.   *Louise Goepfert-March: Das Tibetanische Totenbuch,* German edition of *The Tibetan Book of the Dead* (Zürich and Stuttgart: Rascher Verlag, 1970).

146   *Martin Buber:* "Ekstase und Bekenntnis"; see note to p. 16 (Buber).

lotus posture: Reaching lotus posture by way of sitting "tailor fashion" is permissible. Of the many descriptions of the lotus posture, the one by Kosho Uchiyama Roshi, the abbot of the Antai-ji monastery near Kyoto, is among the most adequate ones: "Sit on a pillow or a rolled blanket, place a somewhat larger pad (another blanket, for instance) underneath that, and cross your legs so that the right foot rests on the left thigh and vice versa. This is called the full lotus posture. If you cannot cross your legs in this way, place only the left foot on the right thigh. This is the half-lotus position. Do not sit in the middle of the pillow or the rolled blanket. Use only the edge. Your knees should be resting firmly on the pad. The body's weight rests on three places: on your buttocks at the edge of the pad and, to the left and to the right, on the sides of your knees. Sit upright and stretch your back as if trying to push your buttocks into the pillow. Hold your neck straight and do not push your chin out! Push upward with your head as if trying to press against the ceiling. Your thumbs should meet above your hands, which are lying open in front of your belly [i.e., resting palms up, one cupped in the other so that] . . . the back of your left hand, which is the passive one, and the palm of your right hand, which is the active one, [are covered]. As soon as you have taken up this position, open your mouth and exhale fully. That will change your entire mood. In order to eliminate the stiffness in your joints and muscles, slowly sway to the left and to the right two or three times; only then take up the motionless position. From that point on, do not move. Even if you feel an itch, do not scratch yourself. Do not pay any attention to the itch; it will disappear by itself. Breathe quietly through your nose. Your breath will go through your abdomen. . . . This posture can be called a unique discovery of the East, as it is the most effective one in dispelling all our personal human thoughts. You will understand this if you think of Rodin's sculpture *The Thinker.* The title *The Thinker* sounds beautiful, but the posture of this thinker is that of a man daydreaming about his illusions: his trunk bent forward, arms and fingers crooked, even his toes are crooked. . . ."

147   *John Blofeld: Gateway to Wisdom* (London: George Allen and Unwin, 1981).

148   *Rainer Maria Rilke: The Sonnets of Orpheus,* trans. M. D. Herter Norton (New York: W. W. Norton, 1942). I feel it important to present the entire sonnet here, as it is a "harmonic poem":

There rose a tree. O pure transcendency!
O Orpheus singing! O tall tree in the ear!

And all was silent. Yet even in the silence
new beginning, beckoning, change went on.

Creatures of stillness thronged out of the clear
released wood from lair and nesting-place;
and it turned out that not from cunning and not
from fear were they so hushed within themselves,

but from harkening. Bellow and cry and roar
seemed little in their hearts. And where before
hardly a hut had been to take this in,

a covert out of darkest longing
with an entrance way whose timbers tremble,—
you built temples for them in their hearing.

149   *Li Pu We:* "Frühling im Herbst" ("Spring in Autumn"), trans. Richard Wilhelm, (Jena, 1928).

Chapter 10

152   *Theodor Adorno: Philosophy of Modern Music* (New York: Seabury Press, 1973).

153   *Count Hermann Keyserling: Das Reisetagebuch eines Philosophen,* 2 vols. (Darmstadt: 1921).

153f.   *Ravi Shankar: My Music—My Life* (New York: Simon and Schuster, 1968).

154   *Gerhard Nestler: Die Form in der Musik* (Freiburg and Zurich: Atlantis Verlag, 1954).

156   *Sometimes . . . I tied my long hair:* Ravi Shankar; see note to p. 153f.

         Ravi Shankar: see note to p. 153f.

156f.   *he saw "many men and women . . .":* see note to p. 153f.

158f.   *John Coltrane:* For more information on John Coltrane and his musical and spiritual position, see the chapter on John Coltrane and Ornette Coleman in Joachim E. Berendt, *"The Jazz Book: From Ragtime to Fusion and Beyond"* (Westport, Conn.: Lawrence Hill, 1982).

160   *Nathan Davis:* at the international conference "The United States in the World," Washington, D.C., 1976, panel discussion.

         Santana means in Sanskrit "the eternally flowing stream of becoming, limited neither by birth nor by death."

160ff.   *Sufi Hazrat Inayat Khan:* See note to p. 38.

163   *Glass Bead Game:* Hermann Hesse, *The Glass Bead Game,* trans. Richard and Clara Winston (New York: Holt, Rinehart and Winston, 1969.) This work has also been published in English under the title *Magister Ludi.*

164f.   *"Organ Playing":* See previous note.

167   *Peter Michael Hamel: Through Music to the Self* (Tisbury, Wiltshire: The Compton Press, 1978).

      Gerhard Nestler: See note to p. 154.

168   *Pandit Patekar:* See note to p. 167 (Hamel).

169   *Siddhartha:* Hermann Hesse, *Siddhartha* (London: Peter Owen, 1954).

170   *"That is the way!":* See note to p. 19f. ("If you blot out . . .").

      nada: See chapter 1, p. 15f.

      Genro: See note to p. 9f.

171   *"If you blot out . . .":* See note to p. 19f.

      Hsüeh-tou: See note to p. 9 (Genro).

      person: Linguistics has two interpretations of the word, one, as described in the text, as *per-sona*, "through the sound." The other interpretation traces it back to the Etruscan word *phersu*, meaning "mask" (Greek *prósopon*). Both interpretations supplement each other. In the theaters of Greek antiquity, the actor's mask had a funnel-shaped mouth opening that amplified the actor's voice. The spectators in the giant amphitheaters, sometimes sitting quite a distance away from the actors, were often able to determine the identity of a mask, of a *phersu*, a *persona* more by its sound *("per-sona")* than by its appearance. Later the identification *per-sona*, "through the sound," was transferred from the actor to "the person" as such.

171f.   *Hermann Hesse:* "Klein and Wagner," in Hermann Hesse, *Klingsor's Last Summer* (New York: Bantam Books, 1974).

Chapter 11

173   *Hafiz:* as told by Sufi Inayat Khan; see note to p. 38.

174   *In Egypt:* My main source for the discussion in this chapter of the sound-based creation of Egyptian and Aztec myth, the Indian Prajapati legends, and so on, is the work of the eminent ethnomusicologist Marius Schneider, especially his study "Klangsymbolik in fremden Kulturen," in *Beiträge zur zur harmonikalen Grundlagenforschung* (Vienna: Lafite, 1979).

175   *Upanishad:* See note to p. 17.

176   *Ernst Schlager: Rituelle Siebenton-Musik auf Bali*, Forum Ethnomusicologicum, ed. Hans Oesch (Bern, Switzerland: Francke Verlag, 1976).

177   *Huan Yi:* related in *The Sound of the One Hand;* see note to p. 20.

177f.   *Sufi Hazrat Inayat Khan:* "The Harmony of Life," in Hazrat Inayat Khan, *The Music of Life* (Santa Fe: Omega Press, 1983).

178   *Alexandra David-Neel: Mönche und Strauchritter* (Leipzig: Brock-haus, 1931).

179f.   *J. R. R. Tolkien: The Silmarillion*, ed. by Christopher Tolkein (Boston: Houghton Mifflin, 1977).

180f.   *Michael Ende: Momo* (Garden City, New York: Doubleday, 1985).

181   *Ancient Indian mythology:* according to Marius Schneider; see note to p. 174.

Part Two

Chapter 1

186   *Bhagavadgita:* "Song of the exalted one"; a philosophical-religious poem from India dating back to the third century B.C.E., in which Lord Krishna expounds the ways of knowledge, action, and devotion to his devotee Prince Arjuna.

187   *haiku* by Basho: quoted in D. T. Suzuki, *Zen Buddhism and Psychoanalysis* (New York: Harper and Brothers, 1960).

188   *D. T. Suzuki:* See notes to p. 97 and 187.

        Hugo Makibi Enomiya-Lassalle: Zen: Weg zur Erleuchtung (Vienna: Herder Verlag, 1973).

190   *smiling and laughing, talking and chirping and giggling:* Her chirping is the aestheticized, almost "musicalized" suppression of the answer that she receives every time she dons the kimono—the answer to the question: How do I bind myself without noticing it? And how do I manage to enjoy both: not to notice the bondage and the fact that it still is a bondage?—the most beautiful bondage in the world.

        The kimono is the sublimation of a deeply Japanese sado-masochistic attitude to sexuality which can be verified at any newsstand in Japan: through its wealth of pornographic magazines displaying an inexhaustible, terrible store of variations of bondage practices. Japan is the only country in the world where sado-masochistic magazines reach circulation figures in the hundreds of thousands. Some of these magazines have attained such a high standard of photography and layout that they themselves have become what the kimono is: an aesthetification of torture, only in a cruder, meaner, less subtle form, but also more in keeping with the times. If they are not depicted naked, many of the bound women and girls (and children!) wear kimonos: the sublimation of bondage as its intensification.

        Mono means "the thing," *ki* means "to put on." A word with the literal meaning "putting on the thing" would never have come into use, if the kimono really represented only all those nice qualities—beauty, charm, grace, preciousness, and eroticism—that one generally associates with it. When do people say "the thing"? Obviously when they do not want to address something precisely. Some years ago, a spine-chilling American science fiction movie entitled *The Thing* featured an unnamable monster that threatened mankind. The closer something is to us, the more we love it, the more precise will the name be that we give to it. Thus, if the kimono were merely all the nice things we associate with it, it would not be called "the thing." "The thing," however, is a fitting name if it stands for something that morals or society (or the subconscious!) force us to put on. "The thing" is a projection by those who really have "a thing": the men, the male human being whose penis, in Western culture as well as in Japan, is "the thing" in the minds of our adolescent daughters—a "thing" that is an object of fear as well as longing, and which is unnamable.

Nomen est omen: Kimono = "putting on the thing." I believe the point is clear: the woman does not like to put into words what she really puts on when she dons the kimono.

193   *Kakichi Kadowaki:* in *Munen Muso: Ungegenständliche Meditation; Festschrift für Pater Hugo M. Enomiya-Lassalle SJ zum 80. Geburtstag* (Mainz: Matthias Grünewald Verlag, 1978).

197   *Danielle and Vadime Elisseeff: L'art de l'ancien Japon* (Paris, 1980).

198   *Elias Canetti: The Human Province,* trans. Joachim Neugroschel (New York: Seabury Press, 1978).

   Vivekananda: In Joachim E. Berendt, *The Jazz Book,* chapter on John McLaughlin; see note to p. 158f. (Coltrane).

199   *Philip Kapleau: The Three Pillars of Zen: Teaching, Practice, and Enlightenment.* Rev. and expanded ed. (London: Rider, 1980).

Chapter 2

201   *Don Ellis:* "The Sound of India," in *Jazz* (Feb. 1967).

202   *In The Jazz Book:* See note to p. 158f. (Coltrane); I am referring here to the chapter "Swing."

203f.   *Ravi Shankar:* See note to p. 153f.

204   *(Verve):* In a departure from my procedure thus far, I feel it is necessary in this chapter, for obvious reasons, to mention record labels. More information about records is given at the end of the chapter.

206   *John Coltrane:* See note to p. 158f.

209   *John McLaughlin:* See the chapter on John McLaughlin in Joachim E. Berendt, *The Jazz Book;* see note to p. 158f.

210f.   *Don Ellis:* See note to p. 201.

217   *Originally all people in India were Dravidians:* The theory turned into certainty when, in 1983, the American anthropologist Walter Fairservis succeeded in deciphering parts of the Harappa culture (approximately four thousand years old). The Harappas lived in the border region between India and Pakistan—in North India, that is, even though their language is related to Dravidian.

219   *Nathan Davis:* See note to p. 160 (Davis).

         James Baldwin: Notes of a Native Son (New York: Dial Press, 1955).

220ff.   *symbiosis:* The topic of symbioses of religions, highly interesting from the standpoint of social and cultural history, has not been studied intensively enough. Religions grow in and through the confrontation with each other: the simple belief in nature of Shintoism through the high level of abstraction of Buddhism in Japan, or Buddhism through the ancient animistic Bon religion in Tibet. There, as in the entire Indian region, Hinduism and Buddhism grew with and through each other.

         One of the most sophisticated and most interesting cases of such growth by interaction of Hinduism and Buddhism was found in the Khmer empire with its capital Angkor Wat, situated in what today is Cambodia. Another fruitful symbiosis is that of Buddhism and Confucianism in China. It often seems as if the teachings of the Buddha fell on especially fertile and solid ground when they met Confucius's pragmatism. And it is obvious that Zen developed beautifully in this symbiosis. Apparently Islam (wherever it has shed the intolerance and fanaticism of its "zealous" prophet, Muhammed) is particularly well suited to such symbioses: with Christianity on Sicily and in Southern Spain; with Hinduism in the ancient Mogul empire of Northern India; with Buddhism and Confucianism in those areas of China that were touched by Islam.

         Christianity, too, is capable of entering into religiously and culturally fertile symbioses, most interestingly with the African Yoruba religion (what arrogance to put it off as superstition!) in Brazil. In fact, the field of religious studies has known for quite some time that Christ's teachings themselves are quite obviously a symbiosis (whose constituent parts have been traced by some scholars all the way to India and Tibet). When following the generally accepted conviction that the best Christians were the early Christians, one should realize that particularly during those times Christianity was "symbiotic" in all directions imaginable: to the Gnostics, to Judaism, to Hellenism, and to the influences coming in from northern Africa, especially from Egypt, and from Asia. The "wisest" New Testament author, the apostle John, was also the "most symbiotic" one.

         If we accept that Western materialism and rationalism also constitute a kind of religion (which they have become, for bourgeois society), you can detect a symbiosis of religions in that phenomenon, too, which has been highly fruitful: with Protestant Christianity. It was the only symbiosis of which Protestantism has been capable. Catholicism is more open; in recent times certain Catholics (such as William Johnston and Hugo Makibi Enomiya-Lassalle; see note to p. 188) have even been able to cross the bridge to Zen. Actually, Protestants should be capable of a much more lively relationship to Zen than Catholics. With its sober character, its reduction to essentials, and its rejection of "cult," Zen *is* a "Protestant" kind of Buddhism.

It often seems as if symbioses (perhaps because they some-how involve an aspect of "competition") bring out the best in a religion while, on the other hand, religions that have been kept totally "clean" tend to degenerate (which today is particularly obvious in certain Islamic countries).

I regret that these thoughts can be entertained in this book only in the form of a note. It would be highly productive to study the topic in much more detail. This topic, too, eludes adequate treatment by "scientific" methods; it has to be experienced.

223f.   *modality:* cf. part 1, chapter 10, p. 159f.

224f.   *John Coltrane:* All quotations are taken from the liner notes to various Coltrane records on the Impulse label.

"Words, sounds, speech": from Coltrane's text to his album *A Love Supreme* (Impulse); see p. 158f.

Chapter 3

228   *Claudio Hoffmann: Smog im Hirn* (Bensheim: Päd. Extra Buch Verlag, 1980).

229   *Carl Friedrich von Weizsäcker: Im Garten des Menschlichen* (Munich and Vienna: Carl Hanser Verlag, 1977).

230   *Robert Kaspar:* "Die Evolution des Lebendigen als Erkennt-nisvorgang," *Umschau* 80/16 (1980).

230f.   *D. T. Suzuki:* See note to p. 21.

231   *Carl Friedrich von Weizsäcker:* See note to p. 44.

taboo reactions similar to those of "primitive" societies: One instance is the code of behavior among scientists; it is particularly obvious in medicine, where adherents of the same scientific school must not be incriminated under any circumstances, even if they have clearly committed a professional error, whereas adherents of other medical schools are subject to attack by way of a standard pejorative vocabulary ("quack," "un-scientific," etc.). The formula-laden communication among physicians, the tacit buddy-type agreement between them, also points in the same direction. Unlike theoretical physics, for instance, medical language does not need technical terms in order to be able to express complicated matters. In the final analysis, medical terms are expressions from everyday language translated into words coming from Greek or Latin roots. It is a kind of language, in other words, whose intention is not communication but camouflage. All this shows behavior patterns that are indeed similar to those of the shamans of "primitive" societies.

232   *Hoimar von Ditfurth: Wir sind nicht nur von dieser Welt* (Hamburg: Hoffmann und Campe, 1981).

Carl Friedrich von Weizsäcker: See note to p. 44.

233   *breast removal surgery:* Christian Bachmann: *Die Krebsmafia* (Monaco: Editions Tomek, 1981).

    Paul Feyerabend: Against Method: Outline of an Anarchistic Theory of Knowledge (London: Verso, 1978).

233f. *Erich Jantsch: Die Selbstorganisation des Universums* (Munich: Deutscher Taschenbuch-Verlag, 1982).

234   *Weizsäcker:* See note to p. 229.

    Erwin Chargaff: Warnungstafeln (Stuttgart: Klett-Cotta, 1982).

235   *Gottfried Benn: Lyrik und Prosa, Briefe und Dokumente,* ed. Max Niedermayer and Marguerite Schluter (Wiesbaden: Limes Verlag, 1962).

INDEX OF NAMES AND SUBJECTS